Freshwater Aquariums

for dummies®

A Wiley Brand

Freshwater Aquariums

3rd Edition

by Madelaine Francis Heleine

Freshwater Aquariums For Dummies®, 3rd Edition

Published by: **John Wiley & Sons, Inc.,** 111 River Street, Hoboken, NJ 07030-5774, www.wiley.com

Copyright © 2020 by John Wiley & Sons, Inc., Hoboken, New Jersey

Published simultaneously in Canada

No part of this publication may be reproduced, stored in a retrieval system or transmitted in any form or by any means, electronic, mechanical, photocopying, recording, scanning or otherwise, except as permitted under Sections 107 or 108 of the 1976 United States Copyright Act, without the prior written permission of the Publisher. Requests to the Publisher for permission should be addressed to the Permissions Department, John Wiley & Sons, Inc., 111 River Street, Hoboken, NJ 07030, (201) 748-6011, fax (201) 748-6008, or online at http://www.wiley.com/go/permissions.

Trademarks: Wiley, For Dummies, the Dummies Man logo, Dummies.com, Making Everything Easier, and related trade dress are trademarks or registered trademarks of John Wiley & Sons, Inc., and may not be used without written permission. All other trademarks are the property of their respective owners. John Wiley & Sons, Inc., is not associated with any product or vendor mentioned in this book.

LIMIT OF LIABILITY/DISCLAIMER OF WARRANTY: THE PUBLISHER AND THE AUTHOR MAKE NO REPRESENTATIONS OR WARRANTIES WITH RESPECT TO THE ACCURACY OR COMPLETENESS OF THE CONTENTS OF THIS WORK AND SPECIFICALLY DISCLAIM ALL WARRANTIES, INCLUDING WITHOUT LIMITATION WARRANTIES OF FITNESS FOR A PARTICULAR PURPOSE. NO WARRANTY MAY BE CREATED OR EXTENDED BY SALES OR PROMOTIONAL MATERIALS. THE ADVICE AND STRATEGIES CONTAINED HEREIN MAY NOT BE SUITABLE FOR EVERY SITUATION. THIS WORK IS SOLD WITH THE UNDERSTANDING THAT THE PUBLISHER IS NOT ENGAGED IN RENDERING LEGAL, ACCOUNTING, OR OTHER PROFESSIONAL SERVICES. IF PROFESSIONAL ASSISTANCE IS REQUIRED, THE SERVICES OF A COMPETENT PROFESSIONAL PERSON SHOULD BE SOUGHT. NEITHER THE PUBLISHER NOR THE AUTHOR SHALL BE LIABLE FOR DAMAGES ARISING HEREFROM. THE FACT THAT AN ORGANIZATION OR WEBSITE IS REFERRED TO IN THIS WORK AS A CITATION AND/OR A POTENTIAL SOURCE OF FURTHER INFORMATION DOES NOT MEAN THAT THE AUTHOR OR THE PUBLISHER ENDORSES THE INFORMATION THE ORGANIZATION OR WEBSITE MAY PROVIDE OR RECOMMENDATIONS IT MAY MAKE. FURTHER, READERS SHOULD BE AWARE THAT INTERNET WEBSITES LISTED IN THIS WORK MAY HAVE CHANGED OR DISAPPEARED BETWEEN WHEN THIS WORK WAS WRITTEN AND WHEN IT IS READ.

For general information on our other products and services, please contact our Customer Care Department within the U.S. at 877-762-2974, outside the U.S. at 317-572-3993, or fax 317-572-4002. For technical support, please visit https://hub.wiley.com/community/support/dummies.

Wiley publishes in a variety of print and electronic formats and by print-on-demand. Some material included with standard print versions of this book may not be included in e-books or in print-on-demand. If this book refers to media such as a CD or DVD that is not included in the version you purchased, you may download this material at http://booksupport.wiley.com. For more information about Wiley products, visit www.wiley.com.

Library of Congress Control Number: 2019947987

ISBN: 978-1-119-60139-5

ISBN 978-1-119-60140-1 (ebk); ISBN 978-1-119-60137-1 (ebk)

Manufactured in the United States of America

C10013654_090619

Contents at a Glance

Table of Contents

Introduction

Welcome to the wonderful world of freshwater aquariums! This updated edition of *Freshwater Aquariums For Dummies* is a handy reference guide for those who want the basics of setting up and maintaining an aquarium system. Everything you need to know to get started on your very own freshwater system can be found right here in this book.

In this book, I tell you about tank styles and equipment, disease prevention and cures, aquarium decoration, maintenance routines, species of fish and their habits, test kits for your water, different types of systems, and tips on working with plants. And much, much more. You're likely to encounter all sorts of equipment and different fish species in pet shops and online, but all you need is the information contained in this book to get you started on the road to successful fishkeeping. After you master the basics, you can venture into new areas of aquarium keeping with confidence.

So sit back and journey into the fascinating world of freshwater aquariums, gathering the basics of keeping your fish healthy and happy the easy way. Your new aquatic pets will love you for it.

About This Book

You may have heard horror stories about your neighbor's aquarium. Or maybe your best friend told you that his new aquarium that was in his second floor apartment is now decorating the downstairs tenant's apartment. Okay, problems happen, but these rare aquarium misadventures can be avoided with a proper knowledge of the basics.

About 99 percent of all potential aquarium problems never occur if hobbyists take the time to find out a few simple fishkeeping basics. Wet floors can be mopped, and tanks can be repaired. Aquarium keeping will still move forward, despite the occasional setbacks encountered from time to time.

It's really very easy to become a successful fishkeeper. All you need is a little bit of help to get you going, which is exactly what this book provides. This third edition of *Freshwater Aquariums For Dummies* gives you good, basic information and the ammo you need to battle any problems that may occur as you live with your aquarium. You can find plenty of information about the following:

>> **Aquarium 4-1-1:** From choosing and finding a good location for a tank and equipment to adding artificial plants and substrate, you can find everything you need to create a safe home for your fish.

>> **The ABCs of fish:** This book includes handy information about the different kinds of fish species to include in your aquarium, behavior and eating habits, and where to purchase your fish. After you have your fish, you'll need to know what food options are available, how to feed your aquatic pets properly, and how to identify, treat, and prevent many common illnesses.

>> **Lowdown on water, chemicals, and plants:** You can discover all things water, including how to set up the aquarium with chemicals and what to do if you have problems. This book also gives you details about live plant species that can make your aquarium more beautiful and also more hospitable for your fish.

>> **Birds and the bees:** Get plenty of helpful information about setting the mood to breed your fish.

>> **So much more:** You can discover how to share your newfound hobby with your others. If you're interested, this book also provides ideas to take your hobby to the next level.

My updates also include fun ways to expand your hobby, new equipment that's available, and a quick guide to a few more advanced systems. This edition also gives you more information on other species of fish and plants.

Foolish Assumptions

When writing this book, I made the following assumptions about you, my dear reader:

>> You're an absolute beginner, have never owned an aquarium before, and never even fed a goldfish.

>> You may have dabbled a little (perhaps you won goldfish at your school fair when you were young), but you have no real knowledge of how to set up an aquarium or take care of fish.

>> You know a little about fishkeeping and want to discover more so you can set up your first aquarium.

>> You've attempted setting up an aquarium, but for some reason, your aquarium had tons of algae and your fish were sickly.

>> You want to start a small aquarium and teach your children some responsibility about taking care of it.

>> You have a small aquarium and want to take your hobby to the next level.

No matter who you are, you can find all sorts of helpful information here.

Icons Used in This Book

If you've flipped through this book at all, you've probably noticed little pictures, called icons, in the margins. Here's what they mean:

TIP

This icon indicates good advice and information that will help you keep your fish healthy and safe.

WARNING

When I discuss a task or procedure that might be problematic, I use this icon. It also points out things that might be dangerous to you or your fish.

TECHNICAL STUFF

This icon flags information that's, well, technical, and you can go ahead and skip that paragraph if you want to.

REMEMBER

When I make a point or offer some information that I feel you should keep with you forever, I toss in this icon.

Where to Go from Here

This book is a reference, not a tutorial. You don't have to read it from Chapter 1 to the end if you just want to get a glimpse of the hobby before you get down to the basics. Just use the table of contents or index to find the topics that interest you and go from there. Start with your needs and interests.

If you don't already own fish and don't know how to set up an aquarium, start with Part 1. If you have a little more background in fishkeeping, maybe you want to check out the species guide in Part 2. Or maybe the chapter on live plants in Part 3 has caught your fancy. Go ahead and skip around. That's what this book is for.

1
Getting Started with Freshwater Aquarium Basics

Understand the basics of aquarium systems so you can set up an aquarium that runs successfully and is easy to maintain right from the start.

Decide which aquarium system is best for you so you can begin simply and move on to more complex systems as your hobby grows.

Find a good location for your tank so your tank will maintain the proper water temperature and your fish won't be disturbed.

Choose an aquarium tank and stand that fit your available space and have plenty of room for the species you choose.

Know how to decorate your aquarium so your tank looks good and your fish feel safe and at home.

Grasp the function of aquarium equipment and figure out which equipment is essential (and which equipment isn't essential) for starting your aquarium.

Chapter **1**

Taking the Plunge: Just the Essentials

S ome of the most pleasurable moments in my live life have involved aquarium keeping. Something special and exciting comes with owning a beautiful tankful of wonderful fish and plants. Most people have either owned an aquarium, lived in a house with a fish tank, or dreamed of putting one together.

Many people think aquarium fish are harder to keep than other pets. This simply isn't true. Everyone pretty much knows how to feed, water, and walk a dog, but many tend to shy away from setting up an aquarium because they worry about the minor details too much. Never fear, consider this chapter your jumping board into this book. It shows you how simple fishkeeping can really be so that you can start on the right foot and be successful.

Focusing on the Tank, Stand, Accessories, and Equipment

If you look at an aquarium from all sides and from the top, you'll quickly see that it's just a glass, plastic, or acrylic box with a bunch of things added to it. It is as simple as that.

You may be asking yourself a few questions like these: What is the function of all this equipment, and how does the tank use them to run? Does it matter which fish and plants I choose? Is there a special type of water in the tank? How do I feed and care for my fish and plants?

You came to the right place for answers. The following sections explain some questions you may have and preview the basics of setting up an aquarium.

REMEMBER

If you have other immediate family members living with you, such as children, don't forget to get them involved in the aquarium decisions as well. By involving others, you can share your new hobby from day one with those you love.

Knowing where to put your tank

People wonder where they should place an aquarium in their home. There are good places and bad places. Place tanks away from direct sunlight and drafts. You also need to take into account household traffic issues and electrical considerations as well to ensure your fish will be safe and happy.

Chapter 3 discusses how certain places in a room can affect your tank's water temperature. You also discover how high-traffic areas have an impact on your fish, how close your water source needs to be to your tank, what electrical supply is required, how much space will be ample to set up the tank that you want, how to fill your tank, and what cleaning options you can use.

Looking at the tank and stand options

Aquariums and stands have several shapes and sizes available in the marketplace, and you may be wondering if you should start out with a small tank or a large tank. In Chapter 4, you find that starting with a larger tank provides a more stable environment for your fish. Don't worry though, you don't have to go crazy and try to set up something that looks like it belongs at SeaWorld right off the bat. Instead, I explore what's best for the beginner.

In that chapter, you also discover the difference between glass, acrylic, and plastic aquariums. I explain what aquarium stand works best for your needs. Chapter 4 also shows you the different styles of tanks and stands that you can buy to suit your individual needs and how to correctly move an aquarium if you ever decide to set your tank up in a different location or in a new home.

Figuring out what (besides fish) to put in your aquarium

When you look at different aquariums, you can see that they contain many different combinations of rocks, decorations, and interesting objects such as driftwood. No big mystery here. Some items are necessary for your tank to run properly, and others aren't.

Chapter 5 shows gravel and/or other substrates are recommended for most aquariums. You also discover the type and number of decorations in an aquarium come down to a matter of individual taste (though some species do well with certain additions such as rock caves), and that you can really let your creativity, decorating skills, and good taste shine.

Considering aquarium equipment

Most new hobbyists get confused when deciding what equipment to purchase. You can choose from many different options. Chapter 6 discusses filters, heaters, lighting, pumps, airstones, thermometers, tubes, valves, tank circulation, and hoods. When purchasing equipment, always buy the best that your budget will allow.

REMEMBER

When setting up an aquarium, don't take shortcuts. You can't rush down to your aquarium store, buy a bunch of stuff, and expect to have fish swimming around in your new tank within an hour. If you take the time to set up an aquarium properly by following a few basic steps, you'll have fewer problems later on down the road.

Determining what you really need

For beginners, I recommend starting out with the basics: a 20- to 55-gallon tank, a simple power filter system, gravel, a heater, food, declorinator, a thermometer, a couple of nets, simple decorations, and a hood with lighting. Often you can find all these things in an aquarium kit for one price. After you become more comfortable with the basics, you can move to larger or more specialized systems.

Caring for Your New Aquatic Pets

Before you're ready to purchase fish, you need to know how to take care of the fish you want. You also need a general idea of the type of fish you'll buy so that you know what types of plants and other items you need and how to set up water conditions that are just right for the species you choose. These sections help you begin.

Eyeing differences in species

A fish's physical makeup (fin shape and size, body shape, color, and so on) and how a fish uses its body in its natural environment are important when determining what type of fish and what type of aquarium you need for that particular species. For example, long, thin, streamlined fish such as danios tend to be speedy horizontal swimmers and love a tank that is long and not tall.

Chapter 7 explains the physical makeup of aquatic species so that you can understand what system your fish will enjoy most. This chapter also allows you to quickly see if there is a problem, such as stress or disease, by observing any deviation in your fish's normal body shape, fin shape, and swimming patterns.

Knowledge isn't only power; it's also the best preventive method on earth for diagnosing aquarium problems before they get out of hand.

Assessing which types of fish are best for you

You have so many choices in aquarium fish that you may wonder, where is the best place to start? Chapter 8 gives you a good selection of popular and easy-to-keep aquarium fish so that you have a many good options to choose from when you begin.

Of course, I only have so much space to discuss the species. It would take volumes to describe all the species available. Chapter 8 offers excellent choices for beginning hobbyists. These fish are inexpensive, easy to find, forgiving of beginner mistakes, and will help get any aquarium off to a good start. You also can read about a few neat *invertebrates* (animals that don't have a spine) to keep your fish company.

Buying fish — what you need to know

The best way to start as a beginning fishkeeper is to develop a good relationship with a local pet store. A quality vendor can help you make decisions on the best way to set up or improve your system. He can also make good suggestions on fish compatibility and lend a hand if your fish become ill.

Chapter 9 helps you figure out how to choose quality dealers and develop good relationships with them. This chapter shows you how to select healthy fish for your new aquarium by providing information on how to evaluate the physical attributes and behavior of fish in a store.

The Internet is a great place to find fish, plants, and equipment for your new aquarium, but nothing beats the wonderful feeling of walking through a tropical fish store and seeing everything up close with a helpful dealer at your side.

Aquarium clubs and societies are another good place to find aquarium stuff. Using a combination of local stores, clubs, and societies, and wonderful dealers online to purchase aquarium fish is always a good choice that will ultimately provide you with the best options for your setup.

Feeding your fish — what types of food to buy

Although you can buy canned fish food, nutrition goes beyond premanufactured dry food. Many species of fish have different nutritional requirements.

Chapter 10 helps you understand basic aquatic nutrition and shows you what and how to feed your fish properly.

REMEMBER

A well-balanced diet for you fish can include prepackaged, frozen food, live food, and in some cases fresh vegetables.

Taking care of sick fish

Despite having the best setup possible, fish will eventually contract disease from time to time. This usually isn't a cause for alarm because many fish illnesses can be cured.

Chapter 11 helps you identify stress, spot common problems ahead of time to prevent disease, treat common illnesses, set up a hospital tank to treat disease, and understand the importance of a quarantine tank to avoid introducing sickness into your main tank with newly purchased fish.

WARNING

Never buy ill fish with the noble idea of taking them home and nursing them back to health. This practice will endanger your other fish and risk upsetting your current system.

Understanding Water, Chemicals, and Live Plants

One of the most important elements of your aquarium is the water that your fish live in. In order to be a successful fish keeper, you'll discover the different types of water, testing methods, types of chemicals to treat it, and the way that bacteria in water stabilizes your tank through a nitrogen cycle. In this section, I also look at putting simple systems together, the different types of live plants that can benefit your tank, and what to do if trouble arises.

Grasping everything water

Adding the right water to your aquarium is extremely important for a good start. Chapter 12 explains the different types of water you can use in your aquarium, the best way to make the water safe, and the way to fill your tank.

Using chemicals to improve your aquarium conditions

Many beneficial chemicals can help you start and maintain your tank. Chapter 13 discusses the chemicals you'll need to start your aquarium, other products that will help you maintain it, chemicals you can use if you decide to keep live plants, and useful medications.

Testing your water

Chapter 14 explains the *nitrogen cycle* (a natural process that makes aquarium water safe over long periods of time). You find out how to start and maintain the nitrogen cycle and how to test your water to keep track of this biological process.

Getting a system going

Chapter 15 spells out a few basic freshwater aquarium setups. I show you step by step how to get your aquarium up and running, so you can successfully become a fishkeeper right out of the gate.

Adding live plants

If you decide that you want to use live plants in your aquarium, Chapters 16 and 17 show you some different plants you may want to consider and how to purchase and transport plants from a dealer, how to maintain them, and how to take care of any problems that arise.

Fixing common problems

Despite best efforts, problem to pop up from time to time. Chapter 18 helps you solve feeding and aggression problems. You also discover what to do when your equipment, tank, and water have issues.

Expanding Your Aquarium Hobby

Setting up and maintaining an aquarium is only the beginning. If you want to expand your hobby, you can do many fun and interesting projects.

Breeding your fish: Yes or no?

Many hobbyists love to breed their fish for fun and profit. If you become really good at breeding, you may even come up with a new color or pattern for the world to enjoy.

Chapter 19 helps you find the right water conditions, feeding schedule, plants, and equipment for breeding fish. It also tells you how to help coax your fish into mating. When you get to Chapter 20, you can discover how to decide which fish to breed, how to select strong breeding traits, what the best ways are to care for fry and protect them from other fish, and how to succeed in this wonderful and challenging aspect of the hobby. This chapter also gives you breeding tactics for several different easy-to-breed species.

Keeping track of your progress

Many hobbyists are concerned about remembering every fish and the problems and success they have had with each species. Chapter 21 helps you cut through the clutter by explaining how to accurately record fish data and photograph your fish for fun, education, and potential profit.

Broadening your hobby

Chapter 22 explains many different ways to expand your hobby by joining aquariums clubs to interacting with others, volunteering in fish-related enterprises, setting up tanks in places that can heighten the enjoyment of fishkeeping for others, entering your fish in a show, writing about your hobby, and teaching kids about aquarium science to ensure the future of the aquarium industry.

Contemplating other types of aquarium structures

This book focuses on freshwater systems so that you can gain a strong foothold on the basics of keeping a successful aquarium. After you master the basics of freshwater aquariums, your choices will become unlimited, and you may want to continue your adventures in the hobby by trying other types of setups.

If so, look at Chapter 23 that gives you a brief overview and a quick guide to the different types systems you can try, including the brackish and marine (saltwater) side of the hobby. This chapter also shows you where to find good information on setting up an aquarium for those oh-so-beautiful marine species of fish and invertebrates.

SHORT ON CASH?

Okay, if you're like me and never have any money, you can still set up a halfway decent aquarium system. Probably the least expensive way to get a small system going is to go to a superstore and buy a freshwater aquarium kit. Grab a few bags of gravel, a bottle of dechlorinator, fish food, a net, and a few plants on the way out the door, and you're ready to go.

Chapter **2**

The Practice of Aquarium Keeping

quarium keeping continues to be one of the fastest growing hobbies in the world, so get ready to dive right in. As this chapter explains, the fishkeeping hobby has been around for a long time, and many types of aquarium systems are available that include freshwater, saltwater, and brackish. The benefits of owning an aquarium are numerous, so keep reading to find out how to start your own amazing aquarium journey!

Imagine: It's eight o'clock at night, and you're just getting home from the office, where you spent the final half hour listening to your irate boss rant and rave about problems beyond your control. Your ears are still ringing, your head is pounding, and your mood is ugly. You walk in the front door of your home, plop down in your best easy chair, and let the healing therapy begin.

Directly in front of you is your beautifully maintained 55-gallon aquarium. In your private underwater world, you can see bright green plants waving softly in the gentle current. The clear water soothes your tired eyes as it swirls endlessly through the tank. A frolicking mix of brightly colored guppies and platys dart merrily through a hole in a piece of driftwood. The smooth pebbles on the aquarium floor gently reflect the dazzling array of fish colors. The faint soothing bubbling from the filter reminds you that there is always a place you can go to relax and get away from it all right in your own home.

Hey, your aquarium sounds fantastic! Can I come over?

Recognizing the Amazing Benefits of Owning an Aquarium

Okay, snag a comfortable chair and travel with me through the marvelous world of freshwater aquarium keeping. People have aquatic pets in their homes for a lot of great reasons. Basically the benefits and advantages are endless. The following are several advantages to having an aquarium in your home:

>> **Fishkeeping is a hobby that the whole family can participate in and enjoy together.** A fish tank is a great way to teach children the responsibility of animal care as well as the biological principles that go with their own species' daily survival. The older generation can also benefit as well — scientific research shows that aquariums can help lower stress and prolong life.

>> **The tanks don't require a lot of space.** Fishkeeping is perfect for apartment dwellers who may be prohibited from owning larger, roaming pets, such as dogs and cats. (Make sure if you're renting an apartment, house, or business building that you have permission from the landlord to set up a tank.) You can match an aquarium to almost any space that you have. You can get a tank that takes up an entire wall in your home or one small enough to fit on your desk — and every size in between. And speaking of desktops, an aquarium in your office is a great way to spend a little bit of time goofing off each day without your boss finding out. Besides, your coworkers will think you're cool if you have a tank that they can come look at.

>> **Fish don't make noises or cause distractions.** They don't bark at the neighbors, caterwaul at the moon, chase the letter carrier, make unsightly messes on the floor, or whimper all night. You'll probably never have to bail an escaped renegade goldfish out of the local pound, either.

>> **If you need to go on a vacation, fish are the perfect pets to leave home alone.** You can feed and maintain your fish while you're away in many ways (I discuss a few in Chapter 10). No need to find all-day pet sitters for your

aquatic friends, because today's aquarium technology allows you to spend your time enjoying your vacation instead of worrying about your fish.

>> **An aquarium encourages your artistic side to run wild.** Aquariums are great because *aquascaping* (decorating your aquarium's landscape) allows you some real hands-on interaction with your aquatic pet's amazing environment. Chapter 5 gives you lots of aquascaping tips.

>> **Fishkeeping is soothing and relaxing.** Nothing compares to dipping your tired arms into nice cool water to do a little underwater planting or rearranging. It beats periodically putting a new collar on your dog and braving the weather to walk her any day.

Furthermore, aquariums can help to calm and soothe pain for people in situations where they need it most. Have you ever been to a hospital or dental waiting room and noticed a cheerful little aquarium system keeping people entertained who are waiting for their turn to enter the torture chamber? I remember being frightened to death at the thought of going to a dentist when I was a kid. While I sat in the waiting room waiting to be dragged kicking and screaming onto a dental chair that promised certain doom, I forgot all my woes as I watched a tankful of playful platys swimming among a beautiful aquascape of live plants.

>> **Daily care and maintenance of a home aquarium is fairly simple and doesn't require a great deal of time or money.** Setting up and maintaining an aquarium is a matter of following basic rules. Knowledge is the key to success, and you're making a good start by buying this book. You can set up a complete aquarium system with a relatively little investment as long as you don't go overboard at the beginning and are content to add to your system as you go along. But if you're like me, you may find yourself paying off several credit cards at your local pet shops, so be careful.

TIP

You can also keep current on future fishkeeping trends by joining local fishkeeping societies, talking to your local fish store manager, and relying on other sources, such as libraries, magazines, and the Internet. A little research can go a long way and make all the difference between complete success and unnecessary failure. Do your homework well and you'll be prepared to handle any aquatic situation.

AQUARIUMS OF OLD

The ancient Egyptians are generally believed to be the first true aquarium keepers. Historical evidence suggests that Egyptians kept fish in ponds as a source of food and smaller species in their homes to impress their friends. (I don't know if they had pyramid-shaped aquariums back then, but I kind of doubt it.)

High-ranking Roman officials are rumored to have kept ponds full of hungry eels. If an eelkeeping official happened to have a politically uncooperative neighbor . . . well, the neighbor may have gotten a fish-eye view of their good buddy's aquatic pets.

From Rome, fishkeeping began spreading in the Far East. Asian aquarists became so fascinated with the common goldfish that they went into aquatic hyperdrive and started selectively breeding them at a rapid rate. Needless to say, they came up with a bunch of cool-looking goldfish.

Public aquariums began to show up in Europe in the late 1800s. Those first aquariums were quite a bit different that the ones today and displayed only a few different species. Later on, expensive glass aquariums were manufactured for the elegant homes of the rich and famous. Unfortunately, because they were heated by open flames or oil lamps, these primitive tanks were unsafe. Often, members of high society with aquariums ended up with a very large pile of ashes where their mansions once stood (and a fish fry dinner).

During these early, dark days of aquarium keeping, hobbyists had to make do with makeshift equipment and scary potions. The situation finally began to improve in the 1900s when fish shows and aquarium societies (fish nerds gathered together in one place) emerged to help the increasing number of hobbyists maintain their tanks.

Today top-of-the-line equipment, caring breeders, and expanding species availability allows anyone to keep a home aquarium with ease. Technology has made it easier than ever to keep your aquatic pets healthy and happy.

Identifying Aquarium Water Systems

Because you're reading this book, I assume that you've decided to start in the freshwater side of the hobby. Good choice!

The aquarium hobby has three general types of systems to set up: freshwater, saltwater, and brackish. Individual types of fish, tanks, equipment, and plants vary dramatically from system to system. Although this book focuses on freshwater systems, the following sections give a brief overview of each type of setup to give you a better idea how space considerations, initial financial outlay, difficulty level, and availability of species may affect your decision to try other systems after freshwater.

TIP

If you choose to have an aquarium that contains all plants and no fish, make sure you feed the plants aquarium fertilizer. The plants also need carbon dioxide (CO_2) through water changes or a CO_2 unit. Ensure that you choose plants that have similar temperature, pH, and lighting requirements, such as anubias, Amazon swords, java moss, java fern, and vallisneria.

Although you can have a freshwater tank with artificial plants, a setup that includes live plants mixed with tropical fish from those particular plants' native region is better. A complete natural setup is a display of nature at its best.

Freshwater systems

The most popular type of aquarium is a *freshwater* system. It's the most practical system for a beginning aquarist for several reasons:

>> **Generally a freshwater system generally isn't quite as expensive to set up as a saltwater system.** Saltwater systems often require extra equipment; (See the "Saltwater systems" section later in this chapter.)

>> **Freshwater fish are generally less expensive than marine fish.** It's much better to work with less expensive fish when you're just starting out and still discovering the ins and outs of the hobby.

>> **Freshwater fish are readily available at most aquarium shops and come in a wide variety of colorful species.** Many hardy species, such as guppies, platys, and swordtails, are easy to keep and don't have difficult special requirements. Saltwater fish are much more sensitive to water conditions and don't tolerate mistakes as easily.

>> **Many varieties of freshwater fish breed quite easily.** Breeding freshwater fish may provide you with opportunities to sell your overstock (don't quit your day job, though) and a chance to experiment with new breeds.

>> **You can have more fish.** You can keep significantly more freshwater fish than marine fish in the same amount of space.

Freshwater systems come in either tropical or coldwater varieties. Each has slightly different equipment requirements and houses different types of fish.

Freshwater tropical aquariums are relaxing

Freshwater tropical aquariums house the majority of retail freshwater fish. If you choose a tropical system, you can set up a *community aquarium* with a variety of species that can coexist peacefully. Or you may decide to try a *species tank* for a more aggressive fish family, such as cichlids. A freshwater tropical aquarium offers a huge number of choices in livestock and plants to suit everyone's individual taste.

TIP

Most tropical freshwater fish are inexpensive and fairly easy to keep, which is why this is the best system for a beginning hobbyist. You can also purchase an aquarium system at many superstores and pet stores in kit form. A kit generally includes a tank, hood, filter, net, food, instruction book, and the heater necessary for a tropical tank. A kit often doesn't include gravel, plants, or decorations that must be purchased separately. Always read the box label so that you will know what extras you'll need to buy to get the tank up and running properly. Pet stores and large retail stores are great places to find these starter kits, which are a good buy for the money.

Popular species of tropical freshwater fish include these items:

>> Angelfish

>> Barbs

>> Bettas

>> Guppies

>> Mollies

>> Platys

>> Swordtails

>> Tetras

And that's just to name a few. You have such a wide variety from which to choose.

Freshwater coldwater aquariums for special fish

A *coldwater aquarium* usually houses special species of fish and invertebrates such as these:

>> Goldfish

>> Koi

>> Snails and crabs

>> White cloud mountain minnows

In their native habitat, these fish normally live in lower temperatures than their tropical counterparts. Large koi are often kept in coldwater ponds. The equipment you need for a coldwater aquarium is similar to that for a tropical aquarium, except that coldwater tanks don't require an extensive heating system. Larger tanks are better for this type of system because coldwater species are generally bigger than most tropicals and consume more oxygen.

TIP

Take special consideration when choosing plants for a coldwater system because many plants can't survive the lower temperatures. Room temperature is a factor in coldwater aquarium setups as well, because many homes are kept very warm which can affect the temperature of your tank. You can purchase a chiller to keep the temperature lower.

REMEMBER

Aside from goldfish, coldwater fish can be difficult to obtain in many areas of the country. Setting up a coldwater system drastically reduces your choices of fish and live plants, unless your local dealer can special order them if she doesn't have them in stock. The Internet is an excellent place to purchase coldwater fish, as I discuss in Chapter 9.

Saltwater systems

Saltwater, or marine systems, not surprisingly, require saltwater. You see marine fish on scuba and underwater nature programs. The most popular ones include the coral reef species such as clownfish and tangs that are often found living in close proximity to various *invertebrates* (animals without backbones, such as anemones), and are often very colorful and quite beautiful. But don't fool yourself, beauty has its price. Saltwater fish and invertebrates that go in their aquariums can be extremely expensive if you're on a budget.

TECHNICAL
STUFF

The saltwater used in a marine system is usually obtained by mixing fresh water with a manufactured salt mix. Salinity must be monitored carefully, because even small fluctuations can cause illness and death. (See Chapter 8 for more on salinity testing.) A good filtration system is important in marine tanks to keep the oxygen levels high and the ammonia levels low. Marine fish have a lower tolerance to ammonia (a fish waste product) than freshwater species do, and an inadequate filter soon leads to disaster in a saltwater tank.

REMEMBER

Gaining a little experience with a freshwater tropical or coldwater system is a great way to get ready to enter the marine side of the hobby. Don't get me wrong. A beginner can maintain a successful saltwater tank, but the lessons can be expensive. I've seen many new hobbyists become disheartened with fishkeeping because they start out with a marine setup that's just too much for them to handle. If you have a close friend who is experienced in saltwater systems, ask her for advice — she may be able to help you get started successfully. You can also check out the latest edition of *Saltwater Aquariums For Dummies* by Gregory Skomal (John Wiley & Sons, Inc.).

Here are three systems I suggest you research further if you're interested in salt-water systems:

>> **A fish-only saltwater system:** A fish-only saltwater system is a setup that focuses on the fish in the system. It's usually decorated with coral skeletons or fabricated coral, which is great for beginners because you can keep all your attention on maintaining the fish without worrying about maintaining live corals and other living decorations.

>> **A fish-only system with live rock:** Often referred to as FOWLER (fish-only with live rock), this system is great to start the marine side of the hobby. You need to have at least a 30-gallon tank. The tank should be outfitted with sand and live rock. Calcium-based live rock is taken from the ocean or cultured in a closed environment and contains beneficial bacteria, algae, and small microorganisms that act as a great biological filter. Clownfish and damsels are often great fish for this setup.

>> **Saltwater reef tank:** This one of the most challenging of saltwater setups for beginners, but it's like taking a vacation at home. This type of system is usually stocked with live coral and invertebrates. Live coral and invertebrates can be sensitive to water conditions, so it requires constant and careful monitoring. Mandarin and gobies are often found in this type of setup.

Brackish systems

The *brackish aquarium* is the least popular of all the three systems, simply because the fish are generally difficult to find in many local pet stores and are usually more expensive than freshwater tropical fish. The water in a brackish aquarium lies somewhere between fresh and marine in salt content.

Here are some popular species for a brackish system:

>> Archers

>> Monos

>> Puffers

>> Scats

The equipment for a brackish system is similar to that for a freshwater setup, but only specific live plants can tolerate a brackish system. Refer to Chapter 23 for steps on setting up a brackish system.

Organization Is the Key to Success

One of the keys to success in almost any project is organizing your goals and ideas. Your choices are endless: your smartphone, your laptop, or a planner you carry around with you. This would be a good time to start using it. If you don't use one and your earliest memory goes back to yesterday's breakfast, then you should probably begin your aquarium project by making a simple list. Even if you have a good memory, go ahead and make a list anyway.

TIP

A good list provides you with a set of short- and long-term goals to help you set up and maintain your new aquarium system. For example, your short-term goals may include purchasing your tank and equipment and picking out a few starter fish. Long-term goals may be breeding your fish and trying different types of systems. By setting a few goals, you give yourself a plan to follow. You can begin your own list of goals as you read through this book.

A little knowledge can spell the difference between success and ultimate failure. I realize that research may bring up frightening memories of school librarians, but there are other practical ways to gain knowledge. You can go online and access current information on the aquarium hobby or check with other fishkeepers.

REMEMBER

Keep researching the type of system you're interested in, even after you have it set up. By researching a fish's natural environment and finding out how and where it lives in the wild, you'll have the knowledge to provide your fish with the best aquarium conditions and environment possible. A natural, stress-free environment promotes long and healthy lives for your wet pets.

IN THIS CHAPTER

» **Focusing on your floor**

» **Understanding household locations that affect tank placement**

» **Finding a water source**

» **Thinking about other household items**

» **Considering space, electricity, and cleaning**

Chapter **3**

Finding a Good Location

When you're looking for a good place to set up your aquarium, keep in mind that your home's physical aspects can have a major effect on its success or failure. Carefully inspect the area where you plan to set up your aquarium to check for a few easily avoided hazards. A little good judgment and patience go a long way.

To start, I examine a few common physical problems that can occur when aquariums are placed in inadequate spots. (Check out Chapter 4 for some of the psychological aspects of tank placement.) If you're like me when I was starting in the hobby, you've probably thought about putting an aquarium on a flimsy breakfast bar no matter what the cost. Well, after a few days of poached eggs floating around in your tank and greasy fingerprints all over the aquarium glass, not to mention that the breakfast bar is sagging under the aquarium's weight, you'll probably be forced to change your mind.

REMEMBER

Nothing is more frustrating than having to move an aquarium because you put it in a place that just isn't working for one reason or another. Aquariums are extremely heavy when fully loaded and must be drained to be moved to a new location. Don't spend a lot of time setting up a tank if you're not completely sure about its location. It's better to take a day or two and look over your options than to just put up the aquarium without any forethought. Start on the right foot if you want to be successful.

Making Sure Your Floor Is Sound

The first thing you need to consider when placing an aquarium stand is the stability of the floor. For safety, it's always better to place your tank and stand on level flooring. If your floor has even a slight unevenness, correct it by putting thin metal shims under a corner or two of the stand to correct it. Ensure the stand is solid and not rocking when you're finished.

REMEMBER

Placing tanks near the corner of a room or against a wall can provide more floor support. Filled aquariums can be extremely heavy, so have a contractor inspect your floor where you want to put a large tank if you're unsure.

Keep the following in mind with these different flooring types:

>> **Carpet:** No matter what you do, carpet will be smashed by aquarium stands. The only thing I've ever found that worked is putting a thick flat rug between the tank and the regular carpeting. If you ever move the tank, this buffer helps bring the original carpet back to life with a steam cleaner.

>> **Concrete:** Placing an aquarium on concrete is ideal.

>> **Hardwood:** A good hardwood floor is a great place to put a furniture-type stand. If you use an older stand with four legs, put small rubber furniture leg mats under each leg to protect the floor.

>> **Linoleum:** This type of floor is a disaster waiting to happen because linoleum tends to tear, buckle, and crack over time, particularly if it's subjected to heavy weight.

>> **Tile:** Hard tile is ideal for furniture-type stands. Be careful putting the old stands with four metal legs on tile because tile can easily crack over time.

The weight of larger tanks and stands can damage soft floor coverings, so take this into consideration before making your final choice.

Taking Room Temperature and Its Effects into Consideration

Most aquariums need a stable water temperature. Extreme changes in temperature can lower your pets' immune systems and increase their risk of contracting disease and even cause your fish to die in a tropical tank. Heaters can keep your water temperature high enough to prevent your fish from becoming floating fishcicles. But if you place your aquarium in a room where the temperature is 20 below zero, your heaters are going to go south for the winter and your aquarium is going to be an ice sculpture. The point is, your heaters can only handle so much.

TIP

One way to help with a room that is slightly chilly and maintain heat is to use two heaters in the tank to lessen the load. I always keep an extra heater handy, just in case one fails. (Chapter 6 examines heaters in greater detail.) Furthermore, place aquariums in a room that is comfortable for you on a daily basis and avoid places like unfinished basements and drafty add-on rooms such as an unheated enclosed porch. Don't place your tank or stand directly over central heating or cooling vents either because doing so will change your tank's temperature.

WARNING

Too high of a water temperature can kill your fish. As water temperature rises, the water loses oxygen. After a short period of time in a hot tank, your fish start gasping at the surface and can eventually die of asphyxiation. Extreme temperatures can damage their scales, fins, and other physical aspects as well. One piece of equipment designed to keep water temperature down is a *chiller*, but it can be very expensive.

The most important thing to remember is that your room shouldn't change the temperature of your aquarium more than a few degrees from the norm (normal temperature depends on the species of fish; refer to Chapter 8 for more specific information).

You may be thinking, "But my house is well insulated." And you're probably right, but two things in even the best-insulated homes can cause temperature fluctuations: windows and doors.

Wicked windows

Windows may seem innocent enough, but an aquarium placed near a window is going to have several problems. When normal, direct sunlight shines on an aquarium, the water temperature can reach lethal levels in a period of just a few hours if the windows have thin curtains or open blinds. Heavy drapes and thick blinds can help block out enough light to prevent this problem if you have nowhere else to put your tank. Consider purchasing blackout curtains to block out a majority of the light around your tank. Older windows also tend to be drafty and can cause dramatic changes in your tank's temperature in a short period of time.

REMEMBER

Placing your aquarium near a window may also promote a tremendous overgrowth of algae. I don't mean a little algae — I'm talking about your aquarium looking like a golf course. Getting rid of the stuff can be difficult.

TIP

Keep an eye on your windows for a day during normal sunlight hours to get an idea of just how far and brightly the sun's rays reach inside your windows. Place your aquarium beyond the outermost limits of the sun's potentially lethal grasp. Putting the aquarium in an area with good air circulation and ventilation can help to avoid hot or cold spots in the tank as well.

Deadly doors

Most homes have two types of doors: interior doors that connect rooms and exterior doors that lead outside. Both types can wreak havoc on your aquarium in different ways:

REMEMBER

» Exterior doors can be extremely drafty. Every time someone opens a door in wintertime, cold air seeps in. It doesn't take long for an aquarium to chill under these conditions especially if a door is left accidently open. Place your tank well away from any outside doors to avoid drafts.

» Interior doors may be safe from cold drafts, but they can be deadly if they hit your aquarium. Most doorknobs seem to be at a perfect level to slam into the glass on many tanks or rock the stand leading to spilled water. I've seen many expensive aquariums broken by a door that has hastily flung open. If you must place an aquarium near a door, open the door a few times to make sure that it has plenty of room to safely clear your tank.

High Traffic Areas, Children, and Pets (Spell D-I-S-A-S-T-E-R)

High-traffic spots such as hallways, entranceways, kitchens, and so on aren't good places for your aquarium. *High-traffic areas* are those places in your house where the carpet is constantly dirty or worn. If you have small children and four-legged pets, that could be 99.9 percent of the carpet. Constant movement along the tank's glass also tends to keep many species of fish continually spooked and hiding. Fear leads to stress. Stress leads to disease. Disease leads to death. This is a simple but all too frequent pattern.

TIP

To avoid freaking your fish out all day, place them in a nice quite spot such as a corner in the living room or den. These types of protected spaces give your fish an opportunity to get used to people occasionally moving around them, without overloading them with constant traffic 24 hours a day.

Children are another major problem for aquariums. Children can tend to get a little wild sometimes. If you have children, I haven't told you anything you don't already know. Even if you don't have children living in the house, you may have neighbor kids, grandchildren, or nieces and nephews who come over once in a while. Aquariums can be great learning tools for children, but youngsters need to be reminded that the fish have needs and wants that have to be considered in the overall scheme of things. Check out Chapter 22 to see what you can do with children to teach them about aquariums.

When you have young children in your home, you childproof rooms by locking up chemicals, putting away sharp objects, and hiding anything that can harm them. You need to do the same thing with your aquarium. Place the aquarium where the kids have a hard time getting at it, such as on top of a large cabinet-style stand in an area you're in frequently. Make sure your aquarium is on a solid stand that won't move easily if someone bumps into it. If your family spends most of its time in the family room, that's a great place to have the aquarium so that you can keep a close eye on it when your children are near.

A few examples of childhood play that can be devastating to your aquatic friends include the following:

>> Tossing a ball back and forth in front of the tank (guaranteed to give your fish whiplash)

>> Floating toy boats on top of the aquarium water

>> Practicing finger painting on the tank's glass

Now, if you were a fish, what would you think of all these situations? A fish may likely think that it's about time to check out and visit that great fishbowl in the sky as it's gasping at the UFO in your home. Give your fish a break by teaching your children to respect their aquatic pet's privacy. Don't allow them to tap on the glass with their fingers or any other object. Remind them that fish are like all other animals on earth and need a little bit of relaxation to wind down. But most importantly, allow them to reap the joy and knowledge of your hobby by teaching them a few simple rules in the beginning to avoid disaster later.

REMEMBER

Don't forget about your other pets. Larger dogs can tip over a smaller tank by jumping up and pushing against them. If this is going to be a problem, buy a furniture-style stand or a stand that has a lip around the edge that the aquarium fits snuggly down into. Cats like to jump on aquariums. Make sure there are no shelves or other pieces of furniture near that a cat can use to get on top of the tank.

CHECK WITH YOUR FAMILY BEFORE PLACING IT

Talk with your family members to ensure everyone is copacetic with placing an aquarium in your home, particularly if it's in a common area. If your friends or family are like mine, they actually enjoy all the neat little sounds that an aquarium makes. They may even find them relaxing. But other people may think your little aquatic setup is downright annoying. Serious hobbyists often consider getting rid of the people before the tank, but if that's not practical for you, your placement options may be limited quite a bit.

Contemplating Your Water Source When Placing Your Aquarium

One important thing to remember when placing your aquarium is the availability of a water source. Nobody wants to spend hours of backbreaking work hauling water around. You need water to fill your tank when you first set it up, and you also need to top off your tank from time to time as the water evaporates. And don't forget those weekly water changes. All that water lugging gets old quickly.

TIP

It's best to use a faucet that other family members don't use often so you don't inconvenience them by using the tap all the time. A faucet in a spare bathroom is an excellent place to work from, if one is near your tank.

You can use several different water options to fill your aquarium, including tap water, bottled water, rainwater, natural water from bodies of water such as streams, and well water.

TIP

Make sure that the water you're going to use is free from heavy metals and other hazardous content. For example, if you're using water from an old well or any other source that may contain large amounts of iron and other metals, take a sample to your local water company or university and see if they'll test it for you to make sure that it's safe for not only your own consumption but also for your fish. Obtain a local city water report if possible, in your area. Check out this link for further information: https://ofmpub.epa.gov/apex/safewater/f?p=136:102.

City water has chlorine, but you can remove it using dechlorinator from your local fish store or by letting the water stand in open containers for 24 to 48 hours. If you use bottled water, don't buy distilled because it has had most of its minerals removed. Water from lakes, streams, and rainwater generally isn't a good idea because you don't know what pollutants it contains. City water is usually a safe bet and the best option. Refer to Chapter 12 for more in-depth discussion about water.

Thinking about Other Household Items

You need to keep in mind a few other things when deciding where to place your tank. These sections discuss them in greater detail.

Furniture and space

Make sure you have enough space in your home to add your aquarium without having to sell any furniture. If you do find the need for more space, casually suggest to your partner that the loveseat is looking kind of shabby and needs to be replaced. While your partner is hauling it away, set up your tank. Talk up how great the new aquarium looks and hope your mate doesn't have the heart to make you move it after you've gone through all the trouble of setting it up.

Put your tank in a clear space where people, household pets, and furniture such as recliners, won't constantly jostle it. Providing a clear space makes it much easier to watch your fish and carry out periodic maintenance.

An easier method is to just make sure that you have enough room for the tank you buy. Measure the intended spot carefully so that you know exactly what size tank you can purchase before you buy.

Electrical outlets and TVs

Check for electrical outlets near the place you want to place your tank. Nothing is more frustrating than setting up a tank only to find out that you have nowhere to plug in your aquarium equipment. Make sure that electrical outlets (you'll probably need more than one, or you'll have to use a power strip with a surge protector) are in good working condition and are close to the tank so you don't have extension cords lying around, which can short, look messy, are difficult to clean around, and can cause people to trip. And make sure your outlets are up to code if they look extremely old or ratty. If necessary, get a professional electrician to install a new outlet.

Consider having a ground-fault circuit interrupter (GFCI) installed. A GFCI protects you from electrical shock by monitoring the amount of power going to the plugged-in device. If water gets in the outlet, the GFCI notices the change in current and promptly cuts the power.

The power outlet should be near the aquarium but not directly behind it just in case there is an aquarium or equipment leak. It's important to have a drip loop, which is basically placing the power cords so that they dip below the wall outlet or power strip and then back up to it. Doing so creates a small loop below the plug or power strip so that water can't run into the source of the electricity. (Chapter 6 discusses equipment.)

The effects a large-screen TV can have on your fish are surprising. Constantly flashing lights can be confusing for fish if their tank is too close to the screen. I noticed my friend's fish darting away from one side of the tank constantly due to a flashy and light intense movie. Try to keep your fish at a respectable angle or distance from your television so they can stop believing they're living in a king-sized kaleidoscope or at a drive-in movie.

Overhead lighting

Some interior lights that are installed in the ceilings of homes can be quite bright and can distract you from getting a good view of your fish due to glare. Close overhead lighting can increase the temperature of your tank as well. Place the tank away from direct overhead lighting whenever possible.

Cleaning considerations

Once in a while, you have to do a little cleaning and maintenance on your aquarium. Leave enough room around the tank so that you can easily reach all sides of it without pushing against the tank itself. Trying to squeeze in behind a tank that is too close to the wall is flirting with disaster. Space also protects your home from evaporation.

TIP

Even aquariums with tight-fitting hoods tend to have drips and dribbles every so often. So one way or another, you have to get behind your aquarium at some point. Make sure when you are setting up your tank that you have plenty of space to take care of any problems that may occur. Only use stands that are waterproof in case you have dribbles.

Chapter **4**

The Tank and Stand

The two largest items that you'll purchase for your aquarium system are the tank and the stand. The available styles, shapes, and sizes are endless. The quality of the construction has improved leaps and bounds. Now newer acrylic and glass tanks are much better than the old steel-framed aquariums that were around when the hobby began. Even if you have a very small space to work with, you can find an aquarium that fits perfectly.

Aquarium stands have also come a long way over the years. The old, ugly, heavy iron stands have now been replaced with a wide variety of beautiful cabinets and fancier metal varieties. Aquarium keeping is truly an art form in itself. With all the variety and colors of stands to choose from, you can easily find one to match your style.

This chapter examines two of the main components of aquarium keeping, the tank and the stand. Choosing the correct stand and placing it in a good location is important for success. Here I examine the different types of aquarium tanks and stands so that you can pick the setup best for you.

Buying a Tank: What You Need to Know

The first step in setting up your new aquarium system is purchasing a tank. But before you go out and actually purchase one, take the time to look at a few of the variables that may affect your purchase. Your aquarium has to fit into your individual situation. (Chapter 3 explains different issues you can consider when finding the best spot for your aquarium.) You have to match your tank to its surrounding environment and to any of your special space needs.

TIP

Stop for a moment and think about the purpose of your tank. Are you setting it up in a common area so that everyone in your family can enjoy it? Or do you want to have it in the privacy of your own office or bedroom? A freshwater *community* tank (one with several species in it) may be more suited to family viewing than a *species* tank (one devoted to one species) would be. If that's the case, you don't want to purchase a 2-gallon tank for your living room, because it would be too small for a thriving group of community species. A tank that size wouldn't make a good conversation piece either. For your crowded office, maybe a thin wall-hung tank would be best. I discuss the different types of aquariums in "Examining the Different Types of Aquariums Available" later in this chapter.

Before you place your stand, think about the following considerations. These sections give you a few tips on where to buy your equipment, what you need to consider concerning cost, and what to you need to know about starter kits.

Water is heavy

Take weight into consideration when choosing your aquarium setup. To determine the weight of a proposed aquarium, multiply the total number of gallons by 10 pounds. That's right, a 100-gallon aquarium weighs around *half a ton*, including water, fish, equipment, and decorations.

REMEMBER

This method provides a good, rough estimate of the total weight of an aquarium with the tank, water, rocks, equipment, and decorations all figured in. Here are a few common aquariums and the weight you need to take into consideration on average:

>> 10-gallon tank, 100 pounds

>> 20-gallon tank, 200 pounds

>> 55-gallon tank, 550 pounds

>> 100-gallon tank, 1,000 pounds

>> 125-gallon tank, 1,250 pounds

As you can see, you really need to make sure that your floor can handle the weight of heavier tanks. Chapter 3 helps you consider which floor type is best. If you're unsure, call a contractor. If you rent, check with your landlord because some landlords and rental companies don't allow large aquariums in apartment rentals.

Watching the tendency to overspend

Before you go shopping, check to see how much money you can spend on your hobby, taking into consideration that even though your aquarium is probably the largest piece of fishkeeping equipment you'll ever own (and the one with the largest price tag if you're buying a large tank), the cost of all the other hardware — filters, pumps, gravel, chemicals, and heaters — adds up quickly.

A larger tank is not only more expensive to start with, but it also requires more equipment. Don't purchase a 125-gallon aquarium if doing so leaves you with five bucks to spend on equipment. It's better to purchase a 20-gallon tank and have more than enough money left over for substrate, plants, equipment, fish, and other essentials.

Checking out starter kits

One easy option is to purchase a starter kit. A starter kit is a system-in-a-box that usually contains *most of* the following:

>> Tank

>> Filter

>> Food

>> Hood

>> Lights

DON'T BE NICKEL-AND-DIMED TO DEATH

If you're not careful, you can go broke purchasing extras for your tank. Skip the fancy decorations when you first set it up and use your money instead to purchase the aquarium you really want and the equipment you really need to keep it running properly. Make sure you figure in the price of filters, lights, gravel, chemicals, hoods, plants, air hose, nets, pH test kits, heaters, medications, and of course, your fish — which you'll buy *after* the tank is set up and ready. Chapters 5 and 6 discuss equipment and extras you need.

Aquariums are really a good value in the long term and generally cost quite a bit less than many other expensive hobbies such as skydiving and bungee jumping. The money you invest in a beautiful aquarium now will pay you and your family back with years and years of pleasure.

- » Heater
- » Fish net
- » Thermometer
- » Water conditioner
- » A beginning aquarium book

Not every kit contains exactly the same things, so read the label carefully. If you purchased this kind of starter kit, all you need to buy afterward is gravel and a few plants to get the tank up and running plus a stand (unless you're using furniture instead). Many starter kits don't have gravel, decorations, plants, or stands, so they're not really complete.

Size matters — gauging space requirements

When purchasing an aquarium, make sure you buy one that fits your residence. If your home is small, purchase an aquarium that you can enjoy without cramping your living space. If you find yourself sleeping on the sofa the following week, you probably miscalculated your free bedroom space.

REMEMBER

To avoid space hassles and a significant other's fury, use Table 4-1 to gauge minimum space requirements (average length by width by height) for various sizes of several standard aquarium tanks. These are *minimum* requirements — I don't figure in the space that extra equipment takes up and the room needed to clean around the aquarium.

TABLE 4-1

Space Requirements for Tanks

Tank Volume	Inches Needed
10 gallon	Regular: 20 x 10 x 12
	Long: 24 x 8 x 12
	Hex: 14 x 12 x 18
15 gallon	Regular: 24 x 12 x 12
	Long: 20 x 10 x 18
	Show: 24 x 8 x 16
20 gallon	High: 24 x 12 x 16
	Long: 30 x 12 x 12

Tank Volume	Inches Needed
	Hex: 18 x 16 x 20
25 gallon	Regular: 24 x 12 x 20
29 gallon	Regular: 30 x 12 x 18
30 gallon	Regular: 36 x 12 x 16
	Breeding: 36 x 18 x 12
40 gallon	Long: 48 x 13 x 16
	Breeding: 36 x 18 x 16
45 gallon	Regular: 36 x 12 x 24
	Hex: 22 x 22 x 24
50 gallon	Regular: 36 x 18 x 18
55 gallon	Regular: 48 x 13 x 20
75 gallon	Regular: 48 x 18 x 20
100 gallon	Regular: 72 x 18 x 18
125 gallon	Regular: 72 x 18 x 22
200 gallon	Regular: 84 x 24 x 25

Taking people into consideration

The people living with you are another important part of the type of aquarium you purchase. Face it, your aquarium is going to make some noise, even if it's outfitted with the most up-to-date equipment on the market. Sure, it won't bark, meow, chirp, croak, hiss, or growl, but it probably will do a little bit of bubbling, rattling, and/or humming once in a while.

WARNING

Children are another important factor in considering the type of system you purchase. If you have small tots in the house, a tank full of piranhas will probably go over with your spouse like a lead balloon. A community tank filled with friendly fish such as guppies and platys may be more appropriate for younger children.

Deciding where to buy

You have a few choices when it comes to where you purchase an aquarium. As a general rule, I suggest buying a new tank to avoid problems like leaks when you're setting up your first aquarium, but be aware of other options as well:

>> **Your local pet shop:** This choice is obvious. The advantages of buying from a dealer are numerous. Dealer tanks usually have a warranty of some kind, depending on the store's policy, and are in good condition. If you have any problems with your aquarium, you can often return it for a replacement or a refund. A dealer can also give you advice and help you pick out your equipment and livestock. The drawback of purchasing from a pet shop is that the prices are usually higher than at retail superstores.

WARNING

>> **Retail superstores:** These usually carry a small line of aquarium equipment, but you don't generally find a whole lot of specialty items. The employees are usually trained in the basics of aquariums at best, so you may end up with bad advice on more complicated systems. Also, I find that the quality of livestock in this type of store isn't the greatest (in fact, it's downright scary sometimes!).

>> **Garage sales:** Shopping at garage sales and yard sales is a fun and practical way to purchase used aquariums at rock-bottom prices. But keep in mind that the aquarium is used and may have some problems. Determining if a tank leaks when it's sitting empty in someone's driveway isn't easy, and most garage sale sellers generally don't promise anything.

>> **Classified ad websites and apps:** You can purchase aquariums from a plethora of websites and apps, such as Craigslist, Facebook Marketplace, OfferUp, and LetGo. They can lead you to a nice aquarium at a nice price, although the same reservations about buying used apply. Buying through an ad, however, may give you a chance to see the tank up and running before you purchase it. Always bring someone along if you're buying from a stranger or meet in a public place.

>> **Online stores and fish clubs:** Many good dealers on the Internet sell standard and custom aquariums. Enter "aquariums for sale" into your favorite search engine to get started. Chapter 8 discusses buying fish on the Internet. You should also check with members of local and online fish clubs (like on Facebook) who often sell new and used equipment at reduced prices.

TESTING AND REPAIRING A LEAKER

One way to test an aquarium for leaks is to fill it with water and let it stand on a piece of newspaper for 24 hours. If the newspaper gets wet, the tank leaks (make sure you aren't fooled by condensation drips). You should always test new *and* used tanks for leaks. To repair a leak, dry the tank and remove the old silicone with a safety razor (please be careful!). Gently wipe the area with a soft, clean cloth to remove any oils from your hands to ensure a good seal. Replace the old sealer with new aquarium sealer. Let the sealer dry for 48 hours before you add any water to the tank.

Before you buy a used tank, carefully inspect it for leaks, glass cracks, and worn silicone. Fill it up and see whether it drips if possible. Check to see that the silicone seal (the goopy-looking stuff in the corners and seams) isn't cracked, peeling away, or missing in some areas. A small break in the silicone can cause the aquarium to leak. Look at each individual piece of glass in the tank to ensure that it doesn't have any cracks, large scratches indicating it has been treated roughly, or chips and breaks. A tank that has been stored in an environment where the temperature isn't controlled for a long period of time could have weakened silicone and may leak. If the aquarium has any of these problems, don't buy it.

If you're buying your first aquarium, avoid buying used equipment such as pumps. An old pump could have frayed or worn wires that might pose an electrical hazard or not work at full volume. After you get a comfortable with how your aquarium equipment works, then you may be okay taking a chance on used equipment. Chapter 6 discusses the types of equipment you need.

Examining the Different Types of Aquariums Available

The high-quality aquarium products now offered by manufacturers are quite mind-boggling compared to the old glass aquariums of the '60s and '70s. The original metal frame tanks were heavy and not pleasing to the eye. Fortunately, nonmetallic materials were developed that eventually replaced heavy-metal frames and inadequate seam adhesives. This breakthrough in aquarium construction was a direct result of complaints filed by fishkeeping enthusiasts who demanded better products — ones that could be used for all types of systems. These sections examine your beginning aquarium options.

Glass aquariums

The all-glass aquariums on today's market are becoming the least popular of all available tanks because of their weight and hard corner viewing angles. These tanks are constructed of plate glass and sealed with a nontoxic silicone. The glass in these aquariums is either *tempered*, meaning it's stronger, lighter in weight, and shatters into pieces when it breaks, or *plate*, meaning it's heavier and thicker but only cracks when it breaks.

The frames on glass tanks are usually hard plastic, come in a wide variety of colors, and are glued onto the rim. Glass tanks don't scratch easily and provide a good viewing area because all the walls are flat.

Some of the disadvantages of glass aquariums include the following:

>> **Style-challenged:** They can be formed into a limited number of shapes — basically, rectangles, hexagons, octagons, or squares. If you really want a tank with an unusual shape, you won't find much to please you in the glass department.

>> **Super heavy:** They're also heavy because the glass used in construction gets thicker as the tank gets larger. This can be a real problem if you want a big tank and have weak floors in your home or if you attempt to move the aquarium.

>> **Easily breakable:** Glass aquariums can break or shatter and leave you with a lot of dead fish and a huge mess to clean up.

Some plate glass tanks can be purchased pre-drilled, which means that they have holes drilled in them for equipment and hoses, allowing you to hide hoses and equipment inside a normal cabinet without having to route everything on the outside of the tank. However, pre-drilled tanks can be quite expensive and are intended more for experienced hobbyists. Having drilled holes isn't necessary for any aquarium setup.

CAN I BUILD MY OWN TANK?

Probably not. Building your own glass tank can be very dangerous unless you really know what you're doing. I don't recommend it for inexperienced hobbyists and craftsmen. It's really safer to purchase a tank at a dealer rather than risk building an inferior product that leaks water like a sieve and turns your room into a permanent water display that could put SeaWorld to shame.

Acrylic aquariums

Acrylic tanks have made a big splash in the aquarium marketplace. These light-weight tanks are available in an amazing number of shapes and sizes such as bubble, half spheres, L-shaped, tubular, triangular, and convex. With acrylic, the shape possibilities end only with the designer's creativity. There is an acrylic tank somewhere out there to please almost anyone's personal taste and desire.

Acrylic advantages

There are a few advantages of acrylic:

>> **Lighter than glass:** Acrylic tanks are easier to move and produce fewer hernias. If your aquarium is upstairs, acrylic may give you the option of having a slightly larger tank.

>> **More stylish:** Many acrylic tanks come with colored backgrounds, which can be quite stunning with the proper tank decoration. The modern look of acrylic tanks you just can't find in a standard glass aquarium. You also get more choices in colors and styles to match the interior of your home or office. An acrylic tank gives any room an upscale appearance and generally looks more expensive than glass tanks.

>> **Much stronger:** It takes an exceptional blow with a blunt instrument to shatter an acrylic aquarium.

>> **Cool shapes:** Acrylic can be shaped into cool bubbles, tube shapes, and other unusual but fantastic-looking aquariums. You aren't stuck looking at four hard corners like glass tanks.

Acrylic disadvantages

Acrylic does have a few drawbacks:

>> **Distortion:** Unfortunately, acrylic tanks have small amounts of visual distortion because of the way the material is bent during construction. They're generally made out of one large piece of acrylic that is heated and bent to shape; this method produces a seamless look that's really outstanding. These transparent corners allow you to view your fish from almost any angle with ease. *Good news:* The visual distortion doesn't bother everyone. Look at a filled acrylic tank at a fish dealer and decide if that material is right for you.

>> **More expensive:** Acrylic aquariums are generally more expensive than their glass counterparts, but they're well worth the investment. These tanks are top of the line as far as quality and workmanship and beauty are concerned. If you have the budget to afford one, you won't be disappointed.

WARNING

» **Scratching:** Acrylic aquariums are quite easily scratched. Be careful when cleaning with rough algae pads, for example, to avoid leaving scratches or smears. Moving gravel around can also damage the surface, and pay close attention when you're moving or adding decorations to the aquarium. If you do purchase one and scratch it, never fear. You can purchase good scratch remover kits available through your local pet shop or the Internet that can handle most simple blemishes caused by carelessness.

Plastic aquariums (bowls and small tanks)

Plastic tanks and small glass fish bowls can usually be found collecting dust on superstore shelves. These types of aquariums are very inexpensive. Not surprisingly, they have more serious drawbacks than any other type of aquarium and really aren't worth purchasing. Plastic tanks are now almost obsolete (kind of like the computer I purchased last year) and for several good reasons:

» **Scratching:** They scratch easily, and there is really no way to repair the scratches.

» **Discoloration:** They often take on a yellowish cast as they age.

» **Limited sizes:** They're available only in small sizes (usually between 2 and 5 gallons), which doesn't provide enough water volume and surface area to insure a biologically stable environment.

» **Distortion:** They suffer major distortion problems due to their odd shapes.

» **Prone to melting:** They can buckle when they come in contact with any heat source, including their own hood and light! Whoever designed these tanks needs to have her little (and I do mean little) gray cells examined.

Often parents buy small glass bowls and tanks under 10 gallon for small children to get them started in the hobby, which isn't a smart decision because these tanks are unstable biologically due to their limited size. They aren't made to hold good equipment, so bad filtration, poor water quality, and sick fish are often the result. Instead, buy your children a 10- or 20-gallon tank to get them started on the right track.

Rimless tanks

Rimless aquarium tanks are made of thicker glass so you don't need a thick frame to support the tank. These tanks have beveled edges, clear joints, and use low iron glass for almost perfect clarity and viewing. They're beautiful, but they come at a much higher price than a standard tank.

Considering Different and Unusual Aquarium Styles

Along with different materials used for aquarium construction, there are also many different styles of construction as well. If you don't want a simple box-shaped aquarium, you have other options to choose from, which I discuss in the following sections.

Wall-mounted aquariums

Acrylic wall-mounted tanks are mounted on your home and don't require a stand. They mount on a wall stud just like a picture or flatscreen TV. These tanks are great if you have small children at home. You simply hang the tank out of their reach, so they can't pull the tank off the wall. Wall tanks are also handy if you don't have a lot of floor space but still want an aquarium. These tanks are so beautiful I'd want one even if I lived in a 12,000-square-foot mansion, which I don't.

Wall-mounted aquariums come in a variety of sizes, are often less than 6 inches wide, and don't require a stand. These tanks also offer a good choice of scenic backgrounds and frame colors. When you look at your wall-mounted aquarium, it's kind of like looking through a window into an underwater menagerie.

Feeding your aquatic pets in your portrait tank is a breeze because these tanks have a feeding hole and in-tank access through an opening at the top. Many tanks come with the hardware to hang them. Remember that these tanks have a small surface area and are thin, so you won't be able to keep huge fish or large amounts of fish in them.

Wall-mounted fish bowls are also available, but I don't recommend them due to their lack of filtration and tiny water volume.

In-wall tanks

These tanks are actually mounted inside your wall and are supported by wall studs (see Figure 4-1). If you want to put up one of these models, find a contractor to install it properly. Make sure to ask the contractor to run the lights to a light switch in your room so that you can simply turn the tank on and off with the flick of a switch. In-wall tanks can be specially made to fit a particular width of wall. Some standard-sized tanks are also available, depending on the homeowner's requirements.

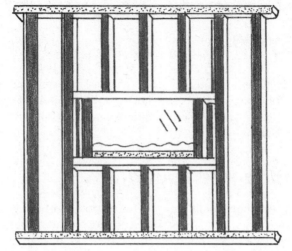

© John Wiley & Sons, Inc.

FIGURE 4-1:
Building an aquarium into your wall is one way to solve the problem of not enough space.

Wall tanks aren't hard to clean because access is left open on one side of the wall, or the top trim piece can be installed to flip open. Follow manufacturer's instructions.

Furniture aquariums

If you would like to combine a piece of furniture with an aquarium, then a furniture aquarium may be just for you. These tanks are built into pieces of furniture such as coffee tables, headboards, end tables, nightstands, lamps, and clocks. Often these dual-purpose tanks can be expensive, but are well worth the money if you can spare it. Use caution when purchasing one of these tanks if you have small toddlers in the house who can easily break or fall onto them.

Tower aquariums

Tower aquariums are simply tanks that are built into the shape of a tall column or tower. These tanks are great for corner spaces and add a contemporary look to any room. The disadvantages to towers is that they can be expensive, and it may be difficult to find tall enough plants to make them look realistic without buying specially made artificial tall plants from the manufacturer. Fast swimming fish don't do well in this type of tank.

Indoor pond barrels

Indoor barrels (often used on patios) can make miniature versions of an outdoor coldwater pond inside your home or on your porch. You need to be careful when considering the overall weight of a small indoor barrel. Consult with a contractor to see if your floors can withstand the strain.

All-in-one tanks

All-in-one tanks are great for beginning hobbyists because they contain everything needed to get started. These systems keep you from having to match filters and other equipment to the tank, because the choices are already made for a balanced system. The entire kit has been designed to work together. These systems have a unified design and are easy to maintain.

The downside to these systems is that failed or add-on equipment can be difficult to replace or add because the system is designed for specific fits. These systems tend to be more expensive than standard models.

Betta tanks and water gardens

In the old days, Betta tanks resembled a glass version of my morning cereal bowl. Today, many new options are available. You can purchase Betta tanks with built-in dividers for keeping two Bettas separated and models with cascading water to house many Bettas. The problem with these tanks is they're extremely small.

A few models of water garden tanks are available that hold one fish and also grows herbs on top for cooking. The drawback to these systems is that they're small and can be difficult to clean properly.

Special tanks from the pros

There are tanks for all shapes and sizes of household living. Tanks can be bought in the shape of a triangle and ones that fit into corners. Companies will build any tank you want, including ones that are large enough to scuba dive in if you happen to live in a mansion and are too lazy to go to any ocean or lake to dive. If you're like me, you'll dream about this tank the rest of your life knowing it's out of your budget range no matter how many garage sales you have.

Bio cubes

Bio cubes are as the names suggests shaped like a cube and come in sizes that usually range from 16 to 32 gallons. Most setups feature superior LED lighting for a dramatic effect. Generally they're used for small saltwater reef or other marine setups, though not all kits include everything you need, like a heater or protein skimmer.

Pre-drilled overflow tanks

Pre-drilled overflow tanks are complicated for the beginner and use a sump system. A sump is a second tank that is placed below the main tank (usually in or behind the stand) and is fed by gravity. The water is processed along the way by equipment such as a trickle filter in the sump and then returned to the main tank. This allows for a clutter-free main aquarium. Look into this kind only after you become an experienced hobbyist.

Choosing the Right Tank

There are many issues you need to address when you're preparing to actually purchase your aquarium. Size, water volume, and shape have a lot to do with the type of aquatic creatures you can actually put in it. Many different tank sizes and styles are available. If you start off with a tank that meets the needs of your individual project or system (a large tank if you want a huge community of fish, for example), you have one foot in the door of success. Consider the following factors when buying your aquarium.

Tank size

If you plan on setting up a freshwater system, purchase a 20-gallon tank to make sure your new fish have an adequate area to provide stable water conditions. A smaller tank is harder to work with, can turn your fish into instant sardines, and will eventually bring you disappointment and heartache. Smaller aquariums are more prone to foul water conditions, which can damage your fish's health. A small tank also doesn't leave much room for adding larger filtration systems, decorations, or extra fish.

TIP

Always buy the largest tank that your budget and space limitations allow within your experience range because increased surface area means better overall biological stability. A large surface area provides good oxygen absorption and carbon dioxide exchange.

Small tanks can be a real problem if you have a power or equipment failure. Due to the small amount of water the tank holds, the temperature and water conditions can drop and deteriorate very quickly. An extended period of lost filtration (usually after several hours depending on your aquarium size) can also foul the water to lethal proportions.

Tank shape

Although having an oddly shaped aquarium is cool, be aware that a few drawbacks go along with these tanks. The shape of an aquarium helps determine the amount of oxygen its water contains.

Vital gas exchange (carbon dioxide for oxygen) occurs at the water surface. A tall, thin tank, such as a tower aquarium, with a small water-surface area, has less gas exchange going on than a shorter tank with a longer, and therefore larger, surface area.

Another factor to take into consideration is that odd-sized tanks, especially if they're really tall and narrow, can be hard to clean or decorate without scuba gear and a body shaped like a pencil. There may even be areas near the bottom that are totally unreachable. You may also find yourself having a hard time locating equipment such as filters and hoods to fit a tank that isn't a standard size if the original part happens to break. (Even if you do find a good match, it probably costs twice as much as the same piece does for a standard-sized tank.)

Carrying capacity

The *carrying capacity* is simply the total number of fish you can keep in your aquarium safely without them going belly up. If you choose to buy a tank that is very tall and narrow, you can't keep as many fish in it as you can in a tank with a larger surface area. It's as simple as that. I'll say it one more time: If you get a fancy tank that has a small surface area, don't count on having a whole bunch of fish.

Picking the Right Stand

Selecting a good aquarium stand can be just as important as picking the right aquarium. A stand needs to be sturdy and strong and look cool at the same time. The one thing that you *don't* want to do is use Granny's antique table as an aquarium stand, because any unforeseen water leaks will quickly ruin that heirloom. A heavy tank can warp the wood on your regular household furniture too. It's always best to use a manufactured aquarium stand built to support a tank's weight and designed to be perfectly level.

Make sure your aquarium fits its stand correctly. If the edge of the tank hangs over the stand, the stand is too small and eventually can cause the aquarium to warp, leak, or break.

Manufactured stands are generally made out of particle board, iron, steel, or hardwood such as maple or oak. Most of these materials make great stands, so it's just a matter of individual preference as to which one you decide to buy. (Okay, okay, I give you a few hints: Just read on.)

Wooden cabinet stands

Stands that include a built-in wooden cabinet are enclosed on the bottom so that you can hide equipment and hoses that generally spoil the overall look of your aquarium system. Chemicals, test kits, nets, and other paraphernalia can be conveniently stored behind closed doors.

Such a cabinet also allows you to buy a bunch of expensive aquarium junk and hide it from your spouse. The only problem with wooden stands is that they can warp under extreme weight if a softer wood is used (placing tanks on it that are too large and hang over the sides), and they tend to bend if they become wet. Make sure that the aquarium you choose matches the stand that you buy to avoid these problems.

But despite the drawbacks, wooden cabinet stands are one of the best stands that you can buy because they look good, will not tip over easily, and often contain shelves for storing items. A good hardwood stand will have a polyurethane finish.

Angle and wrought iron stands

You have two choices with iron stands:

>> *Angle iron stands* are welded together and have a bulky look to them. They'd look great in a medieval castle. Angle iron stands can also leave nasty marks on your floor (if water gets on the metal and then sits stagnant on the floor under the stand) or carpet (the weight of the tank pushed onto small legs instead of spread out over the entire length of a cabinet stand, can leave indentations in the carpet that are almost impossible to remove).

>> *Wrought iron stands* are made of thinner metal than angle iron and are a little bit fancier.

I've always found that no matter which one you buy that they always have an unfinished look to them and rust if undetected water leaks onto them.

Aluminum stands

Aluminum stands are made to withstand great amounts of weight, are light-weight, are easy to assemble, and are pretty much waterproof. Many companies make these made to order, so you can choose your style, add shelves to store your equipment, and get the exact look that will suit your style. These can be more costly than other stands, but they're well worth the few extra dollars that you'll spend.

Do-it-yourself stands

You can purchase a few stands and assemble them easily with a few household tools. The pieces are usually made of pressboard and include at least one shelf. These stands aren't as strong as manufactured ones and may warp or buckle if they get wet.

TIP

One option is to head down to the hardware store, buy some sturdy hardwood lumber, such as oak, and build an aquarium stand yourself. You may find out that a homemade stand costs as much as or more than a manufactured one. But if you have the know-how, an interesting idea, cool tools, and the energy to turn off the TV and head out to the garage, go for it. Make sure the stand you make is firm enough to support the weight of the tank and is level. You can test the stand by adding books or other heavy materials to it. Add enough books to equal the total weight of the aquarium that will be sitting on it (see "Size matters — gauging space requirements" earlier in this chapter for aquarium weight estimation).

Material-based stands

Material-based stands are made of any man-made material that isn't metal or hardwood. Examples include fiberboard and acrylic stands. Fiberboard stands often come damaged from shipping and can be a real pain to assemble. They're probably the weakest of all the stands. This material can fall apart if it gets too wet.

Bow-front stands

A bow-front stand has a semicircular shape in the front to properly support bow-front shaped tanks (tanks that are convex in the front). I personally love the shape of these stands, but it all comes down to personal choice. A bow-front stand tends to have a little less storage underneath than a standard rectangular one.

Moving an Aquarium

Never try to move an aquarium all by yourself, no matter how small it is. Any aquarium should always be lifted by a minimum of two people. You can cause yourself physical injury, and damage the silicone, walls, and frame of the tank if you attempt to haul your tank around by yourself.

TIP

A good way to get help moving an aquarium is to put on a dirty apron, throw some flour on yourself, call your couch potato neighbors, and tell them you want them to try out an exciting new recipe. When they arrive, tell them that your aquarium is blocking the way to the food supply. (Works every time.)

REMEMBER

When you're ready to move your tank, make sure to unplug all equipment and then remove it from the aquarium. Don't remove the heater until a cool-down period of at least 15 minutes to avoid shattering it. Fill a plastic bucket with water from the aquarium and place the fish in the bucket. Drain the rest of the water. Before you lift the aquarium, remove any large rocks or other heavy decorations, which can shift positions and break the glass.

Never lift your tank by grabbing the top of the frame. Lifting an aquarium by its top frame can damage and break the sealer or glass, eventually causing water leaks. The proper way to lift an aquarium is to place your hands (and your hungry neighbors' hands) beneath the bottom corners of the tank.

Chapter **5**

Aquascaping Your Aquarium: What to Add and Not Add in Your Tank

A *quascaping* simply means decorating your aquarium with different types of rock, wood, plants, substrate, and other objects. Arranging the gravel, sand, other aquarium floor coverings, and various available objects can be fun and gives you a good chance to show off your personal creative talents. I can think of no greater joy than creating a pleasing arrangement of rocks, plants, and *substrate* (material that covers the bottom on your tank) for my fish to enjoy. Your fish will appreciate a proper setup as well.

Designing the inside of your tank can be one of the most enjoyable aspects of the aquarium hobby. Imagine beautiful plants swaying gently in the water as colorful fish dash playfully between shimmering rocks and uniquely shaped pieces of wood. What an exciting sight! Your aquarium is your own little personal aquatic world that is just waiting to be shaped into an amazing underwater scene by your creativity.

But although aquascaping, also referred to as *gardenscaping*, can be a real blast, certain types of substrates, rocks, and wood are suitable only for specific aquarium setups. You need to know what to buy before you begin randomly throwing things into your aquarium. This chapter can help you make good choices that will keep your fish happy and healthy.

Many hobbyists choose to set up heavily planted tanks with few fish. Others prefer a simplistic layout with many aquatic species. The choice is yours, of course. If you use your imagination and follow a few simple decorating rules, you can quickly realize that the possibilities are endless.

REMEMBER

You want to create an environment that is good for your fish and pleasing to the eye as well.

Taking Clues from Your Fish's Natural Environment

The first thing to do when aquascaping any aquarium is to take a close look at the native environment of the fish you're planning to keep in your tank. For example, freshwater fish are much happier and healthier in an aquarium full of plants, driftwood, and rock than they are in one with coral and shells — which you generally use in a marine setup. Different types of systems have different aquascaping elements.

WARNING

The following list gives you a few good ideas about which substrates and decorations are most often used in different types of systems:

>> **Freshwater community tank:** Pebbles, igneous and shale rocks, artificial or live plants such as anubias or sword plant, artificial plants, and driftwood with standard fish shop gravel for substrate

>> **Freshwater Amazon rain forest aquarium:** Pea gravel, bogwood, sword plants, cabomba, and hairgrass

>> **Freshwater Amazon rain forest acid pool:** Mixture of pea gravel and coal, bogwood, fanwort, and milfoil

>> **Freshwater Southeast Asia aquarium:** Aquatic soil and silver sand, small stones and pebbles, bamboo, and hygrophila

>> **Sandy river aquarium:** Fine gravel and silver sand, shale rocks, curio type wood, and cryptocoryne

>> **Brackish Costal Stream from Central America:** Pea gravel, silver sand, driftwood, stratified rocks, vallisneria, and cabomba

>> **Marine community tank:** Live rock (rock that has invertebrates attached), aquacultured or man-made dry rock, and dolomite with coral sand and live sand (pre-cultured sand that contains biological organisms for filtration) for substrate, algae, such as grape plant, for decoration, and invertebrates such as anemones and tubeworms

>> **Marine coral reef:** Aquacultured or man-made dry rock, coral sand, live rock, clam shells, live coral, and tubeworms

Getting the Lowdown on Substrates

Substrates come in many different shapes and sizes to suit the needs of each type of aquarium. You can find substrates in grades from fine to coarse and in different shapes such as smooth or chipped. The actual size of substrates can often vary from vendor to vendor, so for the sake of this chapter, I use the following terms:

>> *Fine* gravel is small like sand.

>> *Medium* gravel is what is found in most prepackaged bags at retail stores.

>> *Coarse* gravel is similar in size to a dime.

The substrate you put into your aquarium plays an extremely important role in its overall biological cycle. In time, beneficial bacteria start growing on top of and throughout the substrate bed and help break down waste in the aquarium water. Substrate is also quite useful for anchoring live plants and for holding down various types of artificial plants, live plants, and decorations. Some species of fish enjoy burrowing through substrate, so keep that in mind as well. Some fish actually sift the substrate through their gills, so make sure your species match the substrate size, so they don't choke on particles that are too small.

Choosing the proper substrate gives you a good start on maintaining a healthy aquatic system for your fish. So, you're probably wondering how to find your way through this substrate mess. Well, read on.

Starting with the basics: Gravel, aqua soil, and fluorite

Many different types of substrate for your aquarium include the following:

Gravel

Gravel is composed of quartz or other lime-free minerals and is chemically inert. *Manufactured* gravel is usually the best bet for a freshwater or brackish tank. It's easily cleaned and widely available in pet stores and supercenters by the bag or the pound. Gravel also comes in many different colors and levels of shininess.

Some gravels are better choices than others. Most manufactured gravel is lime-free (so it doesn't change the water chemistry by raising the pH and hardening the aquarium water) and very inexpensive, which makes it one of the most popular substrates.

Of course, gravel is a completely inanimate substance and doesn't provide any type of nutrition for living aquarium plants. So, if you decide to use live plants in your freshwater or brackish setup, you have to supply extra nutrition for them by using plant plugs or liquid food. (Chapter 16 explains all that.)

Aqua soil

Aqua soil is rich in nutrients and organic acid and is good for growth in an aquarium with live plants. It's also good long term because it doesn't tend to disintegrate and carries a pH between 6.7 and 7.0.

Fluorite

Fluorite is a clay gravel with pores in it. This substrate is good for any aquarium, but it's often used in planted tanks.

Thinking about pH with your substrates

Putting the right substrate in an aquarium setup is just as important as providing the correct water conditions. One important point to remember is that some substrates can affect the pH of your aquarium water, so make sure to buy the correct type for the species that you own (if in doubt, check with your local dealer on what substrate works best for the fish and plants you are going to choose). Many live plants also have requirements in gravel size, so check with your dealer to find out what is right for the species you plan on putting in your tank. Refer to the previous section, "Taking Clues from Your Fish's Natural Environment" for more information.

For example, marine dolomite raises the pH of aquarium water to an alkaline level, and therefore is unsuitable for most freshwater tanks that contain fish who prefer more neutral pH levels. If you put dolomite in your freshwater tank, your fish will do the backstroke permanently. Standard aquarium gravel doesn't affect the water's pH, and therefore isn't suitable for a marine setup that requires a consistently higher pH level.

TIP

If you're not sure how much calcareous material (such as snail shells and sea-shells) a substrate contains, perform this simple test: Add a few tablespoons of vinegar to the test pile of substrate and if it has calcareous (that is, containing calcium) material, it will fizz. If it fizzes, don't put it in your freshwater tank, or you'll end up with hard alkaline water.

Crushed coral (pieces of dead coral gathered from coral beaches) and shells raise your water's pH values as dolomite does and shouldn't be used in a freshwater setup (with exceptions like African cichlids who like the higher pH and hardness produced by coral).

Knowing which substrates to avoid

Get all substrate materials from a reputable fish dealer so that you know that it's pure.

WARNING

No matter which substrate you choose for your aquarium, make sure that it's safe for all the fish in your tank. Sharp edges on gravel can damage your fish's body. Jagged surfaces can be especially injurious to bottom-dwelling species that continually dig in the substrate. If your bottom-dwellers look like dartboards, check your substrate carefully and remove any pieces that look like they have sharp edges.

Never use marbles or glass flakes

Several types of familiar items sometimes found in a beginner's freshwater aquarium aren't really suitable for a fish's natural environment. Never use marbles, glass flakes, or other such materials to cover the bottom of any aquarium. Marbles are quite large and allow debris to become trapped between their surfaces, which can eventually lead to water fouling and diseased fish. Meanwhile, glass flakes are dangerous because they can have sharp edges that can damage the skin and gills of your fish.

Stay away from disco gravel

Brightly colored or neon gravels take away from the natural beauty of your fish and should be avoided if it all possible. Neon gravel tends to make your fish look like they're in a made-for-TV movie about a bad night on a disco floor. Neon gravel also tends to reflect a lot of unnecessary light upward into the water, which can be an annoyance to your fish and cause their colors to look washed out.

Keep an aquarium's colors simple and natural looking for the best results. You can get away with a few cool plastic decorations such as treasure chests and scuba divers if your heart is set on those items, but shocking-pink gravel is too much of an eyestrain for both you and your fish (if you wake up one morning to find your fish sporting sunglasses, you know you need to tone down your gravel). Neon gravels may also keep your fish from spawning and make them shy away and hide in corners.

Being aware of gravel size and the perils of sand

Choose the size of your gravel carefully to avoid water fouling. Avoid the larger-shaped materials because they allow food and waste to fall between the pieces, where they can cause serious water problems in a short time because they're hard to vacuum out and reduce water flow. If you use an undergravel filter (refer to Chapter 6), choose a medium-size substrate (the size of regular bagged aquarium gravels) so that the plastic plates don't get clogged with gravel that is too fine. If using sand, a hang-on-tank power filter would be a better choice.

REMEMBER

Gravel with a particle size of ⅛ inch works best for most setups.

Larger granules also have a cumulatively smaller surface area because of their shape and don't allow space for the growth of the proper bacteria for biological filtration. In other words, if you think you can break a window at 10 feet with a piece of your aquarium gravel, then it's too large for your tank and might be better used to pave your driveway.

TECHNICAL STUFF

Small-grained substrates such as sand quickly clog the water flow in your aquarium if they slip down into the undergravel filter plate and can subsequently cause a rise in waste. If you decide to use sand in your aquarium, lay it down in a very thin layer, have a mesh plate beneath it to stop it from falling through into the filter, or use a filtration system more suitable to sand like a canister filter that has the impeller farther back in the water flow path.

TIP

If you can't find the right size of substrate at your local pet store, either order some on the Internet or wait until it becomes available from your dealer. A little bit of patience can definitely save you many headaches in the future.

Adding new substrate to your system

Before adding gravel to a freshwater system, clean it thoroughly by rinsing it under fresh water. As you clean, carefully check for and remove defects such as extremely large clumps, foreign matter, and sharp pieces in the gravel.

The amount of substrate required for a freshwater tank varies not only with the size of the aquarium, but also with the type of filtration used:

>> If you have an undergravel filter, you need a 2- to 3-inch layer of substrate in order to create a proper bacterial bed.

>> If you're not using an undergravel filter, use only an inch of substrate to cover the bottom of the tank.

>> If you plan on using live plants, you may need to add a bit more substrate to make sure that the plants stay anchored and don't float up to the top of the tank.

On average, a standard, rectangular aquarium needs about a pound and a half of substrate per gallon of water. It should be obvious that this rule doesn't work for a tank 2 inches wide and 18 feet tall. You'd end up with a column of gravel that would look great as a pillar on your front porch. Use common sense when adding gravel depending on your tank's shape.

Slope the gravel by making it slightly higher in the back or on one side so that debris will tumble down and collect toward the front glass. Sloping also makes vacuuming and cleaning easier; it also creates a more natural habitat appearance. A few well-placed rocks or plants can help to keep the slope from flattening out as it slowly slides forward.

Using established substrate

You can add established substrate that already has good bacteria if you have a trusted friend or dealer who can supply it. Using established substrate also helps speed up the nitrogen cycle in the tank.

Considering Rocks, Wood, and Artificial Plants

Using rocks, wood, and artificial plants is a great way to add a natural-looking environment to your aquarium. Normal, everyday rocks that come from a quarry are generally used for freshwater setups. Rocks and hardwoods also provide hiding and spawning areas for your fish, and you can easily find artificial plastic or silk plants at most retail pet stores to add that realistic touch to your aquarium if you don't want to use live plants. These sections give you some more insight into your options. (Refer to Chapter 16 for more information about live plants.)

Whatever you choose is up to you. Decide what's best for your particular lifestyle, budget, and aquatic species. Remember, plan before you buy.

Rocks for freshwater tanks

Rocks are a great way to break up the total bottom space into individual territories. Establishing territories often prevents fighting among fish. Squabbles often break out during spawning or feeding times. Some individual fish may also be more aggressive than others, so having a few rocks in your aquarium can provide shelter if needed never hurts. However, make these territories temporary and change them around periodically to keep boundaries on the move.

You can purchase several varieties of rocks including granite at your local aquarium store that are safe to put into any tank. These rocks are pre-cleaned and won't crumble. You can also pick up a little slate while you're at the store. Rocks such as slate, granite, and red lava rock don't change the water conditions in your aquarium and promote a pleasing and natural layout. You can also find worn rocks along riverbanks and streams. Make sure you thoroughly clean any rocks you find by boiling them in hot water and allowing them to dry in the sun before using them.

When adding rocks to your tank, make sure that you try to distribute them throughout the substrate. Although adding rock is rarely a problem, your glass can become stressed and prone to cracks if you pile a very heavy load of rocks on one side of the tank. Natural riverbeds have small rocks strewn around the bottom and small clusters of larger rocks on the sides.

Wood for a freshwater tank

Wood is a wonderful way to add a natural look to your home aquarium. Most retail fish stores sell driftwood, branches, and small hollow logs. They may be real wood that has been sealed or artificial pieces that usually look as good as the real thing. In today's market the choices seem almost endless.

Keeping wood from floating

If you haven't bought a pre-sealed piece of wood from a retail store and have found some nice-looking driftwood, you may run into a floating problem. Nothing is more aggravating or unsightly than a big chunk of wood floating all over your aquarium. Plus, floating chunks of wood may cause aquarium and equipment damage and put dents in your fish, which won't make your fish happy. You can fix it in some cases, so don't toss that beautiful piece out simply because it's bobbing to the top of the water.

Here are a few examples of different types of wood available:

» **Bogwood:** *Bogwood,* which is one of the most popular types of wood for the home aquarium, is discolored due to tannins found in the bog from which it came. The tannins aren't harmful and will turn the aquarium water a tea color. Bogwood is often used in Amazon setups, but if used in a standard setup, the discoloration can be kept to a minimum with water changes.

» **Mopani:** This wood originates from the African Mopani tree and often has a gnarled appearance. It's very hard and heavy and is good for reducing pH and softening hard water.

» **Redmoor:** Redmoor has a reddish tint and a gnarled appearance. It should be presoaked to make sure that it sinks to the bottom of the tank.

» **Rosewood root:** This wood is very thick and resembles the roots of a mangrove tree.

WARNING

Avoid using any type of evergreen wood in your aquarium due to the large amount of resins. Don't use willow because it rots quickly.

REMEMBER

If your driftwood tends to float, you have a few options:

» **Pre-soak it in water until it's saturated.** Saturated wood usually stays on the bottom of the tank.

» **Anchor the wood.** Anchoring wood keeps it from floating or being knocked around by the fish in your tank. Use an aquarium-safe silicone sealant when anchoring. Consider these two choices:

- Attach it to a rock or piece of thin slate. Try this out if wood still floats after being submerged for 24 hours.

- Use plastic suction cups to attach driftwood to a rock in your aquarium. Just add the cups to the wood using aquarium-safe silicone. You can buy suction cups at most hardware and aquarium stores.

If all else fails, remove the wood and look for another good piece that is less buoyant.

TIP

Don't lean rocks against the back glass of the aquarium, because doing so can cause *dead areas* on the rear surface. These tightly enclosed areas don't allow for proper water circulation in the tank and will contribute to uneven heating and water fouling.

Buying wood

Although driftwood is beautiful and helps create interesting scenes in your aquarium, it can be extremely expensive if you buy the stuff from the retail store. If you're on a budget, you have the other options that I mention in this chapter. Any wood not manufactured for aquarium use should be cleaned properly before use. The best way to do so is to boil the wood in water for a couple of hours. This process also removes most tannins and helps the wood become saturated so it will sink to the bottom.

If you do want to buy your own wood, you still don't have to break the bank to do so. I've found that local woodworker's shops often carry small pieces of driftwood at much more reasonable prices. Other good places to check for driftwood are second-hand shops and yard sales. Often people have a piece that they picked up while on vacation sitting around for years just taking up space and then decide to sell it for cheap once they tire of storing it.

Safely sealing wood

Because several types of wood (*bogwood,* for example) contain tannins that produce acidic conditions, not all woods are suitable for every type of system. Bogwood lends itself best to systems that contain species that prefer soft conditions that are slightly acidic.

TIP

If you're not sure how a particular piece or type of wood will affect your aquarium conditions, the safest thing to do is to seal it with polyurethane varnish. Use at least three coats of this sealer, allowing each coat to dry before applying the next. The varnish keeps wood from releasing any products that can affect your water conditions. You can seal an interesting piece of wood from the wild with polyurethane varnish as well.

Plastic plants

The appearance and variety of artificial aquarium plants have really improved over the years. You can easily find plastic plants in all different colors and sizes to suit your aquarium size and layout. If you don't want to crowd the appearance of your tank, buy small plants for the front of the tank and larger plants for the back, just like you would for live plants.

Many artificial plants are now manufactured with attachments such as caves and rocks. These types of decorations may incorporate hanging gardens, substrate caves, and interesting bundles that are bound together in large groups. Most of the time, these combo decorations don't cost much more than single plastic plants.

Artificial plants do have the following advantages:

>> **Are easy to clean:** If you have algae problems or water that is accidentally fouled, you can clean plastic plants by running warm water over them and then gently wiping them with a moist cloth. That little sprayer attachment on your sink works wonders for this job as well.

>> **Are easy to care for:** Many people don't have a lot of extra time to spend trying to keep live plants in good condition, so plastic plants are a great substitution if you're constantly on the go. Artificial plants don't require sunlight, so if you have a busy schedule, you don't have to worry about the amount of light they receive. This is especially helpful if you don't have timer-based lighting that turns your lights on and off automatically at pre-set intervals.

>> **Last forever:** Artificial plants don't die or affect the chemistry of your tank. Dead plants can make a mess quickly, so plastic plants are a saving grace to many. Young children often benefit from use of plastic plants because they can devote their time to learning how to care for their fish first. All artificial plants tend to show wear in time, but most will last years.

>> **Aren't edible:** Plastic plants can't be easily eaten or torn by more aggressive species of fish. Nothing is more heartbreaking than to have your beautifully planted tank destroyed by your beloved aquatic pets. If you have species that are natural nibblers or havoc seekers, consider artificial plants so that you don't have to purchase new live ones on a regular basis, which can quickly get expensive.

>> **Are easy to move:** Artificial plants can be easily moved around you clean or redecorate your tank. Just gently remove them from the substrate by the base and don't worry about tearing the leaves or damaging the plants. Most artificial plants have a hard-plastic base that aids in keeping them under the gravel.

>> **Have a wide variety:** You have many more choices of colors and sizes available if you use artificial plants because not all fish stores carry live plants on a regular basis.

On the flipside, artificial plants do have these disadvantages:

>> **Can look fake:** Poor quality plants can look fake and ruin the look of your tank. Always buy the best quality plants that your budget will allow.

>> **Expensive:** Artificial decorations can cost more than the real thing.

>> **Fish may not like them:** Many species that like to nibble on plants won't like your artificial ones. Furthermore, artificial plants don't aid in chemical filtration or reduce algae like live ones do.

Contemplating Other Aquarium Decorations

Okay, I have to admit that I've been tempted once or twice to take a few frog statues, oversized rocks, and other decorations out of our yard and put them in an aquarium. But this isn't really a good practice. These sections guide you about which other decorations are suitable (or not) for your aquarium.

Keeping safety first

A wide array of decorations is available for you to add to your aquarium. Your best bet for safe decorations is to purchase pieces from a reputable aquarium dealer or other retail store. I can't emphasize this important point enough. Unsafe decorations can kill your fish, ruin your aquarium conditions, and cost you a lot of money and heartache.

WARNING

Stuff from your yard often contains all sorts of parasites and other nasty things that can cause disease in your tank and foul the water. And it may not be safe to use non-aquarium rocks, wood, and plastic sunflowers for standard aquarium use because many contain harmful dyes and paints or fall apart once they sit in water. Despite the fact that the small rotting wagon wheel would make a great centerpiece in your 250-gallon cichlid tank, it's not worth the trouble.

WARNING

Statuettes and toys that you find around the house may contain internal parts made of metal, which can cause destruction in a tank. Dyes and other surface materials can produce ill effects on freshwater fish and other species.

Eyeing plastic divers and other oddities

Plastic divers (see Figure 5-1), dead pirates, bobbing turtles, treasure chests, mermaids, sunken ships that bubble, castles, nasty-looking skeletons, and mutant oysters may be fine and dandy in the safety department (except some do have sharp edges!), but you need to *exercise a little control* when buying these items or your aquarium may end up looking like a scene from *Toy Story*.

Manufactured decorations sold in aquarium shops are quite safe for freshwater tanks, but they tend to become a little unsightly if you cram your tank with lots of them and will turn your naturally behaving fish into crazy toddlers in a heartbeat.

FIGURE 5-1:
This type of piece won't help your fish get in the mood.

Nothing is wrong with incorporating one or two of these pieces into a tank if you surround them with plants or small rocks to make them blend into the scene. Just use a little common sense and don't overdo it.

REMEMBER

Artificial items like plastic scuba divers don't help much when you're trying to get your fish into the spawning mood, either. Be honest, would you feel romantic with a larger-than-life man with a knife standing over your favorite make-out spot? I didn't think so. If you really want to see a ton of these toys floating, diving, and bobbing up and down, set up a small aquarium just for decorations and leave the fish out of it.

Aquascaping Tips and Tricks

As you decorate more and more tanks, you'll eventually discover how to see what looks good and what doesn't. Practice makes perfect, as they say.

Aquascaping can turn a bare tank into a real showpiece. Aquascaping provides a feeling of safety for your aquatic friends, helps to cover up bare spots and equipment, and enriches the overall look of your aquarium. Creating a beautiful tank also helps to educate family and visitors on species and their natural environments and provide your fish with a natural-looking habitat in which they'll flourish.

REMEMBER

Here are some tips that can help you understand the basics of good aquascaping:

>> **Clean.** Keep your water and aquarium glass clean so that your aquascape really shines. Nothing ruins a good scene quicker than dirty water and particles floating all over the place.

>> **Don't make everything symmetrical.** If you looked at the natural environment of your fish, you wouldn't find stones set exactly 2 inches apart or a lake with only one type of plant grouped in bunches of three for miles.

>> **Make rocks look natural.** Pile a few small stones together and then put one off to the side as if it had tumbled down from the pile over time. Use stones that are similar in the extent that they have been worn over time by water movement. For example, avoid putting one craggy rock in the middle of a bunch of smooth stones.

>> **Pay close attention to color.** Not all rocks in nature are the same color, because they've been bleached by water and sunlight. Add a few odd-colored stones to enhance the appearance of a grouping.

>> **Plan, plan, plan.** Sit down and draw a plan on paper before adding any substrate or decorations to a tank. That way you get a better overall feel for the layout you want. You don't have to draw anything really fancy, just plot out a simple schematic for where you want to place everything and adjust it as you go along. Save your final schematic in case you ever have to completely break down the tank for moving or other reason.

Take the overall size of your tank and fish into consideration when making your plan. You want a layout that is filled with life but not overcrowded. Fish need open spaces as well as hidden areas so that they can feel secure and have a place to exercise. Don't be afraid to do a dry test run and place everything around the tank so you can get a good idea of what the best final layout will look like.

>> **Add the water first.** Don't aquascape a tank without water, because after it's added, plants will spread out and look different. Try filling the tank halfway to aid in determining how something will really look.

>> **Research.** Check library books or go online for pictures of your species' geographical environment for ideas on how you can aquascape a setup to look and feel natural.

>> **Have a focal point.** Have at least one main point of interest in your aquascape such as an unusual, beautifully shaped rock or a stunning plant. Group other objects around to highlight the point of interest and guide your eye toward it naturally. Take advantage of a point of interest by using it to tell illustrate a natural area. For example, a hollowed-out log can make a great

point of interest for natural breeding if it's surrounded by broad-leafed plants that shelter it.

>> **Think natural.** Try to use wood and stones from the same region for aquascaping. Don't mix apples and oranges. Keep it natural instead.

>> **Think outside the box.** Why not use aquarium-safe silicone to add small stones to the back wall of the tank in the shape of a rock hill? (Make sure the rocks are close together to avoid dead spots in water flow.) Let your imagination run wild. Try turning your true creative talents into a reality by experimenting with different techniques.

>> **Avoid crowding.** Don't cram your tank with so much aquascaping that food will become trapped and foul the tank. Leave enough space to vacuum the tank as needed. Keep in mind that your plants will need to grow as well. Leave enough room for them to flourish naturally.

>> **Suit aquascaping to species.** Some species such as many cichlids can quickly tear up and destroy a beautifully aquascaped tank. Make sure the plants and rocks you choose match the personality of your fish. For example, large fish such as pacus don't seem to like large plastic objects such as divers and will pull them up. Goldfish may eat live plants. Plecos will dig up plants that aren't buried deep in gravel.

IN THIS CHAPTER

» **Understanding filtration systems**

» **Looking at heaters and thermometers**

» **Bubbling over with air pumps**

» **Sorting through all those neat gadgets**

» **Lighting up your tank**

Chapter **6**

Selecting the Equipment and Other Stuff Your Aquarium Needs

n the wild, a fish's environment functions without equipment for one basic reason: Mother Nature takes care of everything. You know the old saying: Don't upset Mother Nature. Well, unfortunately people have done just that by placing their wet pets in a small, enclosed aquarium environment. That's why at home you need to replace the natural systems that people have taken away by placing fish in captivity. This chapter explains some equipment you need to keep your aquarium running smoothly. An aquarium's equipment is the lifeblood of the whole system.

In nature, the sun heats the ocean, river, and pond waters and the seasons regulate them. In your home aquarium, you duplicate these effects by using a heater, thermometer, and artificial lighting.

In the wild, currents remove fish waste and rain replenishes the water. Natural bacteria help eliminate waste, plant debris, and other undesirable materials. At home, you accomplish these necessary tasks with filters, water changes, and other specialty equipment.

Aquarium equipment is vital to the health of your fish. It also helps keep your water crystal clear so that you can enjoy the view.

Taking the Mystery out of Filters

Filters play an essential role in performing mechanical, biological, and chemical functions in your aquarium. Some filters cover only one function; others may do two or three.

The three main functions of a filtration system are to

>> Promote the nitrogen cycle (which removes unwanted ammonia and nitrites from your system) by providing a medium for bacteria growth.

>> Remove debris and waste from the water.

>> Aerate the aquarium's water by producing water flow and bubbles. By adding these bubbles, oxygen goes into your tank, and eventually CO_2 is removed at the surface through gas exchange.

When you check out the astounding number of filters at a pet shop, you'll probably want to reach for the aspirin by the time you get to the second or third shelf. But don't worry, filters really aren't as complicated as they may first seem.

REMEMBER

There are three types of aquarium filtration, and whatever main system you decide on needs to incorporate all three of them:

>> Mechanical

>> Biological

>> Chemical

You accomplish this balance by combining different filters or by using one that performs all three kinds of filtration. You may not use all three sometimes, such as in the case of a hospital tank (refer to Chapter 11). A hospital tank allows you to cure fish away from the main tank population.

REMEMBER

Filters are one area where you shouldn't skimp and purchase the most inexpensive one you can find. Good filtration is a must, so don't be afraid to spend a few extra bucks buying good filtration equipment.

Mechanical filtration

Mechanical filtration removes solid wastes and debris suspended in the water by passing it over materials, such as synthetic foam or nylon fiber floss, which captures small particles. Basically you're removing dirt and other bad floating materials from the tank with mechanical filtration.

In time, this same filter can perform biological filtration when the surface area of the filter medium (the foam or floss) becomes covered with beneficial bacteria. The medium is usually contained in a small cartridge that slips inside of a power filter unit, sits inside of a canister, or is added in bulk form from a bag or box, as with an older corner filter.

A few popular mechanical filter types include

>> Canisters

>> Power filters

>> Corner filters

Mechanical filters come in many different sizes to accommodate the many different tank sizes. When you go shopping for filters, I suggest purchasing Penguin, Ehime, or Whisper products, because in my opinion they're the cream of the crop.

REMEMBER

A good filter cycles your tank's water volume at least eight times per hour. Mechanical filters are rated on the number of gallons of water that flow through them every hour. If you look carefully at a filter box, you can usually find a gallons per hour (GPH) rating. Manufacturers generally indicate on the label which size tank the filter is designed for.

TIP

If you have a tank larger than 10 gallons, you may want to have more than one filter running even if your filter covers all the requirements for taking care of your water. For example, you could have two power filters or a canister filter and a power filter. There is nothing wrong with mixing two different types of filtration system or having multiples of one type. As a general rule, I always have at least two filtration systems on each of my tanks just in case one fails.

Biological filtration

The main purpose of *biological* filtration is to provide a home for the bacteria that changes ammonia into nitrites and then nitrates. The function of nitrifying bacteria is to convert deadly ammonia (produced by fish waste) and food debris into less harmful *nitrites,* and then into even less harmful *nitrates* which can be removed with water changes. This amazing biological purification process is also known as *detoxification* or the *nitrogen cycle.* Chapter 14 talks a lot more about it.

The bacteria are everywhere naturally (air and water) in small amounts. By adding fish and food, the bacteria have the nutrition required to establish a larger colony. The filter medium provides the perfect nesting place for them to multiply.

You can turbocharge a small filter by adding biological media such as BioHome bio filter media.

REMEMBER

Large filters don't necessarily mean better biological filtration. What counts is the amount of surface area on the medium. The larger the total surface area of the medium, the more bacteria your system and fish have to use in the fight for good water quality.

TIP

Filters that have alternative media, so that you can replace one part without losing it all, are better than the completely disposable type where you lose the whole bacteria colony when you throw the only source of filter medium away. This modular design is a great filter system to use.

The filter box or instructions indicate which parts of the filter you need to replace and when to replace them. For example, a power filter with biowheels (see the section "Power filters" later in this chapter for more on biowheels) would be better than a power filter that only has compact floss and carbon pads that have to be replaced when the pad becomes clogged or the charcoal is no longer active. The reason for this is that the biowheels retain beneficial bacteria even though you're replacing the pads.

Chemical filtration

Chemical filtration takes place through mediums such as *activated zeolite* and *activated charcoal,* which absorb chemicals and dissolved minerals as water passes over them. Proper chemical filtration helps keep your aquarium water clean and sparkling.

You generally find activated charcoal in corner, undergravel, replaceable uplift tube heads, corner filters, canister filters, and power filters. Replace the filter medium according to the manufacturer's instructions. You should replace the medium once a month in most cases.

Sifting through Filtration Systems

You need to know what types of filters are out there and how they work. Technology is advancing rapidly, and a few new systems combine the best aspects of several different filters. The ultimate choice is up to you, so read to see which type may benefit your setup.

REMEMBER

Self-cleaning filters are in development. The aquarium industry is always changing, and manufacturers are consistently coming up with better equipment so keep your eyes open.

Undergravel filters

The *undergravel* filter has been around for a long time. Starter kits used to have this type of filter, but they're becoming obsolete because better filters are on the market. You can combine a good mechanical/chemical filter combo (such as a power filter) with an undergravel unit and have a good complete setup. However, the problem with these filters is they can become clogged easily.

An undergravel filter pulls water down through the gravel and the slots in the plates and returns it to the tank via the airlift (uplift) tubes. During this process, ammonia is broken down as the water passes over a colony of beneficial bacteria living on the substrate's surface and in the space beneath the plates. Debris is trapped along the substrate bed, making it easy to vacuum away. Periodic vacuuming is a must with this type of system to keep the bed from becoming clogged. (If you don't vacuum, eventually your substrate bed looks as if a mudslide hit it.)

REMEMBER

Undergravel filters are great for systems that don't have big rocks or decorations to block large sections of the gravel bed. Blocked plates create dead spots on the filter. A regular, store-packaged gravel substrate is best for this system because smaller substrates will fall through, and larger ones can hide big chunks of debris (your lost golf balls, uneaten fish food, and your child's hidden leftovers). Set the undergravel filter in place before adding the substrate (usually gravel).

Sponge filters

A *sponge* filter provides biological and mechanical filtration. This type of filter is simple in design and, when attached to an air pump, draws aquarium water through a large sponge that acts as a medium for bacteria to gather on. Sponge filters are good to use in quarantine and hospital tanks because they have no chemical filtration that can ruin the effectiveness of medications you may be using. They also quickly build up a biological bacteria medium for new aquariums.

Sponge filters are useful in fry tanks and aquariums with small fish because they eliminate the danger of youngsters getting sucked up into standard filtration units. However, sponge filters only take care of biological filtration and a small amount of mechanical filtration so they're inadequate for use in large main tanks. One other problem with a sponge filter is that it makes your aquarium look kind of like the junk shelf underneath your kitchen sink because it takes up room inside the aquarium.

Corner filters

Corner filters, also referred to as *submersible* filters, function primarily as mechanical filters but also provide biological and chemical filtration. This type is one of the oldest filtration systems known to the aquarium hobby. Corner filters were originally designed for the small aquariums that were the staple of aquarium-keeping years and years ago. Generally, the original clear plastic filter was shaped like a small square box and contained an airstone that pushed water through a layer of charcoal and floss with the help of an air pump. The floss removed debris, whereas the charcoal provided biological filtration.

Fortunately, corner filters have really come a long way in the last decade or so. The newer corner filters are much quieter; many come with swiveling spouts to change flow direction and water flow adjusters to change the power of the water flow. You can also find corner filters that have a clogging indicator that will show you when the filter media needs to be maintained. These types of filters are still weak compared to others.

The old corner filters rested on the gravel bed inside the tank (if you could manage to keep it from floating all over creation and back by weighting it down with small pebbles or gravel). They generally required a pump and air-line tubing to run them. You can hang corner filters today vertically and horizontally on the glass walls. The downside is that they still take up room in the tank and can only be hidden using strategic placement of plants and other aquarium decorations.

One of the better submersible filters is the Marineland Internal Polishing filter that has a diatom filter option to help clear green or discolored water.

Power filters

Power filters (also known as *hang-on-back* filters) are cool because you can use them for mechanical, chemical, *and* biological filtration. A power filter runs on electricity (with an internal motor so a pump isn't needed) and usually hangs on the outside of the aquarium, so it doesn't distract much from the view. Power filters are box-shaped and come in a variety of sizes to meet the needs of different-sized tanks (see Figure 6-1). These units usually have one or two slots on the inside of the unit that hold removable fiber-coated filter pads and are easy to assemble. The inside of these pads usually contain charcoal.

TECHNICAL STUFF

A power filter hangs on the back of an aquarium and sucks up tank water through an intake tube, which hangs inside the aquarium. The water passes over the filter pads and filter media (which house biological colonies that provide biological filtration) and then returns to the water surface. The charcoal in the pads work as chemical filters, and the fibers pick up debris before it clogs the media.

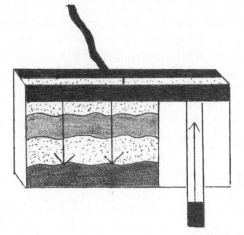

FIGURE 6-1:
A power filter draws water in, passes it through charcoal, and returns it to the tank.

Clean the pads on these filters by rinsing them with dechlorinated water and replace them every month so that you have fresh charcoal. Unfortunately, replacing the pads destroys the biological colony, but there is enough remaining in the aquarium and other parts of the filter to repopulate quickly.

REMEMBER

Some power filters contain *biowheels,* which rotate so that they come into contact with both the water and beneficial oxygen in the air, and never really need to be replaced unless they break. This wheel keeps the bacteria colony alive even if you change the internal pad. Biowheels combos are the best type of power filters to buy.

You can use power filters in any type of system. I recommend buying the largest possible for your system to keep the chemical filtration at a maximum.

Canister filters

A *canister* filter provides biological, chemical, and mechanical filtration. This type of unit is extremely popular with hobbyists and is often used in larger aquarium systems because they do such a wonderful job of keeping the water in good condition. A canister filter contains several media compartments (baskets) that usually contain sponges/foam blocks, carbon (charcoal), and some type of ceramic medium. The aquarium water is drawn through the filter via hoses attached to a high-pressure pump.

Canister filters are capable of turning over several hundred gallons of aquarium water per hour and have an internal motor to accomplish this task. Most canister filters sit on the floor beneath the aquarium, but some models attach to the back of the aquarium glass (hence, hang on tank, also known as HOT). You can adjust the filter's output to any part of the tank that meets your personal desires.

A canister filter can be very large, bulky, and unsightly, so make sure you have a place to hide it in the aquarium cabinet or behind the stand so that your house doesn't look like a water-processing plant. These units are expensive compared to most other filters and aren't the easiest type to set up, but overall they provide the best filtration possible.

They also have the ability to run additional equipment through the outlets such as ultraviolet sterilizers, inline heaters, and chiller units.

Fluidized bed filters

A *fluidized bed* filter (or *suspended particulate* filter) is one of the best biological filters on the market. The only drawback is that this type can be costly and requires a pre-filter to remove particles. But if you happen to make a few extra bucks selling some fry, it's well worth the investment to purchase one of these units.

Fluidized bed filters are extremely compact and use sand, silica, or plastic as a filter medium. The sand is continuously kept wet by water flowing through it and has a huge surface area where a large colony of nitrogen cycle beneficial bacteria can grow and multiply, as mentioned earlier in this chapter. A water pump pumps the water through the medium. This type of filter improves oxygenation because the sand is constantly tumbled in a stream of water at a high speed that creates what is known as a *fluidized bed.* Sand grains move with the water flow to create a high-quality transfer between the water and the bacteria present.

Another important feature of fluidized bed filters is that they respond quickly to any rise in the aquarium water's ammonia levels.

WARNING

A fluidized bed filter really only covers biological filtration, so if you use one you must *also* have mechanical and chemical filters working in conjunction with it in order to balance your overall cleaning system.

Fluidized bed filters are great for planted tanks because they don't remove as much CO_2 from tanks as many other filters do. Make sure the sand bed doesn't become stagnant in the event of a long power failure.

Diatom filters

This type of filter uses *diatomaceous earth* to filter aquarium water to a very clean and polished state. It can capture even the smallest of dirt particles. Due to the super clean water this equipment produces, it will help to lower diseases such as fin rot, velvet, ich, and other problems caused by microorganisms. You can hang this type of filter on the tank or place it on the floor.

The only drawback to diatom filters is that they're expensive compared to many other filters made for the same size aquarium. But if you can afford them, they're well worth the money. One good option is the Marineland Magnum Internal Polishing filter that runs the old Magnum 350 diatom cartridge.

Wet/dry filters

As the name suggests, wet/dry filters use a mixture of water and air to clean the water and are usually used in larger tanks. In the first step, waste is removed from the water after it's passed through an initial filter. On the second step, a filtering chamber aerates the water and passes it through another filter.

A wet/dry filter requires more maintenance because the media must be replaced to avoid buildup of wastes, and it has a higher rate of evaporation. This filter is mainly for biological and mechanical filtration, so you'll need an additional type or combination filter to take care of the chemical filtration in your aquarium.

Natural filtration with plants

Long before artificial filters appeared on the market, nature had its own special way of taking care of everyday cleaning. *Plants* act as natural filters and complement the manufactured units in your home aquarium.

Freshwater plants help biological and chemical filtration in the home aquarium. These aquatic marvels remove ammonia, nitrates, and CO_2 from the water with relative ease. In aquatic systems, plants take in inorganic molecules and CO_2 from the aquarium water and return oxygen and organic molecules for your fish's benefit as long as the plants have enough light to carry out the process of photosynthesis during daylight hours.

EYEING POND FILTERS

Most pond filters are just glorified canister filters in box form. Some pond filters are even disguised as flowerpots. Some models go directly in the pond, whereas others rest on dry land. These filters turn over massive amounts of water, which is essential for a healthy, well-planned pond system.

The only problem with a pond filter is that you have to have a pond to put it in. (Putting a good pond in your backyard will probably be on the same wish list as the swimming pool you always wanted.) You can, however, buy a small pond kit that fits into a barrel, which you can place in your home or on a porch.

An underground filter's best friend — powerheads

A *powerhead* is a cool piece of equipment that isn't really classified as a filter, but it can help increase an undergravel filter's output and efficiency by drawing water up through the tubes at a faster rate than most air pumps with attached airstones can. A powerhead is nothing more than an electric motor-driven pump sealed in hard plastic that you can insert into the top of the uplift tubes of an undergravel filter system. You can also hang powerheads on the tank (or buy a fully submersible model) to provide good circulation in your aquarium. Some models come with internal filter pads as well.

TIP

You can place a submersible powerhead in the tank's dead areas, such as behind large rocks, to help revitalize the water flow.

The really neat thing about powerheads is that they have adjustable valves to regulate the airflow speed (thus increasing or decreasing the water flow's speed and force). This little valve is convenient (not to mention fun to play with) in smaller tanks when you want to cut down the flow to keep the tank's inhabitants from being blown all over the aquarium or permanently embedded in the glass walls. Powerheads also have a rotating outflow that you can turn to direct the water flow to a specific area in your aquarium (or turn the outflow straight up and have your whole family shower at the same time).

REDUCING THE NOISE

All aquarium equipment will make a bit of noise now and then. Thankfully, today's aquarium equipment is much quieter than the stuff from the early days of the fishkeeping hobby.

If your filter equipment is making too much noise, you may need to replace it or have the motor (if it has one) fixed by a professional at an aquarium store. Save the directions that come with the filter because many models have parts that you can easily replace by following the manufacturer's instructions.

Gauging Heaters and Thermometers

If you plan to set up any type of tropical freshwater system, you need to have at least one heater. These sections examine the main types of heaters for your aquarium.

Submersible heaters

As their name suggests, you completely submerse these heaters in the aquarium water. Ideally, place them in a diagonal line across the rear piece of glass, so that heat flows evenly throughout the tank.

A submersible heater has a watertight glass tube containing an electrical element wound around a ceramic core. A small red or orange light lets you know whether the heater is on or off. At the top of the heater is a temperature adjustment valve you use to raise or lower the heat. Submersible heaters usually have an internal thermometer that you can see through the glass tube. You simply rotate the adjustment valve so that the temperature line moves to the temperature you want to set for your species. Other models have temperature lines (similar to markings on a measuring cup but in degrees) built in with the control knob. The heater automatically maintains the temperature you choose.

WARNING

Make absolutely sure that the heater is a submersible model before you put it completely underwater!

Nonsubmersible heaters

Nonsubmersible heaters hang on the outside aquarium frame with the glass tube hanging in the water. The adjustment valve sits above the water line. This type of heater generally doesn't have an internal thermometer. You make adjustments in small increments by turning the valve and repeatedly checking the temperature. This is the older style of heater.

Digital heaters

Digital heaters are great because they're easy to read. Most of them not only show you the current temperature but also the target temperature. The heater is submerged in the tank, and the digital temperature controller hangs outside of the aquarium. Some models have a small microphone-shaped unit with an LED display that is fully submersible.

Heating your aquarium: Thermometers

The rule for determining which size heater your aquarium needs is to allow 5 watts of heater per gallon. For example, a 50-gallon aquarium needs at least a 250-watt heater.

The safest arrangement is to keep two heaters operating at the same time just in case one unit happens to fail. If one does fail, you can divert disaster by having the second heater, which can keep the water temperature from dropping while you replace the failed unit. The aquarium heaters can be placed on opposite side of the tank. They don't need to be the same type of heater.

WARNING

Never remove a heater from the aquarium without letting the whole system sit for at least 20 minutes *after* unplugging the heater. Likewise, never turn a heater on for the first time in an aquarium until *after* you let it sit in the water for at least 20 minutes. Doing so could cause the heater to shatter.

If your heater doesn't have a built-in thermometer, you can purchase one separately. Extreme fluctuations in water temperature can cause disease or death, so it's important to closely monitor the thermometer readings. You can find a ton of good information on what temperature is correct for many species in Chapter 8. Thermometers are inexpensive and come in several varieties:

>> **Hanging thermometers** hang from the aquarium on the inside of the aquarium glass. This style of thermometer is composed of a capillary tube containing mercury that moves up and to display the temperature.

>> **Stick-on thermometers** are flat and adhere to the outside of the aquarium glass. Degree panels light up as the temperature changes, displaying the current water temperature. The two disadvantages of stick-on thermometers are that they're permanent (can't be moved from place to place) and they can be hard to read in rooms with low lighting.

>> **Floating thermometers** slowly cruise around the aquarium and display the current temperature with a mercury line like home thermometers that hang on the wall. (Unless you're used to watching tennis, you may get whiplash trying to read one of these.)

>> **Digital thermometers** run on batteries and measure the water temperature with a probe that can be attached inside the tank with a suction cup. Many models also display the room temperature.

>> **Wireless thermometers** use a radio wave signal to send the water temperature from a remote sensor to a unit with a digital readout. Some models allow you to have several sensors sending information to one display unit.

TIP

Monitor your aquarium's temperature at least once a day to make sure there are no equipment problems. I like to check it every morning when I turn the lights on. Another option is to purchase a heater controller that will sound an alarm (sent to your phone) if the tank water gets too hot or too cold.

Making Bubbles with Airstones and Pumps

One of the big advantages of having an aquarium is that it makes a bunch of cool sounds. Air bubbles produce a great tone and can be soothing. After you figure out your filter system, it's time to have a little fun and create a few cheerful bubbles. The following sections address a couple of optional pieces of equipment. Including them in your aquarium depends on your individual tastes.

Air pumps

Air pumps (used to run some filters and decorations) usually have some kind of bubble or current outflow that is fun to watch. An air pump (see Figure 6-2) is kind of a jack-of-all-trades. They can power filters, airstones, and several types of plastic decorations. When added to an undergravel filter, a pump drives air through the airstone in the uplift tubes via tubing. The air is then broken up into small bubbles as it passes through an airstone and up the tube.

FIGURE 6-2:
An air pump adds bubbles to the water, helping gas exchange at the surface.

© John Wiley & Sons, Inc.

TIP

An air pump should always sit above the midpoint level of the aquarium to avoid water backflow (which can ruin your pump) if electrical power is lost. For example, if your aquarium is 12 inches tall, the pump should sit higher than 6 inches measured from the bottom of the tank.

However, the easy solution to this problem is to buy a checkvalve. The *checkvalve* is a small plastic cylindrical object that allows water or air to flow in only one direction, so that any backflow of water won't damage your pump. The checkvalve is added to the air-line tubing.

Air pumps come in a variety of different sizes to suit almost any piece of aquarium paraphernalia that needs one to run.

Airstones and other bubble makers

Airstones are inexpensive little tube-shaped artificial stones used to split the air supplied by the pump into small bubbles. These bubbles help increase water oxygenation. Airstones are generally made of ceramic or perforated wood-based materials. Airstones can be short and round or tall and thin. The tall stones tend to emit a finer stream of bubbles than the shorter ones do. Replace them when they become clogged.

You attach airstones to one side of standard air-line tubing and attach the other end of the tubing to the air pump. You can use airstones in undergravel filter tubes and corner filters or just put them in the tank.

A couple other bubble-making options are as follows:

>> **Bubble disk:** A *bubble disk* is a large airstone that looks like a plastic flying disc. You simply connect the disk to an air pump with tubing and then slip it into the tank. The disk makes a large stream of bubbles, which can aid in water circulation. Bubble disks may become clogged with algae after a while, but you can clean them by rinsing them gently under clear water. Fish love swimming in and out of the bubbles.

>> **Bubble curtain:** A *bubble curtain* is long and emits small columns of bubbles all the way down the surface. Many come equipped with LEDs that change colors and can give the aquarium a dramatic affect.

BUBBLE WANDS: NO MAGIC, JUST HASSLES

A *bubble wand* is long and shaped like the concrete thing you run into with your front tires when trying to park your car at the store. To create a big bubble stream in your aquarium, you can purchase a *bubble disk.*

Stay away from *bubble wands.* These delicate little stones are shaped like rods and usually have suction cups attached to the back of them so that they can be mounted on glass. The problem with bubble wands is that they can become clogged and stop functioning quite quickly. Bubble wands break easily, so you may end up trashing half the decorations in your tank trying to remove one for cleaning. They also tend to float constantly unless you have something heavy to weigh them down. I don't think I have ever owned one that worked properly after two days.

Connecting Tubing, Valves, and Tees

Air-line tubing functions like the veins and arteries in the human body. Without your veins and arteries, your internal organs would just kind of lie there, lifeless, because they have nothing connecting them — nothing keeping the lifeblood flowing. The same applies to the air-line tubing and your aquarium equipment; therefore, a supply of good air-line tubing is an absolute must.

Here I mention some of the other important elements of your aquarium system. At first, you may think that some of this equipment is unnecessary, but everything has its place. Even if you don't use everything, some of these extra gadgets are nice to have lying around just in case of an emergency. Besides, the more fish junk you have, the better you look in the eyes of other hobbyists.

Air-line tubing

Air-line tubing connects equipment such as corner filters, airstones, decorations like divers and moving ships, and bubble disks to an air pump. Tubing is really a necessity — not an option — if you want to power any decorative object that needs it. Furthermore, it's useful with undergravel filters. Even if you have nothing in your aquarium that runs off tubing connected to air pumps, it's always a good thing to have on hand. Air-line tubing is a great way to siphon water from the tank if you don't have a hose.

Stick with the rubber type of tubing manufactured from a silicone/rubber-based material; it provides greater flexibility and is much easier to work with. Rubber tubing is blue-green in color and blends in nicely with the natural tint of the aquarium water. Rubber tubing is pliable, simple to maneuver around decorations, and doesn't crack easily when it begins to age.

Stay away from older tubing (the standard clear stuff you purchase at your local pet store). Standard tubing tends to crack as it ages, turns yellow, and bends out of shape (even when it's still new, right out of the package) when you set it over equipment connections. Because it's rigid, older tubing also tends to pinch and kink easily, which can diminish or completely cut off the airflow to your equipment. Working with old air-line tubing can be as frustrating as untangling a cheap garden hose.

You can purchase tubing in different lengths. The diameter of most tubing is standard; however, you can purchase mini tubing with connectors (that will connect mini tubing to standard tubing) because a few aquarium decorations have extremely small connections in the back that are too small for standard tubing.

You can also buy air-line suction cups that attach to the inside of the aquarium glass. You simply push your air-line tubing into the plastic clip on the suction cup and to keep your tubing in place so it doesn't float in the tank.

Gang valves and tees

You can split the air from an air pump in several directions with two cool gadgets:

» You use *gang valves* to run several pieces of equipment or decorations off one air pump. A valve usually hangs on the back of the tank and is made out of plastic or brass. The air-line tubing from the pump hooks into one side, and the tubing directed toward decorations and equipment is connected to one of the multiple outlets on the valve. You can adjust the strength of the airflow coming out of the valve for each piece of equipment simply by turning the individual shut-off nozzles.

» *Tees* are usually made of plastic or copper and are shaped like the letter T. A tee splits a single air source in two opposite directions.

Both the valve and tee are inexpensive, although the gang value is better because it has the ability to feed air to numerous decorations and equipment as needed. You can adjust individual air flow with knobs by each air-flow outlet.

Creating the Best Lighting

Unless you can see in the dark like a cat, you need a little bit of lighting for your aquarium. Your fish probably weren't born in a black hole either, and they'll be much happier if you provide them with a little daylight. Without light, your fish can't see their food or each other and may miss the mark by a fraction of an inch when they spawn. The following sections help you make some important lighting choices.

REMEMBER

Live plants in an aquarium require light in order to photosynthesize, manufacture their own food, and expel oxygen beneficial to your fish.

Some *hoods* (a top that fits over the upper edge of the tank) have a built-in light (full hoods); others don't. If you purchase a unit that has a light built in to it, you can change the bulb when it burns out or put in a bulb that better suits your needs. Some built-in lighting is made of flat LEDs and doesn't need to be changed. Check the manufacturer's instructions so that you don't end up with a meltdown due to excessive heat build-up if you use an older unit with a standard light bulb. Also make sure that the hood fits the tank correctly to prevent water loss from evaporation and the escape of any high-jumping fish.

TIP

If your light isn't connected to the hood, such as a strip light, and sits on top of a glass cover (called a *canopy*), you can experiment a little bit by moving the light around to see which position illuminates the tank best. The main advantage of strip lights is that they provide you with the freedom to add more lighting later on; full hoods don't. The disadvantage is that when moisture collects on the glass or acrylic beneath it, it tends to dim the light because it can't fully penetrate like normal clear glass or acrylic.

WARNING

Make sure the lighting system is unplugged when you put it on top of your tank. Don't plug the unit in until you're sure it's stable! You (and your fish) can be electrocuted if lighting falls into your tank.

Looking at bulb types

You have several bulb options to consider:

» **Actinic blue** bulbs produce long-wave ultraviolet radiation. This type of lighting is great for plant growth but also produces an abundance of algae if you have it on a lot. It's used often in marine tanks.

» **Fluorescent lighting** is great for aquariums with live plants. These bulbs last a long time, don't emit excessive heat, and have an even spectrum of light. There's a fluorescent light to match almost any system you plan to set up. Even though they continue to burn, fluorescent lights often begin to dim and lose a portion of their power after about six or seven months. This type of bulb brings out the natural colors of your fish and plants.

» **High-powered mercury vapor lights** can hang over aquariums and are often used to light deep tanks. Mercury vapor lights are a little short in the green and blue wavelength department and may need supplemental lighting to complete a full spectrum. The cool thing about mercury vapor lights is that they usually retain 90 percent of their original capacity over a period of several years.

» **Metal halide lights** produce a pleasing effect in your aquarium because they have a high red and yellow spectrum and are bright. Unfortunately, they're expensive. These are great for heavily planted freshwater tanks because they're made to produce properties similar to natural sunlight.

» **LED lighting:** Light emitting diode (LED) is an efficient and inexpensive lighting option for your aquarium. LED lights last longer than traditional lighting, use up to 85 percent less electricity, and come in a wide variety and mixture of color combinations to create the effect you want in your aquarium and to complement any type of fish and plant setup you have. Some models can be run on phone applications. LED lights are much cooler than other lights because they're energy efficient.

» **Tungsten (incandescent) lighting** is used in household lamps. Tungsten lighting isn't good for aquariums because it's too hot, burns out quickly, produces excess algae, has a limited spectrum, doesn't show your fish's colors well, and distributes light unevenly. You may see colored tungsten lights in your pet store, but avoid them. You'll often find these in all sorts of 1960s disco colors, including red, blue, and green.

REMEMBER

Whichever lighting you choose, make sure to purchase it from a pet store. Even though a hardware store can sell you a replacement bulb that fits your hood, these bulbs weren't intended for that purpose and won't provide good lighting.

LIGHTING EXTRAS

You may come across some of these lighting terms:

- A *power center* enables you to regulate the lighting schedule on your aquarium. You can set the time you want your lights to come on and off and forget about having to remember to do that as you are rushing off to work.

- *End caps* fit over the prong end of your fluorescent aquarium light tube like a sock. They're made of rubber and protect your lights from getting rusty or damp in the connection area.

- *Ballast kits* allow you to plug lights into sockets that you can clamp onto your reflector using lamp clips.

- *Sleeves* are colored materials that slip over your aquarium bulbs to give a different color effect (such as orange, green, purple, red, or blue) to your water.

Making a hood choice

The best hood/lighting system for you depends a lot on your personal taste. Some hobbyists swear by one certain type of lighting and hood combo, and others swear by another. Here are a few types of lighting systems you can choose from:

Eclipse

The Eclipse hood made by Marineland (www.marineland.com) is probably the coolest setup ever invented. (In fact, everything this company makes rocks.) This system is a hood that contains lighting *and* filtration. Using the Eclipse leaves lots of space on the back of the aquarium, so you can move it closer to the wall as well. You can also put the tank in the middle of the room and give a good 360-degree view as well.

The downside is that you have to remove the hood to gain access to the tank, and don't forget to keep dreaming if you want one to fit a very large aquarium.

Standard full hoods

This is a regular hood that covers the top of your aquarium and has one or more lights in it. There are usually a few small slots you can remove from the back of the hood to allow you to hang things on the tank.

Strip lights

Strip lights can be used to add extra lighting to a tank or to replace hoods. You can buy them to fit across the top of your tank. This is basically the light fixture unit without the rest of the hood.

Fan-cooled hoods

Fan-cooled hoods have built-in fans to make sure that you have optimal temperature in your tank while providing proper lighting. The fans also help to increase
the longevity of the lights.

Hanging lighting

You can purchase lights that hang above the tank. These lights are usually halide
or LED and are suspended by wires that are usually included with the lights. Halide can be extremely hot and difficult to hang depending on where you are placing
them. LED is a much better choice.

Reflective lighting

You can experiment with hanging lights to achieve *reflected* lighting (lighting that
is bounced off another surface such as a wall or ceiling).

The sky is the limit, so have fun creating new lighting schemes. Make sure that
whatever you do is safe and secure and provides your fish and plants with the light
they really need.

HOT RODDING YOUR AQUARIUM

Hey, I'm a fish nerd, and naturally I have a few toys. Car nerds get expensive hubcaps
and awesome paint jobs, so I make sure to have my own little wish list, too. In fact I wish
I had *more* of the equipment on the following list:

- *Ultraviolet (UV) sterilizers* kill parasites and bacteria in your aquarium water. These
  units contain an ultraviolet lamp, which you need to change two or three times per
  year. The UV unit sterilizes nonbeneficial bacteria and parasites (that are harmful to
  your fish) so that they can't reproduce.

  They can be expensive. ***Beware:*** Looking at an UV light can damage your eyes! Be
  careful when installing this unit!

- *Pump timers* allow you to hook up several aquarium pumps to the device so that
  you can control the output of each to create the type of low wave patterns you
  want.

- *Carbon block CO_2 units/fermentation units* release CO_2 into your live plant aquarium
  without using chambers or any type of bottle gas. You can set the unit to release
  the amount you want. You can also purchase units that use sealed fermentation
  canisters to create CO_2. These units have a buffer that protects them from extreme
  temperature changes that can affect the production rate.

2

Taking a Closer Look at Fish and How to Care for Them

Examine fish anatomy to understand how your wet pets move, breathe, and eat.

Decide which type of fish to buy for your new aquarium and find out know which species go well (and don't go well) together.

Investigate fish dealers to ensure you purchase good quality stock that is free from illness.

Feed your fish the right stuff so they show their best colors, develop normally, and live happy healthy lives.

Understand fish diseases to be prepared to help sick fish return to good health if a problem arises.

Set up a hospital tank so that you can treat your sick fish in a separate area away from the main aquarium.

IN THIS CHAPTER

» Moving

» Breathing

» Sensing

» Drinking

» Identifying

Chapter **7**

Fish Anatomy 101

F ish are truly amazing creatures. They have been roaming the earth's waters for almost 450 million years and have adapted themselves over time in order to thrive in their watery environment. A species' body shape, fin length, and other physical characteristics have been specially formed through evolution to meet the needs of different types of habitats. As you find out more about a fish's physical makeup, you increase the odds of becoming a successful fishkeeper with that species.

By becoming familiar with the physical characteristics of aquatic species, which this chapter explains in detail, you can purchase fish that are healthy, spot problems easier, recognize disease quicker, and set up the proper habitat for them. Figure 7-1 shows the main parts of a fish.

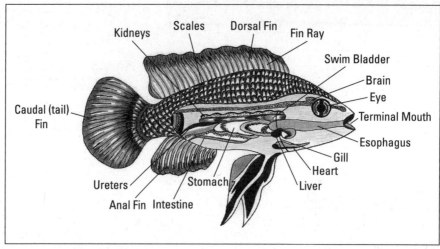

FIGURE 7-1:
Try to get to know the most important parts of a fish.

Understanding What Makes a Fish Go

At one time or another, everyone has stood transfixed, watching aquarium fish glide effortlessly through the water and wondering how they navigate through their liquid environment with such ease. What makes a fish swim better than humans do? The answer is really quite simple.

Fish have a set of fins (six or seven of them, depending on the species) that they use for locomotion. They also have a cool organ called a *swim bladder* that helps them stay afloat (otherwise they would sink; see the section "The swim bladder" later in this chapter for more).

Fish have evolved to conquer their watery environment with adaptations that have created the perfect aquatic swimming machine. By contrast, even using rubber fins, humans can achieve only a pale imitation of their aquatic friends.

To understand what makes a fish go, you must first understand each fin's function. Each individual fin has a specific job to do, and the combined effort of all of a fish's fins is what propels it through the water and helps it navigate smoothly. Fin functions are an interaction of muscle power and sheer grace.

The dorsal fin

The *dorsal fin* is located along the back of the fish between the tail fin and the head. This is the classic fin you see slicing through the water in the movie *Jaws*. If you happen to see a *Jaws*-type fin while swimming in the ocean, you may want to take up beach volleyball for a while. Fortunately for your peace of mind, the dorsal fins on your aquarium fish generally remain underwater.

The dorsal fin provides lateral stability so that your fish can swim in a straight line. The dorsal fin also helps in sudden turning and keeping the fish from rolling.

Controlled swimming conserves energy. A fish that can't swim well doesn't live long because it can't compete for food with its tankmates. Each fin consists of a series of individual rays (fin segments, some soft and some hard) loosely bound together by a membrane web.

The caudal fin

The *caudal fin* (also known as the *tail fin*) is responsible for sudden forward movement (bursts of speed) and very fast swimming patterns. Fish also use their caudal fin to slow forward movement and to help make turns. This fin produces the majority of a fish's physical power.

Lengthening the caudal fin of many species (such as the goldfish and betta) for show purposes through artificial selection (breeding for a specific trait) produces a slower-moving fish. Fish with very long caudal fins probably wouldn't survive long in the wild. A 3-inch goldfish with a 6-inch caudal fin dragging in the gravel like the train on a wedding dress is bound to have a few swimming problems.

Sadly, many species of fish have been selectively bred to have caudal fins that are so long or unusually shaped, the fish struggle just to stay upright in the water. Fish that have truncated (Chinese fan-shaped) fins can dash quickly even though they normally swim slow and easily. Fast-swimming fish generally have forked fins; rounded fins are found in slower-moving species. If you do decide to breed, don't rebreed fish with fins that are of little use to the species and ones that will produce unnatural swimming traits. (Refer to Chapter 19 for more about breeding.)

The anal fin

The *anal fin* is located on the underside of a fish between the pelvic and caudal fins. The sole purpose of this fin is to provide stability — it keeps your fish from rolling over in the water and going belly up. In some species, the anal fin has developed into a double set of fins that are fused together at the base of the fish's body.

TECHNICAL STUFF

In species such as the freshwater guppy, the male's modified anal fin acts as a sexual organ and is known as a *gonopodium*. This rod-shaped organ inserts sperm into the female's *vent* (female organ) during spawning. Many species of characins, such as tetras, have small hooks on their anal fins that attach them to their mate during breeding. If you do decide to breed, don't rebreed fish with fins that are of little use to the species and ones that will produce unnatural swimming traits.

The pectoral fins

Pectoral fins provide stability as a fish moves through the water, hovers, and makes slow turns. These paired fins are located near the bottom of the fish, directly beneath the gill openings (one on each side). Pectoral fins help with navigation, maintain depth, and are constantly in motion. They also assist the fish brake.

Many species use the pectoral fins to incubate their eggs with water during the brooding period. Many flying fish have adapted their pectoral fins into wings so that they can jump and take short flights through the air. Some species of catfish can lock their pectoral fins into a rigid stance when defending themselves from predators. *Locking* turns a normally flexible fin into a solid-unmovable fin that prevents other fish from attacking vulnerable body parts and can allow them to tightly wedge their bodies into holes in rocks so they cannot be pulled out by predators.

The pelvic fins

Pelvic fins aid fish in braking, stabilizing their bodies, and changing directions. These fins are located in front of the anal fin on the abdomen of the fish (one on each side). Other uses of the pelvic fins include searching for food, carrying eggs, sticking to rocks, and fighting. These fins are usually smaller in open water species like the freshwater platy, and larger in some bottom-dwellers.

These fins are often called *ventral fins* because of their position on the body near the small body-cavity opening on the bottom of the fish. Some species such as marine gobies use these fins to help them stand on the substrate. Other fish use them like suction cups to attach themselves to aquarium decorations.

The adipose fin

A few species of fish such as tetras and some catfish have an extra fin called the *adipose fin,* located on the back between the dorsal and tailfin. Hobbyists often refer to it as the *second dorsal fin.* Scientists haven't found any physical reason for this fin to exist, although recent studies suggest this fin could be used for sensory purposes to help navigate turbulent waters. Either way it looks cool, so why not?

Swimming movement

The special body shape of fish helps increase the overall efficiency of their swimming movement. A fish's body is usually tapered at the head and tail and bulky in the middle (like many people during midlife). This tapering allows fish to slip through the water without much effort. So, maybe if people can find a way to live in their bathtub, they'll have it made.

Looking carefully at your fish, you may notice that most of them swim with little or no effort, which is surprising because water is much more resistant than air. But water's liquid form supports a body's weight as the body moves. Because your fish's weight is suspended in water, it needs only a small amount of energy to overcome the force of gravity — as opposed to the effort humans must exert as we move through atmospheric air on dry land.

TECHNICAL STUFF

A fish's muscle force is achieved through energy created by short fibers that run throughout the fish's entire body. These numerous fibers move in sequence and create physical energy in a series of s-shaped curves. This energy is then transferred to the tail to provide locomotion. Finally, the caudal (tail) fin pushes all the water surrounding it backwards, which in turn propels the fish's body in a quick forward motion. This sequence of events allows the fish to move through the water without creating any turbulence, which would slow it down.

Breathing In and Out — Respiration

Just like humans, fish require oxygen for survival. Fish use oxygen that they strip from the water (or air in some species) and produce carbon dioxide (CO_2) as a waste product. Any living plants in your aquarium use this CO_2 and eventually expel oxygen back into the water. Chapters 16 and 17 give more details about live plants. Not all aquarium fish breathe the same way. Here are a couple of different methods that fish use to get the vital oxygen they need for survival.

The gill method

Unlike land animals, most fish don't get their oxygen from air. Instead, fish take their oxygen directly from the water through their gills. Gills are lined with a large number of blood vessels that help retrieve oxygen.

Gills are similar in structure and form to human lungs, except that they're a whole lot more efficient. Although fish remove up to 85 percent of the oxygen from their aquarium water, humans obtain only about 25 percent of the oxygen in the air they breathe by comparison, so water quality is important! (Of course, if you live in a crowded city, your oxygen consumption may drop to about 2 percent.)

Water enters a fish's mouth and passes across the gills where the oxygen is extracted by the gill filaments. The oxygen-depleted water is then quickly discarded.

Fish with high energy levels who are extremely active, like the freshwater danio, must constantly keep swimming in order to force water through their gills and obtain oxygen. Species of fish with high energy levels would eventually suffer asphyxiation if kept in a small aquarium that restricted their swimming movement. You don't want to live in a sealed elevator with 20 other people. Neither do your fish.

REMEMBER

Make sure that your tank is large enough to provide ample swimming room for your aquatic friends. Know your species well so that you can provide the correct shape and size of tank to suit their needs. Chapter 4 discusses the different sizes of aquariums you can consider.

WARNING

When moving fish from one location to another, remember that gills are made out of fine tissue that can collapse if removed from water. The gills are structurally supported by the weight of the water itself. Keeping your fish in water as much as possible while moving them is important to avoid causing any damage to their gills, bodies, and fins, which can be crushed by lack of water support.

The labyrinth organ method

A certain group of fishes (known as the anabantids), found in Asia and Africa, are able to breathe air directly from the atmosphere, using a specialized organ called the *labyrinth*. The labyrinth, located inside the head behind the gills, has evolved over time to take oxygen directly from the air as a supplement to extracting it from the water. These fish can survive for a short time out of water as long as they're kept moist, though I don't recommend that you try.

Anabantids include bettas, gouramis, and paradise fish. In the wild, many of these fish live in dirty, poorly oxygenated waters full of strange-looking creatures (not unlike a good day at your public pool). These fish tend to have wide bodies and enlarged fins.

The physical shape of the labyrinth organ gives rise to its name, which literally means *maze.* The labyrinth contains rosette-shaped plates that have thousands of oxygen-absorbing blood vessels, which gather air that is inhaled. The inhaled air is then trapped inside a group of folds (which resembles a sponge) and is eventually absorbed into the main bloodstream.

Anabantids can survive in a smaller aquarium space than that which is normally provided (usually 10 or more gallons) because they can extract oxygen from the air. However, this doesn't mean that anabantids can or should be kept in crowded conditions or extremely tiny tanks. Even though they have the ability to breathe "extra" air, they still add as much waste to the water as their tankmates and need proper space and filtration for healthy living.

You'll often see betta fish for sale in small jars. The reason many dealers do this is to keep the males separated so that they don't fight. However, doing so isn't a good practice for you to pick up and use. Don't keep labyrinth fish in small bowls or hanging vases for decoration purposes. Give them a good healthy aquarium environment with plenty of room instead.

REMEMBER

Anabantids can develop diseases brought on by crowded tanks with bad water conditions, just like other species. Poor water conditions can deteriorate or damage their scales. Take my word for it; they'll be healthier and happier in a proper aquarium. Provide anabantids with the same high quality filtration, heating, and other proper conditions as is standard with other tropical fish. They'll like you a lot better too.

Getting Acquainted with the Senses

Like humans, fish have five senses: taste, sight, hearing, touch, and smell. Fish use all these senses to locate food, communicate with one another, attract mates, and avoid bigger and meaner fish. Fish have been known to learn to do without one or more of their senses when they're injured or born with a physical defect. I've seen fish in the worst possible physical condition continue to survive. Think how great they can look and feel if humans keep them in the best possible condition! These sections delve deeper into these five senses.

Sight

Here are some fun facts about fish eyes:

>> Most fish have the ability to see in two directions at the same time. This physical phenomenon is known as *monocular vision*.

>> Fish can't completely focus both their eyes on a single object at the same time.

>> Fish don't have eyelids and sleep with their eyes wide open, resting in a hypnotic state.

>> Most fish are nearsighted and see clearly only about a foot away. So, if you stand across the room, smiling and wildly waving both your hands to entertain your fish, don't hold your breath waiting for them to respond. Instead, wiggle your fingers a few inches from the glass.

The lateral line system

Fish have an interesting system known as the *lateral line,* which helps them locate objects in their path and in their surrounding environment that they can't see normally due to their limited eyesight (see Figure 7-2). This line is incomplete in some species. The blindcave fish use this system to navigate, and killifish use it to help locate insects above the surface of the water.

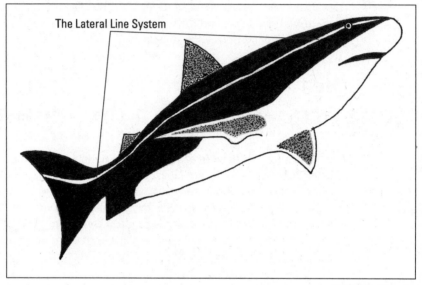

The Lateral Line System

FIGURE 7-2:
The lateral line system is a different kind of sensing system from your own.

The lateral line is located on both sides of their body and runs from the back of the eye to the base of the tail fin. These lines are composed of small *neuromasts* (receptors) that contain *cilia* (very fine hairs) in fluid-filled canals. These canals detect vibrations in the water, and the vibrations form an image inside the fish's brain.

The eyes

A fish's eyes are often large to compensate for the poor lighting conditions that exist under water. Usually the eyes are located on the sides of the head, and some species can rotate them 360 degrees. In certain species that live in areas of total or semi-darkness (such as the blindcave fish), the eyes are absent altogether. Over time, the eyes have been selectively removed through the evolutionary process.

REMEMBER

Some fish do have the ability to see a few colors at various depths, but they have great difficulty adjusting to rapid light changes because their iris works slowly. For this reason, fish may panic when an aquarium light is suddenly turned on or off without warning in a room that is still dark. So if you turn on your aquarium light right after you get up in the morning and then notice that your fish are stuck to the ceiling, you probably frightened them a little bit.

Within the human eye, the shape of the lens is constantly changing in an effort to achieve proper focus. The lens in a fish's eye remains the same shape, but focuses with help from special ocular ligaments that actually move the eye forward and backward in its socket.

Scientific testing has indicated that aquarium fish can eventually recognize human faces over time. I can personally attest to this fact as my own fish do cartwheels on the glass when they see me walking by the tank because they know I feed them.

Hearing

Fish don't have complex ears like humans because sound travels in water much faster than in air, so by evolution standards complex ears weren't needed. Fish ears are composed of a simple inner chamber. Vibrations picked up from the environment are passed over sensory components, which generate sound. Fish also use their lateral line to detect sounds, and some species like carp use their swim bladder like a hearing aid.

Most *ichthyologists* (fish experts) believe that a fish's swim bladder works together with the components of the inner ear to distinguish specific sound patterns in some species.

Smelling

Smell plays an important role in detecting food and prey and in locating a suitable mate. Fish take in smells through their nostrils (called *nares*), which are connected to their olfactory system instead of the throat like in mammals. This olfactory system isn't completely joined with the respiratory system and acts as a separate unit.

Tasting

Fish have taste buds on their mouths, lips, and, in special cases, on their fins. The complete range of taste for fish is extremely short, so they must constantly forage through their environment in hopes that they can find the food they need to survive. Catfish have evolved *barbels* (whiskerlike appendages) that contain taste buds for locating food in cloudy or dark water.

Feeling

TIP

The old argument as to whether fish can feel pain or not has been at issue for many years. I'd really hate to find out that my fish could feel pain if I did something that caused them harm. The safest bet is to assume always that your fish can feel pain and treat them with respect and great care just like you would any other pet.

Comprehending Osmosis and the Salt-to-Water Ratio

Osmosis is a simple process by which a fish maintains the correct salt-to-water ratio in its body (see Figure 7-3). Through osmosis, water molecules constantly pass through semipermeable membranes in the fish to equalize the amount of salt to water throughout its body. Osmosis is one of the main reasons freshwater fish can't live in saltwater and vice versa. (As with every other rule, there are a few exceptions to this one.)

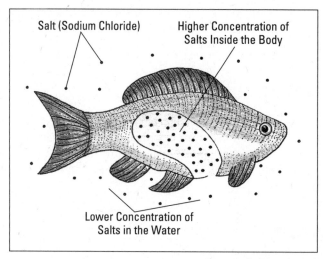

FIGURE 7-3:
Osmosis in a freshwater fish.

© John Wiley & Sons, Inc.

When osmosis occurs, fish need to regulate the water that enters into their bodies. Freshwater fish and marine fish are completely different when it comes to maintaining the correct water-to-salt ratio. Here I delve deeper into the ratio for freshwater fish.

Fish that don't drink water

The salt concentration in the body fluids of freshwater fish is higher than the salt content of the water in which they live. For this reason, water is always being drawn into their cells by osmosis. If fish didn't have a means of getting rid of this excess water baggage, they would burst like a balloon that has been filled to a point where it has exceeded its air capacity or they would resemble the human body after Thanksgiving dinner.

Water is removed by the kidneys in the form of very dilute urine in freshwater species. Specialized salt-absorbing cells located in the gills move salt from the water into the blood. Very small amounts of salt that are present in commercial fish foods also help aquatic species remain in balance. The amount of salt passed into a fish's body is so small that it doesn't require much energy to get rid of it.

Fish that need to drink water

Just in case you decide to keep marine fish after you have become acquainted with freshwater fishkeeping, you should know that they have the opposite problem when balancing water and salt in their body's cells. Saltwater fish have a lower salt content in their bodies and must constantly drink water to replace that lost by osmosis to the saltier environment around them. If saltwater fish didn't constantly drink water, they would eventually die from dehydration.

Saltwater fish excrete small amounts of urine. They also rid their bodies of excess salt to maintain their overall osmotic balance. Check out the latest edition of *Saltwater Aquariums For Dummies* by Greg Skomal if you're interested.

Recognizing Traits to Identify Fish

A fish's life, habits, and movement are completely dependent upon its overall body form and size. When you look at the mouth structure and fin design of each species, you can discover many clues to help answer questions about the way a fish survives, eats, and moves through water.

REMEMBER

Discovering how a fish's physical form evolved over a long period of time to guarantee its survival in different aquatic environments helps you recognize unfamiliar species and can give you an immediate idea of what their aquarium requirements probably are. Although this isn't a scientific rule, it works about 95 percent of the time.

When you look at your fishes' body shape, location of their mouth, and other general taxonomy, you can get a better understanding of their natural environmental needs so that you can set up the best tank possible for them to live happy healthy lives.

Body shape

The specific shape of a fish's body can tell you about its natural habitat and swimming range and help you set up the right aquarium for it. The streamlined body of a zebra danio, for example, allows it to slip smoothly and effortlessly through open water with quick bursts of speed. You won't find danios living in stagnant swamps in the wild.

Other types of fish have different body shapes that help them in their native environments. For example, the tapered shape of a discus lessens water friction and helps the discus conserve its energy as it quickly slips between obstacles (such as tightly packed roots in its native environment) to catch its prey. You find this fish living in areas with sunken tree roots and other types of natural barriers.

Round-shaped aquatic species, such as fancy goldfish, are slow swimmers and tire quite easily. You find these species living in slow-moving waters.

Fish that are flat on their ventral (bottom) side, such as the cory, spend the great majority of their time moving along the substrate bed in your home aquarium.

Taxonomy

Scientists classify fish as such because of their unique traits that separate them from other animals. The fish in your aquarium are *cold-blooded*. All this means is that their body temperature depends on the water temperature around them. Metabolic rate also plays a role in body temperature — active fish have a slightly higher body temperature than lethargic fish. On the other hand, mammals such as whales and dolphins aren't fish because they're warm-blooded and are required to come to the surface in order to breathe. Most fish don't need to breathe air because they have the ability to extract oxygen from the water around them.

Scientists classify animals into large groups that have similar physical attributes. This system is called *taxonomy. Ichthyologists* (people who spend their time studying fish) place aquatic species into several categories based on physical traits so that they can, for example, differentiate fish from other aquatic animals.

TECHNICAL STUFF

Scientists classify bony fish as having a backbone *(vertebrae)*, a small skeleton that protects and supports body weight and internal organs, fins, rays made of cartilage or bone, gill respiration, separate sexes, and a brain case. About 90 percent of the world's fish are bony. The common fish you find in your freshwater aquarium are bony fish.

Mouth location

The way a fish's mouth is shaped and the direction it points have quite a lot to do with the manner in which it feeds and the range (top, middle, or bottom) of aquarium water in which it spends most of its time:

>> **Top feeders:** Aquatic species such as the hatchet fish have an upturned mouth, indicating that they're top feeders who scoop up flakes and floating food on the water's surface in the aquarium. This upward-turned mouth is also known as a *superior* position.

>> **Midwater feeders:** When the mouth faces straight away from the fish's face, it's known as a *terminal* position and is common in species that swim in midwater, such as goldfish and platys. These species feed by picking off food as it sinks.

>> **Bottom feeders:** A turned-down mouth (*inferior* position) is found in many bottom-dwelling species such as catfish. These fish feed along the gravel bed, off the glass walls of the tank, and from flat rock surfaces and plant leaves.

Scales

Most fish have a body covered by scales that overlap each other like roof shingles. *Scales* are formed of transparent plates that protect the body from injury. These thin structures also serve to streamline for efficient gliding. A slimy mucus layer covers the tops of the scales to provide smoothness and protect against invading parasites and infection.

Not all fish have scales, however. As usual, there are a few exceptions.

Here are a few types of scales found in bony fishes:

>> **Ctenoid scales** have tiny little teeth on their outer edges.

>> **Cycloid scales** are smooth and round.

>> **Ganoid scales** have a diamond shape and can be found on species such as gars.

Scales grow out from the skin and generally have no color. Scale color comes from pigment cells located in the skin itself.

The swim bladder

Hypothetically, most fish should sink to the bottom of your aquarium because they're slightly heavier than water. The swim bladder helps fish overcome this problem. In other words, the swim bladder is similar to a buoyancy vest used by scuba divers. The swim bladder is an organ filled with gas that helps fish maintain their vertical position in the water instead of sinking. The organ may be lacking in some bottom-dwellers. The walls of the bladder contract and expand to regulate the correct amount of gas to stay afloat.

Internal gas adjustments through the use of a specialized duct allow fish to remain suspended with little or no effort. A gas gland introduces gas to the bladder to increase its volume and increase buoyancy when it excretes lactic acid that allows gas in the blood to diffuse into the bladder. To reduce buoyancy, gas is released from the bladder into the bloodstream and then expelled by gills into the water.

When a fish moves to the bottom of an aquarium, its swim bladder automatically compresses, and the fish sinks. To correct this problem, gas must be added to the swim bladder to achieve buoyancy again. When a fish decides to move toward the top of the tank, its upward movement releases gas from its swim bladder. Otherwise, the fish would be forced to expend too much physical energy to move to a higher depth.

Color and its purpose

Pigment cells (known as *chromatophores*) in the skin are responsible for a fish's color. Different shades of colors in fish warn off predators and attract mates. The social use of this physical attribute hasn't been lost in the captivity of the home aquarium. Many species of freshwater and brackish fish have adopted new colors that have appeared through selective breeding and use them to their own advantage in mating and aggression displays.

Lighting that is too low or too high in your aquarium can dull a fish's color. Poor diet and stress can also lead to reduced coloration.

WATCH OUT FOR UNETHICAL PRACTICES

Be aware of unethical treatment or practices that you see so you and pass that knowledge to other aquarists to help keep undesirable species and activity out of the hobby.

Several artificially colored aquarium fish often pop up on the market. These fish don't come by their brilliant colors naturally; instead dealers dye them. Dying causes disease, stress, and death (up to 80 percent) mortality rate for those injured fish during the process. How do disco fish and other types of artificially colored species get that way? It's accomplished by several methods:

- **Injected dye:** Fish are injected with dye through the method of sticking needles under the skin. This method often produces many puncture sites that can become infected long after the fish are shipped and relocated to a dealer or home aquarium.

- **Dye dipping:** The fish are put into a solution that strips away their slime coat so that dye can be absorbed. The fish are then put into another irritating solution in order to encourage the slime coat to regrow.

- **Tinted food:** The fish are fed food with tint added to it. After the fish stop feeding on this food, their color starts to slowly fade away in your aquarium. These fish often suffer from growth and health problems.

The barbaric practices used to color these fish should be eliminated from fishkeeping. When hobbyists buy these types of artificially colored fish, they're supporting these dealers and encouraging them to continue doing what they're doing. Don't buy these fish, and educate and encourage other hobbyists to not purchase them either. If everyone stops buying these artificially colored fish, then the dealers will eventually go out of business.

Another problem fishkeepers need to be aware of is dealers who give bad advice. Many chain stores don't properly train their employees to sell fish, and many family-owned business don't pay close attention to the advice they're giving. When you encounter them, try to correct them.

Years ago, I walked into a fish store that had bettas in tiny plastic bags that were tied up with rubber bands. The bettas had just enough water in the bag to keep them wet, and most of them looked extremely ill. I explained to the dealer that this practice wasn't good. Despite breathing air, bettas have the right to a comfortable tank with good water quality and natural decorations just like any other fish. I pointed out that there were several tanks in the store with community fish that could house the bettas.

Chapter **8**

Figuring Out What Kind of Fish to Buy

When you go to purchase your new fish, you need to have a general idea as to which species can survive in your particular type of system. Otherwise, you may end up with a bunch of marine fish floating at the top of your freshwater aquarium because you bought saltwater species. You simply can't mix apples and oranges in aquariums. Save that combination for Sunday's fruit salad.

This chapter gives you a general overview of major fish families and shows you where they fit into each type of aquarium system. This chapter also helps you understand special dietary and social needs of many species. Most of the fish listed in this chapter are excellent choices for beginners. (I give you plenty of warning about those that aren't.)

TECHNICAL STUFF

This chapter presents you with many scientific names. A scientific name is usually based on Greek or Latin and uses two words. The first word is the *genus* (a group of related species) that the fish fit into. The second word is the *species* (a group of animals that can interbreed) within that genus. The species name is sometimes the same as the person who first described the fish. A named ending in *i* means that a man first described the fish. A name ending in *ae* means that a woman first described the species. Because no one could pronounce half of these strange names, a common name (like guppy) is also given to each fish.

TIP

All you need to do is to memorize a few common scientific names so you can look cool around other hobbyists.

Looking Closer at Freshwater Fish

The freshwater aquarium system doesn't require any marine salt (however, some species, such as mollies, enjoy a teaspoon per 5 gallons added) and generally requires some type of heater unless it's a coldwater aquarium. This type of system also usually contains plants and has gravel for substrate. Here are a few example of freshwater fish you may want to consider for your aquarium.

Anabantids

The anabantids are a group of fish native to African and Asian waters. These fish have a specialized organ called a *labyrinth* that helps them breathe atmospheric air in the low-oxygenated waters of their native environment. This doesn't mean you should keep them in an aquarium that lacks aeration. If you do, your fish will eventually become ill due to poor water conditions.

Anabantids are generally peaceful species that swim in the middle to upper levels of the aquarium tank. They're easy to breed.

Betta or Siamese fighting fish (Betta splendens)

The Asian Siamese fighting fish, also known as the betta (see Figure 8-1), has been bred for years to develop strains that have long flowing fins and bright colors.

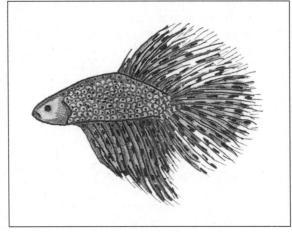

FIGURE 8-1: A betta lives on average two to three years and grows to about 3 inches in the home aquarium.

WARNING

Males of this species are aggressive toward each other so you should only have one male per tank. The betta is a beautiful fish that has a special organ in its head (called the *labyrinth organ*) that allows it to breathe oxygen from the air at the water's surface. Good tankmates include cories, danios, angelfish, kuhli loaches, and schools of harlequin rasbora.

Bettas build bubble nests by blowing air from their mouths in the form of bubbles that cling together in a mass. If you want to spawn them, they should be kept at a temperature of 76 to 83 degrees F. The betta is omnivorous and swims in all levels of the tank. Bettas enjoy being fed floating foods and freeze-dried bloodworms. Remember that bettas aren't overly active, so they won't eat as much as more robust varieties.

Climbing perch (Anabas testudineus)

This amazing fish can live several days without water and has been known to travel across land in its native environment as it moves from pond to pond. Keep climbing perch in water near 80 degrees F and provide plenty of shelter for them (rock caves and so on). This fish should be kept with its own kind. The climbing perch grows to 10 inches in length, is carnivorous, and swims in all levels of the tank. A climbing perch requires a tank of at least 125 gallons and is a good choice after you've mastered a few of the easier-to-keep species.

Paradise fish (Macropodus opercularis)

The beautifully striped and speckled paradise fish is native to China and South Korea. When frightened, the paradise fish loses its color quickly. Paradise fish build bubble nests for spawning and prefer a temperature of 75 degrees F. The paradise fish is carnivorous and swims in all levels of the tank, and generally grows to lengths of between 3 and 4 inches.

The paradise fish is aggressive and should be kept with other paradise fish in a group and with hardy tankmate species of its own size. Some males constantly fight with each other. Good tankmates include loaches, tiger barbs, danios, gouramis, and red-tailed sharks.

Cyprinodonts and livebearers

The *cyprinodont group* is also known as *toothcarps* because they have tiny teeth. This group contains both live-bearing and egg-laying fish and contains some of the most popular and classic community fish (guppies, platys, and swordtails). Cyprinodonts are friendly, easy to breed, and swim in all levels of the tank.

Guppy (Poecilia reticulata)

The Central American guppy (as shown in Figure 8-2) is an amazing little fish. It has been the staple of many community aquariums since the hobby began. Guppies are available in a wide variety of colors and fin shapes. Many hobbyists have started out by keeping guppies as aquatic friends. This fish rocks! The guppy is omnivorous and swims in all levels of the tank. Though often inexpensive, don't overlook the beauty of these little fish because they can provide years of joy as you watch their very active lifestyle and mating rituals.

The male's anal fin has evolved over time into a specialized organ called a *gonopodium* (a rodlike extension), which it uses to internally fertilize a female's eggs. Guppies are best kept in a well-planted tank in a ratio of one male to every three females.

The guppy should be kept in water that has a temperature of between 78 to 82 degrees F. Guppies do best with one tablespoon of aquarium salt added for every 5 gallons of water, but adding it isn't essential. Guppies do well with flake food and are highly appreciative of frozen brine shrimp as a treat.

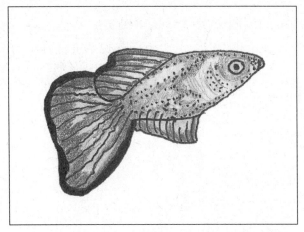

FIGURE 8-2:
Guppies get along with a wide variety of fish.

Good tankmates can include swordtails, ghost shrimp, glassfish, white clouds, and cories.

Killifish (Fundulus)

Although most killifish prefer soft, acidic water, a few species can be kept in a community aquarium. The killifish swims in the upper to middle levels of the tank and is carnivorous. Killifish should be kept in schools (three or more fish).

Platy (Xiphophorus maculatus)

Platys sport some of the most beautiful colors of all freshwater fish. This hardy species, which is native to Mexico, Honduras, and Guatemala, breeds easily in the community aquarium and is extremely peaceful. Platys have been developed extensively through commercial breeding and can be found with different fin shapes and in almost every color imaginable. The platy is omnivorous, swims in all levels of the tank, and is easy to breed.

Keep your platys in the same salt conditions as the previously mentioned other livebearers and let them enjoy their water temperature in the 78 to 82 degree F range as well. Good tankmates include angelfish, mollies, swordtails, cories, and pleco. The platy will grow to 3 inches and live several years.

I have to admit that this is my favorite species of fish, simply because of its beauty, cheery round body shape, and amazing colors. The platy also seems very alert to the owner's presence, and I have had many that would swim up to the glass to greet me. You simply can't help but love this amazing little fish that comes in such fascinating varieties as the Mickey Mouse Platy, Marigold Platy, Calico Platy, Painted Platy, Wag Tail Platy, and Sunburst, just to name a few. With fish sporting cool names like that in your aquarium, how can you go wrong?

Sailfin molly (Poecilia latipinna)

The sailfin molly (refer to Figure 8-3) is a beautiful species native to the brackish waters of the United States and Mexico. The male's dorsal fin, when erect, looks like the sail on a ship. Keep mollies in a well-planted tank and provide extra vegetation in their diet.

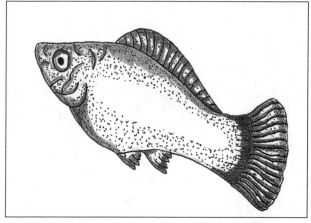

FIGURE 8-3: Mollies come in a huge variety of colors and patterns.

© John Wiley & Sons, Inc.

This species can be aggressive toward smaller fish, but it generally makes a great community member. Good tankmates include cories, swordtails, angelfish, tetras such as the red serapae, and platys.

Mollies enjoy slightly salty water, so you can add about one teaspoon of salt for every 5 gallons of water to make them happy. Keep the water between 78 to 82 degrees. The sailfin molly is omnivorous and swims in all levels of the tank and generally grows up to lengths of 4 inches during its three-to-five-year lifetime.

The one thing I really like about all mollies in general is that they come in such an amazing variety of colors and patterns (marble, patches, metallic, tricolors, and so on). Their round bodies are cool to watch as they make their way through your aquarium.

WARNING

Make sure that the other species you keep with livebearers can tolerate the extra salt before you add it to their aquarium. If not, mollies can live well without it.

Striped panchax (Aplocheilus lineatus)

This great community fish is also an aquarium jumper, so make sure your aquarium hood is secure. This egg-laying species uses plants for shelter and to spawn, so provide plenty of plants. The panchax is carnivorous, requires live food, and swims in the upper level of the tank.

Swordtail (Xiphophorus helleri)

The swordtail (as shown in Figure 8-4) is native to Mexico, Honduras, and Guatemala and is a brightly colored fish that makes a good addition to any community aquarium.

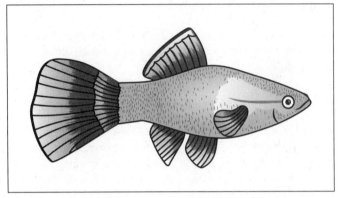

FIGURE 8-4: Swordtails are active community fish.

The males of this species have an elongated caudal fin extension that resembles, not surprisingly, a sword. Male swordtails, like guppies, have a gonopodium (see the preceding "Guppy (Poecilia reticulata)" section) and prefer heavily planted tanks.

Swordtails are extremely active and should be kept in water that is slightly hard (has high mineral content such as magnesium, calcium, and sulfates). The water temperature should be kept between 78 and 82 degrees F. Like other livebearers, the swordtails do well by having one tablespoon of aquarium salt added for every 5 gallons of water in the tank. The swordtail is omnivorous and swims in all levels of the tank.

If you want to breed this fish, you should have a ratio of one male to three females for best results. Having more females helps to ensure that breeding will occur and will keep the male from harassing one female constantly. Harassment can lead to stress, illness, and death.

Swordtails can reach average lengths of up to 5 inches in captivity and will live three to five years in good water conditions.

Catfish (plecos, cories, and one special Cypriniforme)

Catfish play an important role in the aquarium system. These species generally feed off the substrate as they gather unwanted debris. Catfish often survive by using their *barbels* (specialized organs used for tasting) to locate the leftovers that fall to the bottom of the tank. Feed them a diet of sinking pellets as well. Many species are *nocturnal* (more active at night), so feed them the sinking food formulated especially for them accordingly. Catfish can be aggressive if they aren't kept with species their own size, and most are omnivorous.

WARNING

It isn't true that catfish just like to eat fish waste. You have to feed them fish food just like all other kinds of fish. Cories like sinking plankton tabs, spirulina, and regular flake foods.

Bristlenose catfish (Ancistrus temmincki)

The bristlenose catfish is a prehistoric-looking member of the *Loricariidae* family. Males of this species carry a double row of bristles on their snouts, whereas the females bear only a single row. The bristlenose's mouth is formed into a sucker disk that it uses to feed on algae in its native habitat. This South American catfish is herbivorous, lives in the lower level of the aquarium, and is peaceful.

Cory (Corydoras species)

Probably the most popular species of catfish for the home aquarium is the cory (as shown in Figure 8–5). Cories come in a wide variety of spotted and striped patterns, are inexpensive, and do a good job cleaning debris (fallen food, dead plant leaves) from the bottom of the tank. The friendly little blackfin cory from South America is one outstanding omnivorous member of this genus that swims in the lower levels. Cories should be kept in schools (at least three) and are easily bred by amateurs. Females are larger and rounder than the males of the species.

They spend most of their time in search of food, so make sure you provide them sinking pellet foods such as algae wafers. These fish can reach lengths of 2 to 3 inches on average in a home aquarium and have been known to live as long as ten years.

Keep their water temperature between 72 and 78 degrees F. Good tankmates include livebearers, rasboras, danios, barbs, tetras, gouramis, angelfish, rainbowfish, and other peaceful scavengers such as the pleco.

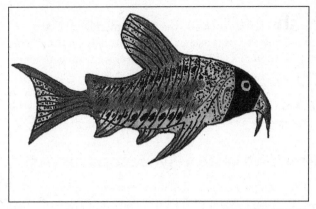

FIGURE 8-5: More than 50 species of cories are great for the home aquarium.

Glass catfish (Kryptopterus bicirrhis)

The glass catfish is a fascinating animal with a transparent body. You can actually see this fish's backbone and internal organs through its body wall. You can even see the food it has eaten before it's broken down by looking through its body.

Keep this peaceful Southeast Asian fish in schools (at least three). The glass catfish is carnivorous and swims in the middle and lower sections of the tank. Make sure you have plenty of live plants (such as Java fern) in the tank for this species because they like to hang around them most of the time. Keep their water clean to avoid disease. Glass catfish don't do well with many medications, so prevention is the key with this species.

The temperature of the water for glass catfish should be kept between 75 and 79 degrees F, and soft water with a pH between 6.2 and 7.0. This fish lives on insects in its native waters, so feed it a diet that includes live foods, such as daphnia. Keep this fish in a group with its own kind because it's a schooling fish in the wild and will become very shy and inactive without others of its own type to keep it company. Never keep one alone without other glass catfish.

Glass catfish are good with most nonaggressive community fish such as guppies.

Suckermouth catfish (Hypostomus plecostomus)

One of the most famous catfish known to the aquarium hobbyist is the suckermouth, also known as the *pleco.* This fish has a leopard-print pattern of spots and can grow to a length of more than a foot, so make sure you have plenty of space for this species to grow. This catfish can be slightly territorial, so good tankmates can include fish that can hold their own, such as larger cichlids.

Suckermouth catfish do well in temperatures between 69 and 79 degrees F and are tolerant of most normal aquarium conditions.

Constantly in search of food, the suckermouth may tear up vegetation if your aquarium is planted as it bashes its way through anything in its path. The suckermouth is herbivorous (it loves to remove algae from your aquarium) and swims in the lower and middle levels of the tank.

If you want smaller versions, you can purchase clown plecos or the bristlenose pleco, which only grow to a couple inches in length.

Upside-down catfish (Synodontis species)

True to its unusual name, the upside-down catfish swims with its abdomen pointed upward. This beautiful little fish from tropical Africa changes its body shading according to its swimming position. The peaceful upside-down catfish is carnivorous and swims in all levels of the tank.

These fish do well in temperatures between 72 and 79 degrees F and have been known to live more than five years. Upside-down catfish grow to lengths of 3 to 4 inches in the home aquarium, have a forked tail and three sets of barbels, and should be kept in small schools. The dorsal side of the fish is lighter in color (used for camouflage), which is the complete opposite of most other species that swim in an upright direction. These fish usually have a beautiful mottled body in earth tones.

If you want to keep your upside-down catfish healthy, make sure you have plenty of plants, rocks, and decorations in the tank because they love to search for tasty tidbits along surface areas. Feed them insect larva and algae discs that they enjoy nibbling.

Chinese algae eater (Gyrinocheilus aymonieri)

This beautiful fish is native to Southeast Asia. Though not a true catfish (it belongs to the *Cypriniformes*), this special little fish has been marketed as a catfish for a long time. It holds on to objects using a sucker-like mouth. This species lives in fast-moving waters in nature and prefers a tank with good movement. Its natural diet is algae so it'll need to be fed plant-based fished food. This fish can grow extremely large in a home aquarium and often becomes aggressive as it matures, so keep it with larger or faster fish, such as danios, tiger barbs, and clown loaches. It survives in a tank that is 65 to 85 degrees F.

Characins

The characins are one of the most diverse groups of fish, including the small tetras and the big, bad piranha of movie fame. Members of this group are characterized by the bones that link their swim bladder and inner ear. Many characins also have a small adipose fin on their top side between the tail and dorsal fins.

Bleeding heart tetra (Hyphessobrycon erythrostigma)

The South American bleeding heart tetra earned its name from its physical attributes. This silver-colored fish has a red spot on its side that makes it look as if Clint Eastwood just shot it at high noon. If you loved the movie *E.T.*, you'll really enjoy this wonderful little fish.

The bleeding heart needs plenty of swimming room and is easily spooked. This semi-peaceful fish (it may be aggressive toward smaller fish) is omnivorous and swims near the middle level of the tank. The bleeding heart tetra grows to lengths of 3 inches and should be kept in temperatures between 72 and 82 degrees F. Make sure you provide plenty of bushy plants for this species.

Like many other tetras, this fish should be kept in a school of its own kind, so that it will feel safe and secure. Bleeding heart tetras will happily eat a wide variety of foods, including brine shrimp, bloodworms, frozen foods, and flakes. When you first get these fish home, they may have a slightly washed-out look (most species will for a few hours to a few days), but they'll gain back their beautiful colors after they have settled into their new home.

Cardinal tetra (Paracheirodon axelrodi)

The cardinal tetra is similar in appearance to the neon tetra, except that its abdomen has a larger area of red coloring. The peaceful cardinal prefers soft, acidic waters (below 6.8 pH) and is omnivorous. This fish swims in all levels of the tank, should be kept in schools (at least six to eight), and should never be housed with any larger, aggressive tankmates. Cardinal tetras will eat almost any food, including flake, live, and frozen.

Glowlight tetra (Hemigrammus erythrozonus)

The glowlight tetra of South America is an interesting little fish with a glowing line running from its eye to the base of its tail and a small adipose fin behind the dorsal. When the lights in the tank are dim, you can easily see the beautiful red stripe running down its side.

The peaceful yet active glowlight tetra prefers soft, acidic water and a well-planted tank that is kept between 75 and 80 degrees F. It's omnivorous and swims in all levels of the tank. Its colors fade if it becomes too stressed.

This species is a schooling fish and must be kept with its own kind in groups of five or more in order for it to thrive successfully. This fish will reach lengths of 1½ to 2 inches and has been reported to live as long as ten years in good aquarium conditions.

Good tankmates for this fish include other small tetras, small gouramis, danios, angelfish, small catfish, and livebearers.

Neon tetra (Paracheirodon innesi)

The South American neon tetra (see Figure 8-6) is one of the most popular and recognizable fish in an aquarium. This peaceful little fish has a blue-green stripe that glitters down the side of its body and a beautiful red half-stripe below that. The neon is omnivorous, swims at midlevel in the tank, needs to be kept in schools (at least six to eight minimum), and is quite difficult to breed in captivity. Males are thinner than the females of the species.

FIGURE 8-6:
Neon tetras can be fed flake food, tubifex worms, and brine shrimp.

© John Wiley & Sons, Inc.

Neons will grow up to an inch and a half in captivity and can live as long as ten years. Keep this fish in water with a temperature between 70 and 78 degrees F and a well-planted tank. This species doesn't do well under bright lighting, so make sure to subdue the atmosphere as much as possible.

Unfortunately larger fish eat neons, so keep them with fish that are peaceful and similar in size such as the cardinal tetra, small community fish such as guppies and mollies, and the glowlight tetra.

Rummy-nose tetra (Hemigrammus bleheri)

The rummy-nose tetra is a peaceful fish that should be kept with other small tetras of equal size. Its name comes from the fact that it has a red splotch of color around its nose and eyes.

This species will eat almost any food offered and should be kept in water that is between 72 and 79 degrees F and softly acidic with a pH between 6 and 6.8.

Serpae tetra (Hyphessobrycon serpae)

This fish takes its name from its beautiful color resemblance to a Mexican *serape* (large shawl), but the spelling has been changed. Go figure. The peaceful serpae is a midlevel swimmer and is omnivorous. It's one of the larger tetra species and can be slightly aggressive with smaller fish. Keep it in a school of six or more of its own species.

Keep the water temperature between 78 and 80 degrees because this fish tends to chill easily. Good tankmates include mollies, swordtails, plecos, and cories. This fish is known to live on average of five to six years.

Unusual characins

There are many different types of characins. The following sections give examples of some that are quite unusual in physical form. Unusual is cool.

Blindcave fish (Astyanax fasciatus mexicanus)

The blindcave fish has no eyes and navigates in dark, underground caves in the wild using its lateral line (see Chapter 7). The body is pink in color overall with a red gill area. Don't overlook this amazing little fish because it's a great asset to any aquarium with compatible species.

This fish grows up to 3 inches in captivity and is an egglayer. A school consisting of five members makes a great addition to the community tank. The blindcave fish is omnivorous and should be kept in waters that are near 72 degrees F with a pH of 7.4. If you're going to keep blindcave fish, make sure you provide them with small caves built out of rocks (or premanufactured aquarium caves) so they can feel secure.

Pacu (Colossoma bidens)

Pacus grow quickly in any home aquarium and are related to piranhas. The big difference is that pacus are mainly vegetarians, whereas piranhas are carnivores. This fish should never be kept in an aquarium that is less than 55 gallons, period. They enjoy a water temperature between 78 and 82 degrees F.

WARNING

A pacu looks like a piranha, grows to the size of your mid-sized car, and can eat you out of house and home. This species can grow rapidly and reach adult lengths of 12 to 30 inches in a home aquarium! These fish have been known to slam against the aquarium glass when panicked, so always provide them with plants or rocks to hide behind.

The pacu is supposed to be herbivorous, but don't bet the bank (or your smaller fish) on it. Many hobbyists have seen them attack and swallow smaller fish, so keep them only with larger species such as oscars, tinfoil barbs, plecos, and knife fish. Feed pacus pellet food that is supplemented with fresh vegetables in small amounts. Pacus swims at midlevel.

Some hobbyists have released this species into the wild after they've realized that it's continually outgrowing their aquariums. Don't do it because releasing them in the wild is detrimental to native species. If you have this problem, donate the fish to an aquatic society, fish store, local zoo, or aquarium that has the means to take care of them.

Silver dollar (Mylossoma pluriventre)

This neat fish resembles a silver dollar in form and color. The silver dollar is herbivorous and may destroy aquarium plants if you have them. These fish are generally peaceful, but a few bad apples can become quite aggressive when larger. For best results, keep silver dollars in a school of five to eight in a species tank.

These fish require lots of swimming space, with a water temperature between 78 and 82 degrees F, and should be kept in tanks larger than 55 gallons because they can grow up to 6 inches in length. Silver dollars are vegetarians by nature and should be fed floating flake food.

Good tankmates for the silver dollar include angelfish, mollies, giant danios, and larger catfish such as the pleco who won't easily be bullied.

Silver hatchetfish (Gasteropelecus sternicla)

The body of the silver hatchetfish body resembles the blade of a large ax. This peaceful South American fish eats live insects and should be kept in schools (of at least three), which will stay near the top of the tank.

This active species requires excellent water conditions to survive and doesn't do well in a dirty tank with little oxygen. The water temperature should be kept between 72 and 79 degrees F with a pH between 6 and 7. This fish requires an aquarium that has plenty of swimming room and does best if provided with current created by powerheads or other equipment.

Good tankmates include tetras, loaches, livebearers, angelfish, and rasporas. Hatchetfish are good with plants (not eating or tearing them up), so don't be stingy. Feed them ample frozen foods, including insect larvae because they feed on them in the wild.

The silver hatchetfish can leap from your aquarium in a single bound using their winglike pectoral fins, so keep a tight lid on your aquarium to avoid this problem.

Three-lined pencilfish (Nannostomus trifasciatus)

This South American species is probably the world's coolest fish. It looks like a swimming number-two pencil due to the dark band that runs from the nose to the base of the caudal fin. You may not find it in stock at pet stores, but you can usually order it.

The three-lined pencilfish is omnivorous and peaceful, and it requires thick vegetation. Add floating plants and dark gravel to diffuse the light so it will feel secure. The temperature should be between 72 and 81 degrees F with a pH that falls between 6.5 and 6.9 for best results.

As they age, the males become darker than females do and will often battle with other males, although not to usually to the point of injury or death.

Loaches

Loaches are an interesting group of species from Asia and India. Loaches resemble streamlined catfish and like catfish are bottom-dwellers that use barbels to search for food. These fish can also extract oxygen from the air by gulping it. Most species are nocturnal, so unless you're up late at night, you may not see them often. Loaches are carnivorous, swim in the lower levels of the tank, and are often shy by nature. They can get very large at maturity, so make sure you have a setup large enough for the species that you choose.

Clown loach (Botia macracantha)

The Indonesian clown loach (refer to Figure 8-7) is scaleless (don't add any medications that don't state on the package that they're safe for scaleless fish!), is striped like a tiger, and spends most of its time peacefully foraging for food near the bottom of the tank. The clown loach is carnivorous and is best kept in a small school of three to five. Loaches often lay on their sides or backs when resting, so remember that this behavior is normal.

FIGURE 8-7:
Clown loaches
will eat just
about anything.

Excellent tankmates include danios, livebearers, small gouramis, cories, and rainbowfish. Try to avoid slow-moving, mellow tankmates because the high activity and darting of the loaches can stress out their aquatic companions. This species has been known to live as long as 20 years in the home aquarium (keep this in mind, because older fish can reach lengths of greater than one foot).

The clown loach tank should be dimly lit and provided with good water current, fine gravel or sand for substrate, and rock caves to match the streams of the loach's natural habitat. This species can thrive in waters ranging from 72 to 85 degrees F. It eats almost anything and really enjoys sinking tablet foods, worms, brine shrimp, and tubifex worms as a treat.

Orange-finned loach (Botia modesta)

The orange-finned loach has a blue-gray body with bright orange fins. Like other loach species, it has small spines on its eyes. This species hides during the day and is shy. The orange-finned loach swims in the lower levels of the tank, is carnivorous, and makes clicking noises to attract mates.

The water conditions, tank setup, and nutrition for this species are similar to that required for clown loaches.

Zebra loach (Botia striata)

The zebra loach is nocturnal in nature and becomes active at night. It's a pretty fish that sports black and greenish tinted stripes. Tankmates can include danios, rainbowfish, gouramis, small cichlids, livebearers, and barbs.

The water conditions, tank setup, and nutrition for this species are similar to that required for clown loaches (see earlier in this section).

African cichlids

Cichlids are native to the Americas, Asia, and Africa. Old World cichlids include species from Lake Malawi, Lake Tanganyika, Lake Victoria, West Africa, India, Sri Lanka, and Madagascar. A few examples of these fish include jewelfish, orange chromides, and mubuna.

Native species like hard alkaline water, so keep the pH between 7.4 and 8.4. Most species (with a few exceptions) tend to be aggressive and are best kept in a species tank with their own kind. Some cichlids require special water conditions; I note them where applicable.

Although many cichlids have a thick body that can grow quite large, a few small varieties are suitable for the home aquarium.

Blue johanni (Melanochromis johanni)

The male of this species has a beautiful, blue-colored body with slightly darker fins and should be fed a diet of vegetable products. Keep the blue johanni in a tank that ranges from 72 to 82 degrees F in water temperature and provide plants and rocks so that the fish can feel secure.

Electric yellow cichlid (Labidochromis caeruleus)

This species is marked by its beautiful and bright yellow color and black-marked fins that make it resemble a thin lemon. This species is less aggressive than most cichlids but can be difficult to find.

The tank setup is similar to the blue johanni. Feed it a diet of both vegetable and meat content such as bloodworms and brine shrimp.

Jewel cichlid (Hemichromis bimaculatus)

The jewel cichlid has a pretty golden color with a dark band traversing its body length. Feed it a vegetable-based African cichlid food and insect larvae, and keep it in an aquarium that ranges from 72 to 82 degrees F in water temperature. Provide plants and rocks so that it can feel secure.

Kribensis (Pelvicachromis pulcher)

The West African kribensis is a generally peaceful, rainbow-colored fish. The kribensis is an omnivorous bottom-dweller. This species can become aggressive during breeding time and should only be kept with other like-size African cichlids and catfish.

Feed it vegetable-based African cichlid food, and keep pairs together in a tank similar to the tank conditions for a blue johanni.

American cichlids

New World cichlids include species from Central America and South America. A few species include oscars, Jack Dempseys, convicts, angelfish, firemouths, and discus.

Angelfish (Pterophyllum scalare)

The angelfish (refer to Figure 8-8) is such a delicate-looking species that you can only wonder how it can possibly be related to other cichlids. Angelfish have long dorsal and anal fins that they use for balance. They come in a wide variety of colors and patterns, including marble, white, and striped. Angelfish are one of the most beautiful and inspiring fish on earth. Just having one of these marvelous creatures is enough to suck you into the aquarium hobby for a lifetime.

FIGURE 8-8: Angelfish make great community fish.

A deep and long tank is best for this peaceful, carnivorous species with a water temperature between 78 and 82 degrees F. Feed this species flake food and toss in some brine shrimp for a treat. This species lays eggs and is easily bred in the home aquarium. Avoid placing fin-nipping mates with them.

Convict (Cichlasoma nigrofasciatum)

If you want to impress your friends with your breeding abilities, the convict cichlid (see Figure 8-9) is the fish for you. This hardy cichlid would breed in a puddle of water during an earthquake if given half a chance. Rabbits can't hold a candle to convicts. Both parents care for their young. The convict is aggressive, swims in the middle to lower sections of the aquarium, is carnivorous, and should be kept in a well-planted *species* tank (tanks that only contain fish of the same species).

The convict gets its name from the vertical black and white stripes on its body that resemble the prison uniforms you see in old movies. This fish is constantly alert, quick, and *very* territorial. Pink convicts are another, quite beautiful variety. This species can get large with females between 4 and 5 inches in length and males 6 to 7 inches in length so make sure you have a tank large enough to keep them healthy. I recommend at least a 55-gallon tank if you want convicts.

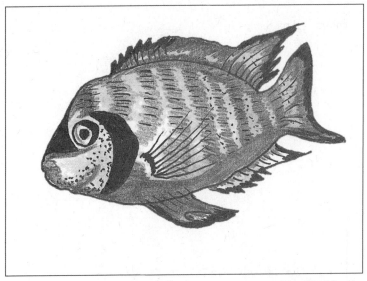

FIGURE 8-9:
Convicts should
be kept in their
own species tank.

Convicts eat any fish food offered to them. Keep them in a tank that has plenty of caves for breeding and hiding and has a water temperature between 68 to 75 degrees F. This species should only be kept with other fish of similar size and bad-boy attitude.

Discus (Symphysodon varieties)

The discus (see Figure 8-10) is the king of the cichlids, the Mona Lisa of the fish world. This flat fish, which resembles a plastic throwing disk, has been commercially bred to produce stunning colors. It's a peaceful and slow-moving species. Not only are discus beautiful, they also are well behaved. Who could ask for more? They're difficult to keep compared to most species because they can be fragile and more susceptible to disease.

These fish are carnivorous and should be kept in schools of at least three to five. They can be fed frozen brine shrimp, cichlid flakes, and insect larvae. They'll grow to longer than 5 inches in a home aquarium. The general rule is to have at least 10 gallons of water for each discus. Discus live in natural waters that have a temperature between 80 and 86 degrees F and a pH of about 4.5 and 6.0.

Discus water must be soft and acidic. Many hobbyists use reverse osmosis (RO) units to mimic its natural waters and combine this in a mix with tap water. However, you also need to add trace elements and minerals (available in liquid form at your pet store) back to the water to make it suitable for your aquarium fish. Discus can be quite expensive, but they're very popular and well worth the investment.

FIGURE 8-10:
Discus are
gorgeous and
well mannered.

Keyhole (Aequidens maronii)

The keyhole cichlid is a pale, peaceful fish with a dark band running through its eyes and a black keyhole-shaped spot on its side. This species usually only reaches lengths of 3 to 5 inches in captivity and should be kept with other nonaggressive fish such as barbs, danios, loaches, catfish, and gouramis. The keyhole prefers a heavily planted tank and is an omnivorous bottom-dweller.

Red oscar (Astronotus ocellatus)

The red oscar is an Amazonian giant (growing to lengths of longer than 12 inches in the home aquarium) who may quickly outgrow your tank, so a 70-gallon tank is a minimum requirement for one or two fish. This animal is carnivorous and eats anything it can fit into its large mouth and will eventually need to be fed cichlid pellet food.

TIP

One cool thing about an oscar is that you can hand tame it to accept food from you.

Oscars spend most of their time swimming in the middle levels of the tank. You can easily fool your friends into thinking that you're risking life and limb by feeding them.

Oscars enjoy water that is kept between 72 and 78 degrees and feel secure with a sandy substrate and rocks. Oscars will tear up plants, so if you do use artificial ones, prepare yourself to a daily routine of replanting them. If you put live plants in your oscar tank, say your permanent goodbyes as you're arranging them because the next time you see them they'll probably resemble confetti.

If kept in small groups, oscars tend to bicker with each other, so keep them in groups of eight or more. Unfortunately keeping this many oscars would require you to borrow a tank from the Shedd Aquarium in Chicago, so prepare to keep a single or two who will fight on and off. Tankmates can include knifefish, large plecos, tinfoil barbs, and other large cichlids of the same size.

Oscars can live a long time with some reports of them surviving more than 25 years in captivity.

Cyprinids

The cyprinids are a diverse family that includes barbs, danios, and rasboras.

Cherry barb (Barbus titteya)

Like its name suggests, this species of barb has a light red iridescent color and is shaped somewhat like a diamond. Even the sides of the fish have diamond-shaped markings. Maybe it should have been called the diamond cherry barb.

If provided with a planted tank and a school of its own kind, the cherry barb is generally peaceful and even timid around other species. Tank conditions are similar to the tiger barb (see the later section).

Green barb (Barbus tetrazona)

The green barb gets its name from its emerald green color. This fish can get slightly aggressive and nip fins. Aquarium conditions and tankmates are similar to the tiger barb.

Tiger barb (Barbus tetrazona)

The tiger barb (see Figure 8-11) is an orange-and black-striped fish native to Southeast Asia. This fish is omnivorous and swims in the middle and lower sections of the tank. Tiger barbs can become quite aggressive and should be kept in a species tank or with fish of similar size and temperament. Good tankmates could include plecos, barbs, rainbowfish, and loaches.

Tiger barbs are territorial, so the larger the tank the better. This species eats almost anything offered, so feed it a mixture of meaty foods and vegetable-based fish food. The water temperature for this species is between 70 and 74 degrees F. Make sure you have lots of plants and decorations to provide them hiding places when they start to pick on each other.

© John Wiley & Sons, Inc.

FIGURE 8-11:
Tiger barbs are aggressive and need a big tank.

Giant danio (Danio aequipinnatus)

This is large version of the danio species and is very peaceful community fish. This fish is a jumper and requires lots of swimming space in waters that range from 72 to 75 degrees F.

Zebra danio (Brachydanio rerio)

The South Asian zebra danio is one of the most popular community fish. The little speed demon makes the top of your tank look like the Indianapolis 500. This omnivorous, torpedo-shaped wonder is gold with blue stripes and is hardy. Keep danio in schools of five to seven in a tank with dense foliage where they can lay their eggs. Danios tend to fade away and die without a school, so give them some aquatic buddies.

The zebra danio is often used as a dither fish. A *dither* fish is an active and peaceful species put in a tank with slower moving species, so that the slower moving species become more active like the dither fish. (Whew!)

The zebra danio will eat almost anything the second it hits the water, so make sure your other fish in the same tank are getting their share, too. Danios can live in water temperature between 64 and 78 degrees F and are extremely tolerant of beginner mistakes.

Harlequin rasbora (Rasbora heteromorpha)

The omnivorous little harlequin rasbora from Southeast Asia has an unusual marking that makes it stand out in a crowd. The body is gold-green and has a dark blue patch that forms a triangle on each side. This fish only grows to about 2 inches. The rasbora should be kept in schools and swim in all levels of the tank.

Good tankmates include angelfish, tetras, danios, catfish, community livebearers, and gouramis. This fish prefers a well-planted tank with waters in between 73 and 77 degrees F and a pH of 6.0 to 6.5.

Freshwater tropical invertebrates

You can buy many of the following invertebrates for your aquarium. *Invertebrates* aren't fish because they lack a backbone.

Freshwater clams (Corbicual species)

Freshwater clams are from Asia and only grow to about 2 inches in the home aquarium. This invertebrate has banded brown and black colors and spends most of its time *filter feeding*. This type of feeding helps to keep your aquarium clean and reduce nitrates as it removes floating particles and uneaten food that is suspended in the water.

Freshwater clams can live in water temperatures ranging between 68 to 85 degrees and are peaceful.

Ghost shrimp (Paleomonetes species)

Ghost shrimp are small (only 2 inches at maturity), have segmented bodies, and are almost transparent except for a colored spot on their tails. This peaceful and delicate creature with ten sets of legs makes an interesting aquatic pet.

This species needs to be kept with passive fish that won't tear it limb from limb. Many hobbyists set up a 10-gallon aquarium just for their ghost shrimp so that they don't have to worry about predators. The reverse is also true: Many hobbyists use them as feeders for other fish.

Ghost shrimp eat almost anything in the aquarium using their tiny claws to scoop it in. They consume waste, algae, and almost any live, frozen, or manufactured food. They're true scavengers.

Singapore flower shrimp (Atyopsis moluccensis)

This beautiful red shrimp is native to Asia and reaches lengths of almost 4 inches in the home aquarium. This invertebrate is able to quickly change colors depending on it surrounding environment.

Singapore shrimp should be kept in aquariums of larger than 10 gallons; they happily feed on aquarium debris by filtering it with special appendages shaped like fans that are attached to their legs.

Ramshorn snail (Marisa cornuarietis)

This peaceful cool gold or cream-colored snail (refer to Figure 8-12) has a shell that looks like a ram's horn. It can live in water temperatures ranging between 70 and 85 degrees F and grows to about 2 inches.

FIGURE 8-12: The Ramshorn is a freshwater snail with a flat coiled shell.

The interesting thing about this snail is that it requires air to breathe. The snail accomplishes this using a siphon that sticks out of the water, like an escaped convict using a reed to breath underwater in an old prison break movie. For that reason you need to leave a couple of inches of open airspace on the top of the aquarium water.

The ramshorn snail is great for cleaning up debris in the aquarium.

Contemplating Coldwater Fish and Invertebrates

Freshwater creatures that live in coldwater tanks don't require heating because they generally live at lower temperatures than tropical ones do. The rest of the coldwater aquarium equipment is the same as for tropicals. However, if you keep fish in an outdoor pond during the freezing winter months, you may have to move them into a warmer area such as a holding tank in your garage until the frigid weather passes. Goldfish secrete a lot of waste, so good filtration is a must.

Although many fish such as the guppy can live in cooler waters, I focus on other nontropical varieties in these sections. In today's market, for example, many beautiful varieties of goldfish will fascinate and amaze you. They aren't your garden-variety feeder goldfish found at carnivals!

Koi (Cyprinus carpio)

Koi *(Cyprinus carpio)* (see Figure 8-13) is a highly colored omnivorous pond fish that is related to goldfish. Because of its large size at maturity (up to 3 feet in length), it's unsuitable for an indoor aquarium. The torpedo-shaped koi requires a good filtration system and many plants, which it uses for food and shade. Champion varieties can be very expensive, but they have outstanding color and beauty.

Koi doesn't do well in acidic water, so its pH needs to be kept between 7.0 and 9.0. Keep the species in ponds that allows it to remain cool throughout the year.

Goldfish (Carassius auratus)

Goldfish are one of the oldest aquarium fish known. These fish were specifically bred from carp for their beauty and have no known natural varieties. All goldfish variations are grouped into the same species, *Carassius auratus*. There are four main types of goldfish:

>> **Common goldfish:** These fish are similar in appearance to the carp from which they were bred, but have more color variations.

>> **Dragon-eye goldfish:** Dragon-eye goldfish have eyes that protrude in the form of telescoping or bubbles.

>> **Egg goldfish:** Egg goldfish have no dorsal fin, are egg shaped, and have double tails.

>> **Wen goldfish:** The Wen goldfish have a fancy style tail and a dorsal fin.

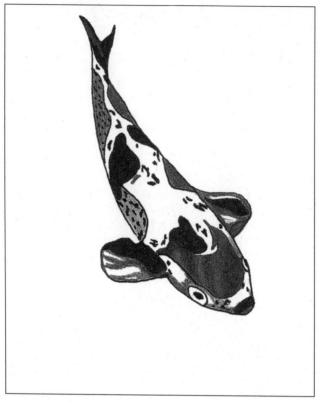

© John Wiley & Sons, Inc.

FIGURE 8-13: Koi get too big for an aquarium, but they're great for ponds.

Because they belong to the carp family, they're hardy. Goldfish tend to dig around in the gravel and will destroy dainty plants. Toss some smooth river rocks into the goldfish tank and watch them flip them all over the place. Keep the water temperature between 65 and 70 degrees F.

Due to their physical makeup, goldfish should have their protein intake limited to no more than 25 to 30 percent of their nutritional intake. The best thing to feed them is manufactured goldfish food. Good tankmates for almost all goldfish species include scavenging catfish, such as the pleco, and other goldfish.

Fancy goldfish have been bred for many physical characteristics, including bubble eyes, split tales, long fins, and unusual head coverings (*growth*). These species can be kept in either a coldwater aquarium or a pond. Either way, these omnivorous fish need a good filtration system and plenty of foliage.

Black moor goldfish (Carassius auratus)

The black moor is a cool-looking goldfish that really isn't gold at all. It's actually black. The body is slightly hunched, and the caudal fin fans downward like a lace veil draped over the top of a glass. Like many goldfish, black moors tend to wobble as they swim, which is quite amusing to watch, and have protruding, velvety black eyes. Keep black moors in tanks of 20 gallons or larger outfitted with either artificial or thick-leafed coldwater plants.

Bubble-eye goldfish (Carassius auratus)

The peaceful bubble-eye is one of the most amazing looking goldfish around. Like the lionhead goldfish, it has no dorsal fin and wiggles to swim. As the name suggests, this fish has huge fluid-filled bubble sacks beneath each eye. As bubble-eyes get older, the sacs grow larger and can become heavy to the point of slowing down their motion and keeping them near the bottom of the tank.

Because they spend a lot of their time near the substrate, make sure that all gravel, rocks, and other aquarium decorations have smooth edges that won't damage their delicate eye sacks. This species also has to be kept with other nonaggressive goldfish. The aquarium should be as large as possible so that bubble-eyes have plenty of room to swim around without risking damaging their eyes on things in the aquarium.

Feed them sinking pellets so that they can easily get their fair share of nutrition. Keep their water slightly warmer (70 to 75 degrees F).

Lionhead (Carassius auratus)

Lionheads resemble a lion in color, have a head growth like a lion's mane, and have thick bodies. These are slow-moving fish (because they have no dorsal fin) that need excellent water conditions in order to avoid disease. Aquarium conditions are similar to those of the black moor. This fish comes in many colors, including orange, white, blue, and black and calico mixtures.

The lionhead can growth to lengths of 10 inches and like other large goldfish requires a lot of tank space to remain healthy and happy.

Telescope-eye goldfish or dragon-eye goldfish (Carassius auratus)

This species of goldfish, which was first developed in the 16th century, has round eyes that protrude outward more and more as the first few months of development pass by. These eyes resemble those of fictional dragons. This gentle goldfish has been known to live up to 25 years in captivity.

This goldfish should be kept in water between 65 and 75 degrees F and should be kept in as large a tank as possible.

White cloud mountain minnows (Tanichthys albonubes)

Originally thought to be extinct in 1980, the white cloud mountain minnow made a comeback through breeding in the aquarium trade. See, you can do something important with the hobby. It's probably one of the most overlooked and most beautiful fish on the planet when placed in a fast-moving river tank.

This species is silver-green in color with a reddish caudal fin. It grows to a length of about 1½ inches. You can keep this minnow in a tank that ranges between 64 and 72 degrees F. Because they do better in schools, maintain them in groups of six minimum.

Coldwater invertebrates

Some invertebrates live in tropical tanks. One fairly common species — the ghost shrimp — also enjoys living in coldwater aquariums. Refer to the previous section about ghost shrimp.

Fiddler crabs (Uca)

Fiddler crabs spend most of their time on the bottom of the aquarium in search of food in nooks and crannies. They're very peaceful and grow up to 2 inches in length.

Florida blue crayfish (Procambaris alleni)

The Florida blue crayfish is a beautiful combination of blue and gray that can live in temperatures as low as 50 degrees F. Keep it in a species tank so it doesn't have to worry about being eaten, and you don't have to worry about them eating other inhabitants. Crayfish are vulnerable when molting.

REMEMBER

Crayfish are good climbers, so make sure your aquarium has a good lid.

Nerite snail (Neritina natalensis)

The nerite snail has a tiger-striped shell and is useful for cleaning up your aquarium. Like all snails, nerite snails need to be placed in the tank after it has been cycled because they're sensitive to water toxins. They also need a tight-fitting lid because they can crawl out and die if they dry out. Make sure they have calcium in their diet to keep their shells strong. This species can live in tanks from 65 to 80 degrees F. Nerite snails only breed in brackish water.

Red cherry shrimp (Neocaridina davidi)

The red cherry shrimp can add a lot of color to your aquarium. Its fire-engine red color is beautiful. The water conditions should be like the community tank setup, but with plenty of moving water. This species likes to feed off algae and live plants and will clean up hard-to-reach areas of the tank. They reach an adult length of about 1½ inches.

Red-clawed crabs (Sesarma)

This species thrives best in cold brackish waters. Red-clawed crabs live to 4 years of age and grow to a length of 1½ inches. This species eats anything you put in the tank and is an escape artist so make sure that you have a tight-fitting lid.

Trapdoor snails (Bellamya chinensis)

Trapdoor snails are also good for cleaning up debris and algae in the aquarium. Keep them in tanks that are free from aggressive fish that will try to eat them. This species can live in a pH of 6.5 to 8.4 and a water temperature between 65 and 82 degrees F. This snail actually hibernates if the water temperature drops below recommended levels.

UNDERSTANDING SETUPS

When your aquarium setup is complete, make sure that you match your fish to it. Using this chapter as a rough guide gives you a good head start. When in doubt about an unfamiliar species, check with your local fish shop owner because some friendly fish have been known to go bad and vice versa. It's better to be prepared with knowledge than face instant disaster.

So much of the road that leads to becoming an expert fishkeeper is dependent upon practical experience as well as knowledge. Sometimes when trying to choose compatible species, you have to experiment a little to see what works best for you and your individual setup. The size of your tank, the number of fish it contains, and the types of decorations in it can all have an effect on how well your tankmates get along.

Thinking about Captive-Bred Species

People tend to think that oceans, rivers, and lakes are an endless realm overflowing with aquatic animal life. But as an ecologically concerned fishkeeper, you must remember that only a small percentage of the world's waters contain the fish that you put into your aquarium. Each year, fish populations decline due to overfishing, the curio trade, and other human interventions, such as pollution and introduction of non-native fish into areas that are altered by their presence. Be it freshwater, brackish, or marine, the problem exists and is worth mentioning.

Often fish dealers offer both *captive-bred species* (fish or other aquatic animals that have been raised in hatcheries for the aquarium trade) and animals that have been caught in the wild. By purchasing captive-bred fish, you can help slow down the elimination of wild species. Most freshwater fish are now commercially bred to one extent or another and are usually less expensive than those caught in the wild.

The bulk of the problem occurs in the marine side of the hobby. Few marine fish are bred commercially because they can be quite difficult to spawn. In the last few years, marine fish hatcheries have made great progress in reproducing many species of clownfish, wrasses, and other types of saltwater fish. At the present time, captive-bred marine species can be a little more expensive than those caught in the wild, but in the long run it's well worth the extra money to help save the natural aquatic resources. Remember this piece of information if you decide to keep a marine tank.

The collection of live coral has also hit an all-time high in recent years. Many areas are now prohibiting collection of live coral because the world's reefs are beginning to disappear due to global warming, pollution, and repeated harvesting for curio shops and the marine aquarium trade.

WARNING

Many marine fish are caught by people using illegal practices and products such as cyanide, which also destroys large portions of any coral reef that it comes in contact with. Purchasing wild animals only encourages wholesalers to continue removing fish and invertebrates from their native habitat.

REMEMBER

So if you have a choice, always purchase captive-bred species (ask your dealer if his stock is captive bred). That way your grandchildren won't have to have an aquarium with plastic fish suspended in it.

Buying Fish Online

Now you have a few good ideas about some interesting and amazing species of fish and invertebrates for your freshwater aquarium. Remember that the species in this chapter are only a drop in the bucket when you look at the total number of fish available. Listing every species would take volumes.

AMAZING FISH FACTS

Fish are truly amazing creatures! Here are a few fun fish facts that you can use to impress your friends:

- Goldfish actually have teeth located in their throat. They can also be trained to respond to sounds at feeding time because they can remember things for several months.

- Some aquarium fish squeeze their swim bladders in order to make noises to communicate.

- A koi named Hanako lived to be older than 200 years old.

- Fish don't get new scales as they grow. The scales they have will grow to produce growth rings.

- Fish need oxygen, so many species will actually drown in water if it lacks enough oxygen to survive.

- Catfish have four times the taste buds that humans do.

- Oscars are very intelligent and have been known to shake their heads and wiggle just like a dog does to get attention. Oscars also enjoy redecorating their tanks by moving rocks, gravel, and other decorations.

- There are more species of fish than all the species of amphibians, reptiles, birds, and mammals combined.

- After giving birth, a female guppy can become pregnant again within a couple of hours.

- Female and male freshwater angelfish look exactly the same physically.

- Scientists believe that there may be more than 15,000 species of fish that are still undiscovered.

- Fish have been around for more than 450 million years.

Some species are easier to obtain than others are. You should patronize your local shop whenever possible, but don't forget that you can go online to find many fish at reasonable prices. Most online companies are good about shipping their stock on time and in good condition, so don't worry about getting what you paid for. Just make sure you check the company's shipping costs (which vary from company to company) so that you can add them into the total cost for your purchase. Also always read the reviews to see what others think of the company.

Chapter **9**

Working with a Fish Dealer to Purchase Your Fish

O ne of the best ways to start out as a beginning hobbyist is to develop a good relationship with a local tropical fish dealer. A quality vendor can help you make informed decisions on the type of aquarium best suited for you, the proper equipment for your new tank, and the best aquatic species for your system. A good vendor can also locate hard-to-find products and can help you with water testing on a regular basis. I can't stress enough the importance of having a regular aquarium dealer that you trust.

Of course, you can do many things as an informed hobbyist to help you start off your fishkeeping adventure with success. Choosing healthy pets from a good local vendor is the best way to start off right, and this chapter can help.

Choosing a Quality Fish Dealer

The aquarium hobby is generally a lifelong addiction. (I'm a promising candidate for Aquariums Anonymous.) Putting this fascinating hobby aside after you take the plunge is difficult. In the years to come, you'll need to purchase fish, replace worn equipment, and keep stocked up on chemicals and proper food. That road will go more smoothly if you have informed people who can offer help and real-time advice along the way.

During the course of your hobby, you also need expert advice on fishkeeping skills once in a while and someone to keep you informed on the newest trends in equipment and other aquarium-related paraphernalia. No matter what your skill level in fishkeeping, there is always something new to learn. This is why you need to find a good retailer who specializes in the aquarium aspect of the pet industry.

REMEMBER

A knowledgeable aquarium fish dealer, especially one who is conveniently located in your neighborhood, can help you anytime you have a problem or emergency with your aquatic pets. Building a personal relationship with this type of merchant also helps you stay informed on aquarium-related issues. For these reasons and more, it's important to make contact with an informed and trustworthy vendor. (Besides, if you get to know a dealer well, you may be able to snag a few freebies as well.)

TIP

The best way to develop a good relationship is through communication. When you find a good dealer, talk to her frequently when you visit. Ask her about her own aquariums and share information. Developing a good relationship with a fish dealer is no different that developing one with a friend.

Searching for a fish store

When you want to buy a house, you don't just purchase the first one you see, do you? No, you look around a bit first. The same principal applies to your aquarium hobby. Look for the best and don't settle for less. There's nothing wrong with checking the gossip in your neighborhood to determine whether the local dealers have a good reputation among other businesses and their customers. Friends, aquarium clubs, and family members are a great place to start asking questions. If you're like me, you'll not only hear all you need to know about local aquarium shops, you'll pick up a few juicy extra tidbits at the same time.

TIP

You can start your search local and then move online. No matter where you look, make sure you check online reviews, such as Yelp and Google, for an overall general clue of how a business operates. You also can check with the Better Business Bureau for complaints against businesses you're considering.

In today's consumer-conscious environment, you can't afford to end up with mediocre service because you were afraid to investigate the references or character of a particular dealer. You can obtain valuable information through this age-old method.

Looking in your hood

The best strategy is to visit as many local dealers and aquarium shops as your time and budget allow. These fun investigative trips provide you with a solid foundation on which you can compare dealers' overall quality of service, livestock selection and condition, friendliness, willingness to help, and prices on fish and equipment. Look for dealers who stock a full line of aquarium hardware and fish. Avoid those who have a small selection of aquarium supplies jammed into a corner in order to make room so that they can specialize in every other type of pet supplies.

In choosing a tropical fish dealer, take into consideration a few important factors (covered in the next sections) before you pledge your loyalty to one particular shop. In fact, I find it best to frequent at least *two* fish shops minimum. It's kind of like having an ace in the hole (or up your sleeve) at a poker game: If one shop goes out of business or has an internal problem that affects your ability to get good equipment or livestock, you're still covered.

After you compare all your local fish shops, choose the two retailers you think can satisfy all your aquarium requirements.

Searching online

You may live in a more rural area and not have a dealer within close business. Perhaps your local dealers don't have a large selection of supplies and fish. If so, you may want to look online. The best way to find a good online fish store is to look for companies that have been in business for many years and have a wide selection of products and/or fish. Most business on the Internet list the number of years they've been in business. Going with an established store is safer. The good news: Nearly all reputable businesses have an online presence. Your options online of available aquarium shops are endless.

REMEMBER

Another good way to find stock is through local aquarium clubs. Hobbyists who are members are often willing to sell good stock. Check out this link: `https://fishlab.com/local-fish-and-aquarium-clubs/`.

The importance of great service

When deciding on the two best local dealers, see whether the employees are friendly and offer good advice. Ask yourself these questions:

>> Do the clerks make every attempt to help you out when you come in, or do they just stand around shooting the breeze?

>> Do the shop's workers take a personal interest in your aquarium?

>> Are they willing to go out of their way to make sure that you find exactly what you need?

>> Are there adequate personnel to provide good service to you even during the peak hours of the day?

If you have to blitz and tackle a clerk to make him talk, then you need to find another place to shop. A reputable and caring owner who takes pride in his business and in providing customer satisfaction makes sure that his shop is well staffed with knowledgeable and caring employees.

WARNING

Employees who stand around and do nothing generally don't have an interest in their employer's business and probably don't have an interest in making sure that you get the stuff for your aquarium either. (Hopefully you won't see those clerks the next time you visit.)

The store's appearance

When you go to an aquarium shop (even if you're checking out a new one that just opened in the neighborhood), carefully inspect all the display tanks for obvious signs of dealer dedication or apathy. If the place looks like the owner couldn't care less about how the tanks look, he probably cares just as little about the rest of his business, including the fish. A visual inspection can tell you quite a bit about a shop's habits. As you look around the shop, check for the following clues that distinguish a good dealer from an uncaring one.

The tanks

Quality retailers understand that the overall condition of their shop makes a big difference as far as customers' first impressions are concerned.

The physical condition of the tanks is a good indication of how well the fish are taken care of on a daily basis. Ask yourself these questions:

>> Are the tanks free of excess algae or do they resemble the Florida swamps?

>> Are the proper mixtures of compatible species displayed in the tanks or does it appear that a bunch of fish have been thrown in a tank to save space?

>> Is the tank water clear or murky?

>> Do the tanks look like they have been properly vacuumed lately?

>> Is the front of the glass clean or does it still bare smudges and fingerprints from the grade school class who visited the shop the week before? Someone who won't even take a couple minutes to clean the front glass doesn't care much about presentation or the impression the shop makes on its customers and usually doesn't care about the health of his fish or his customers' best interests either.

>> Are the shelves full of merchandise, neatly stocked, and organized, or is everything dusty and just tossed together on one shelf?

The fish

A good quality retailer has good quality fish. No exceptions. If a dedicated dealer isn't happy with his suppliers, he quickly looks for another who can provide high-quality fish. While you're browsing through a store, see whether the dealer's fish are swimming boldly (out away from the decorations) in the open spaces of the aquarium or hiding in the corners with their face smashed against the glass.

Fish that hide in corners usually have health problems after you bring them home. If the fish in the shop look like they just swam through a waste dump, find another pet store.

Here are some things to ask when examining fish:

>> Do the fish look generally healthy?

>> Do the fish have sores or are they missing scales? If so, avoid buying them.

>> Are the fish all lurking at the bottom of the tank or gasping at the surface and look distressed? If this isn't normal for the species, there could be a problem. (Check out Chapter 8 for more information on where species like to hang out.)

>> Does the dealer have many artificially colored fish? If so, run away. (Refer to Chapter 7 for more on artificially dyed fish.)

>> Are the fins erect?

>> Do the bodies display proper color?

>> Do the fish have a good shape and are their bodies correctly formed for the particular species?

>> Do all the merchant's fish appear to be in good health or just a few?

>> Has the dealer shown honesty by turning the lights off or putting a sign on sick tanks to indicate diseased fish — or is the store just selling fish in bad condition?

The equipment

Sometimes your equipment will wear out or fail, and you need to replace it. Make sure that the dealers you choose have an adequate supply of equipment and parts. Nothing is more frustrating than having to run from store to store to find a simple piece of equipment such as a net, pump, or filter, or be forced to pay high prices for an overnight Internet delivery.

Make sure that your dealer has a wide selection on hand. If not, make sure the shop can order needed supplies and get them in within a reasonable amount of time.

Chemicals and food

Does the shop have a good supply of chemicals, medicine, and foods available? You may not have time to wait for a dealer to order medications if your fish are really ill — it's much better to have it available when an emergency arises. Check to see if the store carries a wide selection of frozen foods as well as food for fish with special or unique dietary needs. Make sure none of the expiration dates have passed.

Dealer Practices: The Good, the Bad, and the Ugly

I classify dealers into good dealers (Do Bees), bad dealers (Don't Bees), and ugly dealers (Wanna Bees). I've seen all types during my years in the aquarium hobby. All I can do is give you a little personal advice as to what to look for when you are trying to determine who is the good guy and who is the bad guy. I can't stress this enough, because if you don't have a good place to purchase fish and aquarium equipment, you may become frustrated with fighting a continual uphill battle to maintain successful aquariums.

Do Bee dealers

A Do Bee dealer helps you find success. Some of the signs of a good retailer are the following:

>> They have friendly, helpful, knowledgeable staff members who answer your questions willingly, go out of their way to help, and who are familiar with aquarium equipment, the different types of aquarium systems, and individual species of fish.

>> They carry a large selection of aquarium equipment, food, medication, and fish on hand — more than one or two brands.

>> They offer free services, such as water testing.

>> They offer some type of guarantee on the fish they sell and the commitment to stand behind the equipment that they sell. A really good Do Bee offers free repair service or your money back on basic equipment that he has sold to you if it doesn't work properly.

>> They offer a willingness to tell you where you can get a certain species or piece of equipment if they can't get it. This includes offering competitors' contact information.

>> They offer autopsies of dead fish to help determine the cause of the disease (if the dealer has qualified staff) and medication advice to help prevent the need for an autopsy.

>> They're genuinely interested in you and your aquariums.

>> The ability to bag fish with oxygen if they're located far from your home.

>> They have signs on the front of each tank giving the name, general water conditions, compatibility, and other information on each fish they stock.

>> The shop is clean, including the tanks.

Don't Bee dealers

Don't Bee dealers own aquarium shops you want to avoid. They're quite easy to spot when you recognize the symptoms of their "I have no business being in the tropical fish trade because I don't really care about my job, or I am just in it for the money" disease. Avoid these dealers at all costs!

You can recognize Don't Bees by the following characteristics:

>> They're willing to tell you to take a hike if you question the quality of their service or livestock.

>> They let you stand around without offering to help you find what you're looking for.

>> They spend a lot of time answering phone calls and leave you waiting for service until they finish yacking.

>> They try to give you a snow job if you ask them a question they don't have an answer for.

>> They try to sell you a bunch of junk you don't need because they believe that you don't know any better.

>> They sell fish they know are diseased just to get rid of them.

>> They use the same net to capture fish in all their tanks without sterilizing it between uses.

>> They have dirty aquariums and a filthy shop.

>> They sell you fish that aren't compatible just to make a few extra bucks (which obviously they don't spend on the upkeep of the shop).

>> They refuse to go out of their way to order any special equipment or fish for you.

>> They don't keep regular store hours and show up whenever they happen to feel like it.

>> They are extremely rough with the fish when bagging them up for transport.

Wanna Bee dealers

A Wanna Bee dealer is the owner of a pet shop who appears overnight and disappears within a few months because he didn't have the proper finances to keep it afloat long enough to establish itself. These dealers sell you poor quality fish and equipment at inexpensive prices to get some money coming in and then simply fall off the face of the earth. If a new shop opens up and you're unsure as to whether you should purchase fish from the new owners, simply wait a few months to see if it stays open. During this time, keep your ear out for information from other customers concerning the quality of the shop.

Developing a Good Relationship with Your Fish Dealer

After you make your final decision and pledge your loyalty to a couple of dealers, try to become acquainted with as many of the employees in the shop as possible. Go out of your way to meet the owner or store manager, who can likely help you with any serious problems you may have.

A great majority of dealers are very enthusiastic when given the opportunity to work with regular customers. After the initial conversation, your aquarium, ideas, or wishes may become as familiar to them as their own personal tanks. Many merchants beam proudly at a customer's first successful aquarium setup (after all, the merchant helped create it). A caring vendor also mourns with you at the loss of your favorite fish. A vendor who can't remember your name after you have been buying from his shop for months probably should be avoided.

TIP

Making the effort required to solidify a personal relationship with your local dealer puts you in good position to receive quality advice and the highest degree of comprehensive service available. When a merchant is familiar with you, the type of systems you own, your special interests, and other personal aquarium specifications, he has a better opportunity to help you become a successful hobbyist.

Selecting Healthy Fish

Whether you find a good dealer or not, you still need to take responsibility for choosing the healthiest fish possible. Starting off with diseased fish is the quickest way to lose interest in the hobby. You always take a risk when you purchase a live animal because unseen problems may manifest later on, but you can improve the odds of success by starting off with the healthiest fish possible. The following sections help you choose easy-to-care for fish that will allow you to become a successful hobbyist right off the bat.

Start simply and do your homework

If you're new to the hobby, investigate and discover as much as you can about fish. Start with some simple hardier fish, such as guppies, platys, and swordfish, for example, which are great for beginners. Don't buy fish that are completely unfamiliar. Just because you're browsing the store and happen to a see a cool-looking fish doesn't mean you should take it home.

WARNING

Stay away from hard-to-maintain-and-feed species of fish such as pacus or oscars. Fish that have special dietary requirements may be too much to handle in the beginning when you're still trying to get the hang of how your equipment works. Wait until you're completely familiar with your system before trying your luck with the harder-to-maintain species of tropical fish.

If you do want to try a more difficult to keep species, make sure you do your research (via Internet sites dedicated to particular species and talking to experienced hobbyists and pet store personnel who keep that type of fish) before buying so that you know exactly what that fish require to flourish.

Look for signs of good health

You can look at several physical characteristics to determine whether the fish you want to buy are in good health. There is never a guarantee of complete success, but if you follow these rules, you increase your chances of getting a healthy specimen. Keep an eye open for the following:

» The body color is rich, not faded or dull. The color should be complete and not missing in any areas (unless it's typical for the species).

» There are no open sores, visible ulcers, boils, or obvious skin problems, such as peeling scales or blemishes.

» Fins are long and flowing, or short and erect. The fish shouldn't have any ragged, torn, or missing fins.

» Scales are flat and smooth, not protruding away from the body.

» The stomach is well rounded, not sunken or concave.

» Girth of the entire body is of normal size, not bloated or emaciated.

» Visible *excreta* (fish waste) should be dark in color, not pale.

» All the fins on the fish's body shouldn't be collapsed or completely clamped shut.

» Eyes are clear, not cloudy or popping out of the sockets.

» No visible parasites, such as ich or velvet.

Know your fish's behavior

A few behavioral characteristics (how the fish acts) are worth taking a look at. Healthy fish should

>> Swim in a horizontal motion, not with its head up or down (except for the notable exceptions).

>> Swim with complete ease, not continually fighting to stay afloat.

>> Swim throughout the aquarium, not lurk in the corners or excessively hiding behind decorations.

>> Breathe normally, not gulp for air or hang around the top of the tank with its mouth gasping at the top of the water.

Understand how big the fish will grow

Check with your dealer to find out how large each individual species will get at maturity. Many dealers carry young fish. You don't want to end up with an over-crowded tank after they're fully grown. For example, I was at a pet shop recently and saw a 2-inch pacu. It was so cute! But this fish can grow to lengths of 10 inches or more, leaving smaller tankmates to end up as Sunday buffet.

If you have any doubts, consult your local dealer. Larger fish are great for some hobbyists, but they do tend to limit your aquarium space and your choices of other tankmates. Here is a list of *average* sizes for many fish in home aquariums:

>> Platy 1.25 inches

>> Tiger barb 1.0 inch

>> Black moor 3.0 inches

>> Swordtails 2.0 inches

>> Dwarf gourami 1.5 inches

>> Cory 1.0–2.0 inches

>> Pleco 2.0–12.0 inches

>> Red serape tetra .05–1.0 inches

>> Neon tetra .05 inches

>> Black molly 1.25 inches

>> Yellow rainbowfish 2.0 inches

>> Pacu 5.0–35.0 inches

Avoid the first fish off the boat

Steer clear of buying any new arrivals your dealer recently received. If the fish are still in a packing crate, that should give you a clue. You should see a large number of bags containing fish floating in the aquariums on the days the store receives new shipments. Most dealers receive new fish on one or two specific days each week. Ask your dealer which days these are. A good dealer doesn't allow customers to purchase fish until he's had sufficient time to *quarantine* them. This quarantine period reduces the fish's stress from shipping and allows the shop's personnel to treat any disease that shows up in the first few days after arrival. The dealer should quarantine in the back of the shop, so if you see those bags floating in purchase tanks, avoid buying them. Most dealers I have frequented have allowed me to look at the arrivals in the back of their shop.

TIP

If you happen to see some fish that really catch your eye while they are still in the bags in the back, ask the dealer to hold them for you until a reasonable quarantine period has expired. Most dealers willingly agree to do that for free or with a small deposit or prepayment. Helpful merchants who take the time to grant such simple requests to provide customer satisfaction are definitely worth patronizing in the future. Stop for a moment and ask yourself one simple question: If I owned this fish shop, would I do this for my customer? If the answer is yes, then you should expect your dealer to do the same thing.

Don't be Doctor Doolittle

WARNING

Never allow anyone, including your dealer, to talk you into buying a sick or ailing fish in the honorable but mistaken belief that you can quickly nurse it back to vibrant health. This is one of the biggest mistakes a beginning hobbyist can make. I've purchased fish that I wanted to save from destruction, but I wasn't a novice at the time. I saved these fish with round-the-clock care, but a lot of experience and time are usually required to get the job done.

Playing Florence Nightingale for aquatic pets only works when you have the proper knowledge and equipment to pull it off. Diseased fish can cause water problems and infect your other fish as well. Don't buy any fish from tanks that the dealer is currently medicating, because diseases can spread to your other fish.

If you notice dead fish floating in a healthy-looking tank, avoid buying any of the livestock from that same aquarium. Don't purchase a fish with an unusually humped back (unless normal for the species) — because this generally indicates old age. A good dealer never allows a customer to purchase old, dying, or diseased fish, but instead tells you that certain fish are being medicated and aren't for sale until the condition clears up.

REMEMBER

Just because a fish has been medicated doesn't mean that it's completely well again. Let your eye be the best judge; carefully inspect any fish for signs of disease, such as torn or clamped fins, white spots or growths, abnormal swimming patterns, or irregularly shaped bodies.

Getting the Right Fish without Going Overboard

To be a successful hobbyist, you need to understand your purchases and which fish are best for you. By now, you know how to spot a healthy fish, but there's more to it than that. You also need to pick fish that are compatible and won't tear each other to bits and turn your aquarium into a war zone. Making a shopping list after researching species and understanding a fish's ultimate size and temperament are two ways that you can avoid disaster.

TIP

When you go to purchase your fish, write down on a notepad or create a note in your phone of the names of all the fish that appeal to you that you haven't yet researched. By writing down the names of the fish, you don't have to remember names (scientific names and even common names can be a little confusing at times) and can go back and find certain tanks quite easily. This can be a real advantage if the shop has several hundred display tanks. When you finish your list, locate your dealer or do research to check to see whether all the species you chose are compatible with each other, don't have unique dietary needs, and don't have special aquarium requirements.

Keep an eye out for other compatibility issues. For example, if you buy a convict cichlid and a guppy, you'll probably find the convict alone and well fed in the morning.

Chapter **10**

Feeding Your Wet Pets — Diet and Nutrition

J ust like their human counterparts, your aquatic pets need proper nutrition so that they can remain active and healthy and live long lives. A proper diet can be found by using most manufactured fish foods, but you can also increase your fish's good health by providing a variety of fresh vegetables and other products that are suited to each individual species. In order to feed your fish properly, you need to know how much to feed, what types of foods different fish require, the different types of food available, and how to feed young fish if you're breeding. This chapter gives you the basic information that you need to understand the complete picture of aquatic nutrition.

Understanding Basic Nutrition

Unfortunately, you can't feed your fish the cheeseburger, fries, and apple pie that keeps many kids happy, so you have to supply other types of food to meet their dietary needs. Fortunately, you can combine many good nutrition sources to form a proper diet for your fish. Aquarium food can be quite varied and includes brine shrimp, dry flake, fresh shrimp, algae, daphnia, pellets, algae wafers, tubifex worms, and beef heart — to name just a few choices. These foods are all good sources of nutrition, but only if they're distributed in proper amounts to the right fish. Tossing an entire beef heart into the tank for your guppy's breakfast doesn't cut it, because it would foul the water and it isn't recommended for that particular species.

TIP

When purchasing any type of aquarium food, the most important rule is to select the finest quality your finances can handle. Aquarium foods aren't really that expensive when you look at the total amount of food you get for the price, so why not purchase the best? Top-quality commercial foods are enriched with vitamins and minerals and help keep your fish in optimal health. Low-grade food promotes poor health and disease.

Feeding your fish can be a relaxing activity and also provides an excellent opportunity for you to check them for any signs of illness. What's more entertaining than observing a bunch of animals pigging out? Watching your aquatic pets interact socially (pushing each other out of the way, stealing food from each other, hoarding the choicest items, turning their noses up at others) can be educational. If you're like me, you probably see the same thing at your own dinner table. At least you don't have to cook for your fish.

Fish need basic nutrients to thrive just like every other animal. But overfeeding and underfeeding will harm your fish, so here are a few ideas on how to feed them properly.

Recognizing what your fish need

What you feed your fish should contain the following components:

>> **Carbohydrates:** These provide energy for your fish and also help them resist disease.

>> **Proteins:** These help your fish build strong muscle and tissue. Fish obtain proteins through a diet that includes meat, fish, insects, and manufactured foods. Proteins are an important factor in promoting physical growth, so it's important to remember that younger fish need a little more than full-grown adults.

>> **Vitamins:** These are vital to your fish's good health. A balanced diet that combines live and processed foods easily supplies the necessary vitamins. A balanced diet includes vitamin A (egg, greens, and crustaceans), vitamin B (fish, greens, algae, and beef), vitamin C (algae), vitamin D (worms, algae, and shrimp), vitamin E (egg and algae), vitamin H (egg and liver), and vitamin K (liver and greens).

REMEMBER

Experienced hobbyists realize that feeding their aquatic pets can be an art in itself (especially if you own an overgrown piranha). With so many different natural and prepared foods to choose from, not only in fish shops but also on the Internet, beginning hobbyists can easily get confused about nutritional issues. Just remember that no one product can satisfy every fish in your aquarium. Variety is always good. But as this chapter shows you, discovering how to feed your fish properly isn't as hard as it first seems. A little experience and practice can make all the difference in the world.

Being aware of overfeeding

You want to make sure that your freshwater fish receive all the nutrition they need. However, you can easily make mistakes until you get the hang of a new feeding routine. One main mistake is overfeeding fish. Overfeeding can lead to obesity and other health problems. If your fish resemble overinflated tires, cut back on the grub. Too much food in an aquarium tank can also build up and foul the water or increase the risk of disease.

Excess food around the edge of the substrate is one sign of overfeeding. This wasted food accumulates on the bottom of the tank, turns muddy brown, and begins to spoil. Spoiled food can cause health problems for your fish if they happen to eat it. If excess food piles up, vacuum the tank, decrease the amount you feed, and try putting the food in a different area of the aquarium.

TIP

Remember that your fish's stomach is no larger than its eye. So, if you dump a half a can of fish food into the tank, you had better hope your fish has an eye the size of a dinner plate; otherwise, you're in for a few problems. Excess food breaking down on the substrate surface can cause an overabundance of harmful ammonia. If you do happen to overfeed, remove the excess with a standard aquarium vacuum.

Underfeeding is just as bad

Because so much emphasis is placed on overfeeding and its polluting effects, many hobbyists don't feed their fish enough. Well, the point is, don't overfeed or underfeed. Feed the correct amount.

Feeding just what your fish need

The general rule is to feed only what your fish can eat in a period of three to five minutes per feeding. This doesn't mean that you have to stand around with a starter's whistle and stopwatch at every meal. Just check to make sure that your fish polish off all the food within five minutes. Another option is to purchase a plastic feeding ring that keeps most dry foods confined to a small area on top of the water. A feeding ring can keep most of the food from quickly falling to the bottom of the tank.

TIP

If at all possible, feed adult fish two or three small meals per day instead of just dumping a bunch of food in at one time. I personally feed my fish twice a day. Juvenile fish and fry need be fed more often to ensure they grow properly, so give them a couple of extra light feedings each day.

It's best to feed your fish at different times of the day, usually morning, afternoon, and/or night. Because many nocturnal fish feed only at night, make sure they receive their fair share.

TIP

It's not a bad idea to make your fish fast one day a week. This is normal in nature. Going 24 hours without food keeps a fish's dietary tract in good physical condition. Some fish need to be fed more than others depending on what species you have. Research the fish that you plan on keeping, so you know the correct amount to feed them.

FEEDING YOUR FISH WHILE ON VACATION

Try to find a trustworthy person to feed your fish while you're away on vacation. A relative or mature neighborhood kid is usually a good choice. To make sure they feed your fish properly, place individual servings in plastic bags, pill containers, or tiny plastic cups so that your substitute knows exactly what to put into each tank. Doing so may sound like a hassle, but it's better than returning home to find your prize goldfish, the size of a basketball, beached on a mountain of uneaten food.

Another option is to purchase an automatic feeder from your local fish shop. These units automatically dispense a certain amount of food (you can choose the amount) at daily intervals that you preset. Models can be purchased that hang on the aquarium rim, whereas others are free standing. Dispensers run on either batteries or AC power, and some models offer both options. Automatic feeders are a great way to feed your aquatic pets the proper amount of food regularly.

Never add a bunch of extra food to the tank before going on vacation. Your fish won't eat the extra food before it starts rotting, and by the time you get home you may have a serious water problem.

Knowing What Type of Eater You Have

One reason many aquarium species face starvation and poor health is because hobbyists who are unfamiliar with a particular species fail to provide the proper nutrition for individual needs. If you take the time to do a little research into a fish's natural habitat and feeding patterns, you gain a better understanding of its individual dietary requirements.

For example, danios need to be fed often because they have high metabolism rates. Their high activity level burns off food quickly. If you have a very clean system, there may not be adequate amounts of natural foods, such as algae, to provide the fish with something to tide them over until their next scheduled feeding. Give danios an extra feeding every day. Here are a few examples of how some species eat (remember, this may vary slightly depending on the age and temperament of your fish):

>> **Heavy eaters:** Tiger barb, swordtail, oscar, convict cichlid

>> **Medium eaters:** Guppy, gouramis, angelfish, cory

>> **Light eaters:** Balloon mollies, bubble-eye goldfish, betta, pencilfish

WARNING

Never feed your fish cat food, dog food, or other types of animal feeds. Non-fish manufactured pet food is difficult for your fish to digest properly, and it doesn't provide the essential amino acids and nutrients they really need.

Just like people, fish can be good eaters or bad eaters. The following hints help persuade those fish that don't want to jump on the scheduled feeding bandwagon.

Taking action when they stop eating

At times your fish simply stop eating. After you panic, stop and ask yourself this question: What caused this sudden lack of appetite? Here are some possible answers:

>> **Incorrect food:** When your fish stop eating, the first thing to do is to make sure that you're giving them the correct food for their species. For example, large goldfish need pellet foods that float. If you're only feeding them algae discs, they won't thrive. On the other hand, bottom-feeding catfish would appreciate the same disc. Top feeders like danios do best on floating and flake foods. If you're feeding them the wrong thing, switch to the proper food immediately. If the problem persists, read on for other causes.

>> **Crowded conditions:** Overcrowding causes stress and encourages excessive competition for food. Normal eaters may become shy or frightened and not get their share of the food.

>> **Disease:** Fish stop eating regularly as they start to drop off physically.

>> **Poor water conditions:** Polluted water and other bad aquarium conditions can have a major effect on your fish's normal feeding habits. Also check the temperature and pH and nitrate levels (see Chapter 14 for more information on this subject) if your fish suddenly stop feeding.

>> **Temperature or weather changes:** Hotter weather may mean a decrease in oxygen in the aquarium's water. If this is a problem, add extra filtration or a bubble producing wand or stone.

TIP

The fact that your fish aren't eating may not be caused by improper feeding conditions. You need to take other factors into consideration as well.

Some fish refuse to eat just because they're picky. There may be no other reason than that. Try different types of food until you find one they like. Generally, fish won't starve themselves though, but why not give them what they like anyway?

Meeting your carnivores' desires

Feed *carnivores* (meat eaters, such as pacu) small amounts of meat and insects to help balance their flake or pellet diet. Carnivores need a good filtration system because they excrete a high amount of waste generated by the meaty foods.

Going leafy and feeding vegetarians

Many freshwater fish need vegetable matter in their diet to flourish and achieve proper growth. For example, most species of freshwater catfish and cichlids enjoy vegetables. You can purchase vegetable fish food at your local aquarium shop. Specific types of vegetable foods such as algae wafers are manufactured to meet the needs of these types of fish.

TIP

If you feel creative, you can try preparing a vegetable supplement at home. You can boil lettuce and spinach leaves until they're soft and then put them on a special feeding clip (available at your local fish store), which holds them at the top of the tank. This clip is similar in design to a clothespin but wider. Chopped-up small pieces of potato, fresh peas, and zucchini are also a welcome treat for almost any type of fish if they are slightly cooked to soften them.

WARNING

If you give your fish fresh vegetables in this manner, make sure you remove all the uneaten food after an hour. Fresh vegetables decay and foul the water when left in the tank too long. Only give them tiny amounts supplemented with standard fish food.

Feeding fish that eat anything that falls into the tank

Some fish are sociable (and gluttonous) and continually try to mooch food by imitating a starving animal. (Nothing new there, my teenagers had that routine down to a science.) These fish also try to eat anything that falls into the tank, including pet food, sandwiches, toys, and your hand. Overfeeding these fish can quickly become a problem because they snag most of the food before the other fish even realize that it's chow time.

TIP

If you have a tank hog grabbing all the food, try feeding less food more frequently, and spread the food to different parts of the tank. You can also suck up some of the floating food with a turkey baster and put it back near shy fish if they aren't getting their share.

Identifying the Different Types of Food

You have many types of foods to choose from in an aquarium shop. Most fish eat just about anything. Most fish can survive on any type of aquarium food, but that *doesn't* mean they'll live up to their full potential if they're fed improperly. By combining different types of food, you can give your fish a head start on good health.

In the artificial environment of an aquarium, *you* need to provide the proteins, fats, vitamins, and carbohydrates that are a part of fish's natural diet. If you don't, your fish won't reach their full growth potential. Lack of proper nutrition also makes them more susceptible to disease. Most foods supply the essentials, but combining different products (such as flakes, cooked veggies, and fresh strips of fish) can ensure your success. Here I discuss the different types of food available and which types of fish they're best suited for.

Prepackaged foods

Fish food manufacturers offer a wide variety of well-balanced foods that are easy to use and store. Prepackaged dry foods generally contain most of the nutrients your fish need to survive. You can purchase dry food in many forms, including flakes that float on top of the water, disks that sink to the substrate for bottom feeders, and large pellets for koi and other types of pond fish. There are large-grained foods for big fish and small foods for tiny fish. You can drop tablet foods to the bottom of the tank or stick them to the aquarium glass (using the afore-mentioned food clip) at different levels to help ensure that the fish at all the different feeding levels get their fair share. Pretty neat, huh?

Flake foods are a good staple that can satisfy most of your fish. You can purchase flakes to meet the need of your particular species. For example, some cichlid flakes contain high amounts of fat and protein for quick growth; goldfish flakes often contain garlic, which inhibits parasites, and the extra vegetables that are a natural part of the goldfish diet. Flakes generally float on or near the water surface and sink as they become saturated.

The moisture level in manufactured flakes should be less than 4 percent of the total product because many nutrients dissipate quickly in aquarium water.

Floating pellets are made for surface feeders; bottom feeders, such as pond fish, can gobble up sinking pellets. Granular foods sink quickly and are generally used to feed bottom-dwelling species. Crisps are made from the same ingredients as flakes but are smaller and are great for picky eaters.

Frozen foods

Frozen foods are usually single organism or mixes of live food, such as brine shrimp, silversides, bloodworms, daphnia, meat, or vegetables. You can purchase this type of food in a variety of forms, such as sheets and cubes.

TIP

Little frozen cubes are a great way to keep an accurate account of exactly how much you're feeding at every meal. You must keep frozen foods from thawing before you need them because after they melt, they can't be refrozen without a major loss of nutrients. Also, melted brine makes your house smell like a shrimp boat. Before feeding, take the frozen food and thaw it in a small cup of dechlorinated water (tap water with dechlorinator added) or bottled water. Dispersing the food in water allows the food to move throughout the entire tank so that aggressive feeders don't get a chance to eat it all before the rest of their tankmates get any.

Freeze-dried foods

Freeze-dried foods contain preserved small crustaceans, shrimp, larvae, and worms. Fish seem to love or hate this type of food, so just keep a little bit around for a treat or emergencies. These foods do lose vitamins when frozen so they must be supplemented with standard food. Commercial vitamin supplements are available that you can mix with freeze-dried foods.

You can purchase freeze-dried black blackworms frozen or live; they're an excellent food for aquarium fish such as discus.

Spirulina

Spirulina is a natural micro-algae that is rich in proteins, helps enhance color, and promotes a healthy mucus layer on your fish's skin. Adding spirulina to all your fish's diets gives them healthier fins and increases their resistance to skin infections. You can usually purchase spirulina in both flake and frozen form. Spirulina has a soft cell wall and can be digested quite easily. It contains fatty acids that are important in proper development of the body's organs and is also rich in A and B vitamins, iron, and calcium.

TECHNICAL STUFF

Research shows that most of a fish's color comes from the food it eats. Spirulina contains a high percentage of carotenoid pigments that give your fish outstanding color, and can be fed in fish that aren't used for show.

TIP

If you want the best of both worlds, you can purchase spirulina-enriched brine shrimp. These shrimp have been fed dry spirulina powder.

Live food — the stuff they really love and want

These days, very few aquarium shops carry live food, making it difficult to find. Your best bet for locating live food and the supplies to culture them is on the Internet. Live food includes the following:

>> Bloodworms

>> Feeder goldfish

>> Feeder guppies

>> Fortified brine shrimp

>> Silversides

Feeder guppies and goldfish are usually used to feed large carnivores such as pacu and Jack Dempseys.

Some people balk at feeding their aquatic pets live fish so do what feels right for you. It may help to remember that live feeding just means going along with the natural pecking order in nature's food chain. Feeder guppies and goldfish are raised in large hatcheries specifically for food purposes — if no one bought them, they wouldn't have existed at all anyway.

Certain live foods shouldn't be introduced into your aquarium because they may attack smaller fishes or fry. These predators include leeches, hydras, beetles, and dragonfly larvae.

Brine shrimp

Brine shrimp (*Artemia franciscana*; see Figure 10-1) are tiny saltwater crustaceans that are appreciated by most fish. Brine shrimp are available frozen, though a few pet shops and Internet companies carry live brine.

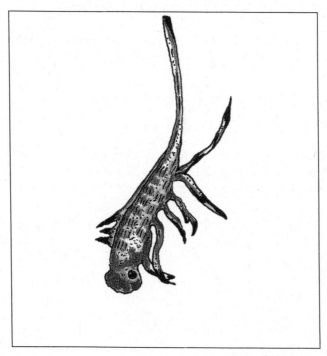

FIGURE 10-1:
Brine shrimp look different and are tiny compared to the kind you get in restaurants.

© John Wiley & Sons, Inc.

If you want to raise your own live food, you can buy a kit at your local pet store and hatch brine shrimp from dried eggs. These shrimp are usually fed to marine fish, but freshwater fish appreciate them as a treat, and they're good for young fry.

TIP

The only problem with hatching your own brine shrimp is the awful smell. Try raising them in a garage or basement; otherwise, your family and neighbors may move away without leaving a forwarding address.

One other important point about brine shrimp: Even though your aquatic pets are in a captive environment, they still enjoy hunting live food. Survival is an important instinct that can't be removed by the presence of four glass walls or by birth in a hatchery. Providing live foods keeps your fish more healthy and active, too. Think about it: If you had to chase down a pig to snag a few pork chops for Saturday's barbecue, you'd probably work up a little bit of an appetite.

WARNING

But along with the good comes the bad, as the old saying goes. Live foods have a higher risk of transmitting disease into the tank than manufactured products do. Live brine shrimp at your local fish shop are pretty safe; however, if you go out to a river or pond to collect live food, you run the risk of introducing disease.

Infusoria

Infusoria (paramecium and amoeba) are small animal protozoans that make an excellent food for small, newborn fry. Infusoria are very tiny and form a cloud when added to your aquarium water. You can culture infusoria at home by soaking vegetable matter (such as a piece of lettuce) in a clear jar of water placed in direct sunlight for at least a week. Check for infusoria when it becomes cloudy by shining flashlight into the jar. The infusoria will appear as small dust-like particles.

Rotifers

Rotifers are small invertebrates raised on farms and can be bought in large fish stores. They're single cell organisms found in nature. Their small size makes them easy to eat and to digest, and they have a very high nutrient content despite their tiny bodies. Rotifers are often used to feed saltwater fish, but many hobbyists use them for freshwater as well.

Tubifex, bloodworms, mosquito larvae, and earthworms (yuck!)

I know these types of foods sound gross, but your fish will love them! You can purchase freeze-dried tubifex and bloodworms in cubes or shredded form to use as a treat periodically. They can cause digestive problems, so don't feed them to your fish regularly. Mosquito larvae provide good health and coloring for show fish, but can be difficult to find. Fish readily accept earthworms, but clean the worms thoroughly with water and chop them up before serving.

Feeding Fry

Young *fry* (baby fish) require a different type of diet than adults because their digestion systems haven't yet matured. The good news is that you can feed many fry special foods available at your local fish shop. The bad news is that young fry need to be fed constantly, so swing by the pharmacy on the way home and grab some drops for your sleep-deprived eyes. Here are some foods you can feed your fry.

Microworms

Microworms (*Anguillula silusiae*) are nonparasitic worms that float freely in water. These worms reproduce in a matter of days.

TIP

You can easily culture microworms at home, and they make a good starter food for young fry because of their tiny size. All you need to do is mix a little oatmeal, yeast, and water in a bowl until it forms a paste. Add a small amount of microworms to the paste from an existing culture (which you can purchase on the Internet) and allow it to stand at room temperature for a couple of days. When worms appear on the sides of the bowl, transfer them to the fry tank.

Liquid, powdered, and growth foods

You can purchase manufactured liquid fry food that comes in a tube that resembles toothpaste. Use this product sparingly because it can foul the water.

Powdered food is used to feed newborn fish. The powder is too small to be used as feed for adult fish, and will end up fouling your tank if not used for baby fry.

Fish food manufacturers make a wide variety of foods to match the growth stages of your young fish. Hikari makes a wonderful line of baby fish foods that are made to fit the growth stages of fish.

Read the labels carefully to choose the correct product for the age of your developing fry if purchasing from a pet store.

Chapter **11**

Recognizing Diseases and Treatments

I f you want your fish to live long and healthy lives, then you need to make sure that they remain as disease free as possible. Many factors, including stress, bacteria, fungus, parasites, chemicals, and poor water conditions, can cause disease. By monitoring your water conditions daily and checking your fish for signs of disease, you can stay ahead of the game and keep your aquatic pets in prime condition.

In order to have happy, healthy fish, first you must do everything possible to prevent disease. Secondly, you must discover how to recognize disease before it gets out of control. Finally, you must know how to properly treat diseases that your fish acquire. This chapter helps you with all these steps.

An Ounce of Prevention . . .

. . . is worth a pound of cure, right? Preventing disease is generally the best way to battle physical problems. Sounds simple, doesn't it? It is. You can provide optimal living conditions for your tropical fish simply by following a few simple maintenance routines.

Keeping abreast of the water and equipment conditions in your aquarium, which takes only a few moments a day, gives you a safety margin to quickly correct any problems that show up. The following schedule gives you a few pointers on watching for signs of disease and other problems such as equipment malfunction.

Your daily review

Maintaining the following daily routine isn't as difficult as it sounds. It takes only a few minutes a day, and after a week or so, it will become second nature — just like grabbing a midnight snack.

Check the equipment

Make sure that all mechanical equipment is functioning properly each and every day. Are the filter systems putting out the optimal flow that the manufacturer suggests? Is the water flowing smoothly or is it running too slow? If the water seems to have slowed down to the point where it resembles a still life painting, check to see whether the filter and tubes are clogged and make sure that the motor isn't wearing down (water flow is slow or the filter is making noise).

Many filter motors can be rebuilt with parts supplied by the manufacturing company that produced the product. If the filter pads are clogged or extremely dirty, replace them or rinse them gently under water until they're clean. The only real disadvantage to replacing or washing filters is losing the biological bacteria that lives on the pads.

Are the air pumps in your aquarium in prime working condition? Carefully inspect them to make sure that they're running properly and not overheating. If the pumps aren't putting out enough air to run the extra equipment and decorations efficiently (you'll know when the little plastic diver turns blue and keels over), you can usually rebuild them by replacing worn diaphragms with parts you special order at your local fish shop. The good news: Pumps are inexpensive now, so just replace your pump if it stops working.

Check the water temperature

Monitoring water temperature is another important part of your daily routine. Any fluctuation in temperature more than 5 degrees from the norm can quickly lead to serious health problems in some species. If the temperature isn't within correct range (your fish are either floating around in the center of an ice cube or have melted into a blob), check to make sure that your heater isn't stuck in the on or off position.

Always measure the water temperature at the same time each day to get the most accurate readings. Replace any faulty heaters immediately.

One common cause of overheated aquarium water is excess natural or artificial lighting. Check the amount of natural sunlight the tank receives every day. If too much natural light is causing the temperature to rise during peak sunlight hours, then you need to move the tank, block out the light with a thicker or darker background, or cover the windows with heavy drapes or shades.

The duration and intensity of artificial lighting can be a problem as well. If a light is constantly overheating your tank, switch to lower lighting or leave the light off longer. Otherwise, your pets may end up looking like floating fish sticks.

Check the fish

After you get up in the morning and savor a few cups of coffee, make a quick inventory of all the fish in your aquarium. If any fish are dead, remove them from the tank and take them to the bathroom for the final flush.

Rotting fish can cause serious biological problems and upset the tank's balance.

If any fish seem to be sick or diseased, immediately transfer them to your hospital tank (I explain setting up a hospital tank later in this chapter) and begin treatment. If you check the health of your fish daily, you can take care of problems before they get out of control.

Monitor the overall health of your fish carefully. Take a close look at their physical condition. Are they swimming normally, or are they consistently lurking in the corners of the tank? Are their eyes bright and alert or clouded over? Are their fins erect or clamped shut and drooping? Do they have a straight spine, or do they look like Quasimodo? Do their bodies have normal, well-rounded proportions, or are their stomachs swollen or sunken? If you can visually identify physical problems, you need to check the aquarium's water and equipment.

Your weekly to-do list

Weekly routines are just like daily maintenance. Choose one day per week to carry out the following tasks.

Check the water

Change at least 15 percent of the water in your aquariums every week. Water changes are a good way to keep the water stable.

WARNING

Cure-all equipment and medications pose a real danger to your fish. When you stray down untried paths instead of using the standard, proven road that you know leads you where you want to be, you run a serious risk of losing your fish.

The water in a fish's natural environment is constantly replaced by seasonal rains, tidal flow, and run-off. But in aquariums, the same water remains in the tank between water changes. Take a moment and pretend that the water in your aquarium is your only drinking supply for the entire day. Would you be comfortable drinking it? Remember, your aquatic pets have to live in it 24 hours a day.

Carefully check your pH and nitrate levels with a test kit each week to make sure that they remain within the range required by your species of fish. If they aren't correct, you can slowly change your pH by water changes or chemicals if your tap pH doesn't match your species (pH should be kept within 2.0 of the required pH). Refer to Chapter 14 for information on testing the pH and nitrate levels.

If chemical tests indicate that your nitrate levels are too high, the best way to fix the problem is to change 20 percent of the water daily until the nitrate levels return to normal. Don't forget to check your aquarium conditions, so that you can identify and correct whatever is causing your nitrate levels to soar higher than the national debt. A few causes of high nitrates include poor filtration, overcrowding, lack of water changes, and chronic overfeeding.

While you're doing your weekly maintenance routine, take time to siphon off any accumulated debris on the substrate's surface area by using a simple gravel cleaner or aquarium vacuum (see Chapter 6). Remove any dead vegetation such as decaying plant leaves from the tank. This type of living debris can quickly cause a large fluctuation in the water's nitrate levels. If you need to use searchlights to locate the gravel in your tank, then the water needs to be cleaned.

Make the fish fast

Ideally, your aquatic pets should *fast* (that is, not be given any food for 24 hours) at least one day per week. I know this may seem difficult and harsh at first, but avoid the temptation to give them treats such as cinnamon rolls and donuts because you feel sorry for them. Fasting often happens in the wild, and it helps clean out your fish's digestive systems and guards against constipation problems. Remember to fast your fish on the same day each week, so they don't go too long between feedings.

Be prepared and know what to look for

Take a close look at all the medications you use for common illnesses such as ich and fungus and make sure you have all the standard treatments (check out the later section, "Identifying Common Ailments and Cures" in this chapter for more). Is there enough dechlorinator (which removes chlorine from your tap water) in your home to make daily water changes if they become necessary? Have you sterilized your hospital tank since its last use? Is it ready? Being prepared can make all the difference between saving your wet pets and losing them.

Aquarium diseases fall into four basic classifications:

>> *Bacterial* diseases often show up as red spots or red streaks and swelling in the eyes or abdominal area. Treat them with a general bacterial infection medications or antibiotics.

>> *Fungal* diseases usually show up as whitish colored patches on the scales or fins. Treat them with a general fungus medication.

>> *Parasitic* diseases appear as small white dots or discolored lumps on the fins and body if external. Treat them with a generalized parasitic cure medication.

>> *Physical ailments* usually manifest in the form of torn fins, poor coloring, and hiding behaviors. You can usually remedy them with improved water conditions, rearrangement of decorations, or removing aggressive fish to another tank.

The section, "Identifying Common Ailments and Cures" later in this chapter, examines some of these in greater detail.

HOW STRESS LEADS TO DISEASE

In your home aquarium, your fish live in an enclosed ecosystem that is very different from and slightly imbalanced compared to the natural stability of their native environment. The majority of health problems that tropical fish experience are the direct result of stress, which is often caused by being moved around, by poor environmental conditions when they're placed in a home aquarium, and by aggression from incompatible tankmates.

Your fish are capable of carrying all types of diseases that generally aren't a threat to their everyday health. These diseases usually remain dormant until your aquatic pets are weakened by fluctuating environmental factors such as unstable temperature and pH, dirty water, and poor diet. When environmental stability problems occur, your fish's latent disease can manifest quickly and cause health problems.

Monthly checklist

Monthly chores are much easier to remember if you mark them down on a calendar. Or you can simply tack a reminder note up on the fridge.

>> Replace all filter mediums that contain carbon. Carbon loses its effectiveness after a period of time. If your filter isn't carbon-based, gently rinse it under a bit of removed tank water to remove debris. Don't use hot water for this task, because excessive heat can destroy the entire beneficial bacteria colony living on the filter. Most important, follow the manufacturer's instructions for all filter mediums.

>> Clean all algae from the glass so that your fish won't think they've gone blind.

Identifying Common Ailments and Cures

The list of common tropical fish illnesses in this section gives you general guidelines for identifying and treating various diseases (refer to Figure 11-1). Keep in mind that several common medications and salt treatments may be detrimental to live plants, some species of catfish, and other delicate or sensitive tropical fish. Treat sick fish in a hospital tank, away from the main population.

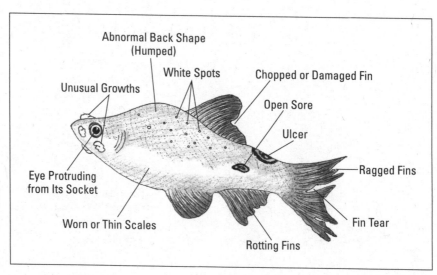

FIGURE 11-1: This poor fish has just about everything wrong with it.

© John Wiley & Sons, Inc.

Common bacterial infection

Symptoms: Blood spots; open sores; ulcers; frayed fins.

Cause: *Aeromonas hydrophila.*

Treatment: Products such as API Melafix bacterial treatment.

Constipation

Symptoms: Reduced appetite; little or no feces; swollen stomach; inactivity. (If your fish haven't left the gravel for over a month, they may be constipated.)

Cause: Incorrect nutrition; overfeeding.

Treatment: Add 1 teaspoon of magnesium sulfate for every 2 gallons of water. Fast your constipated fish for several days. Improve your fish's diet by feeding live foods frequently.

Dropsy

Symptoms: Swollen body; protruding scales; fish looks like a pincushion.

Cause: Organ failure from cancer and old age, bacterial infection or poor water conditions.

Treatment: Treat with API Melafix bacterial treatment after adjusting the water conditions to their proper state and hope it's bacterial or from poor water conditions. Organ failure and cancer can't be cured. Improvement of water quality through water changes also provides a little relief to afflicted fish. Complete recovery from dropsy is rare.

Fin rot

Symptoms: Reddened or inflamed rays; torn, choppy, ragged, or disintegrated fins. Your fish may look like it just swam through an electrical fan.

Cause: Fin rot is a highly contagious bacterial infection that, in its advanced stages, can completely erode the fins and tail all the way down to the body. Bad water quality and fin injuries are usually the main causes of this disease. Fin rot is frequently followed with a secondary fungal infection.

Treatment: Spot treat infected areas with gentian violet and use *proprietary medication* such as SeaChem Kanaplex. Add 1 tablespoon of aquarium or marine salt for each 5 gallons of water. Remove activated carbon from all filters during the medication period. Frequent water changes are necessary to help improve water conditions.

Fish louse

Symptoms: Disk-shaped parasites attach to the skin. Ulcers often develop close to the area of parasitic attachment. Bacteria or fungus problems may follow after.

Cause: *Crustacean* parasite. After feeding on the skin, the adult parasite leaves its host and lays gelatin-like capsules full of eggs on the substrate and aquarium decorations. Often the eggs don't hatch until the aquarium temperature rises and may stay in the tank for extended periods of time.

Treatment: Remove all parasites from the afflicted fish using a small pair of tweezers. Dab any wounds using a cotton swab dipped in commercial Mercurochrome. Remove water from the main tank and sterilize all decorations and substrate. In other words, start over.

Freshwater velvet

Symptoms: A golden-velvet or grayish-white coating on the body or fins. If your fish has velvet, it looks like it has been sprinkled with gold dust. This disease is very common among certain species such as bettas.

Cause: *Piscinoodinium* parasite. The adult parasites attach themselves to the skin of tropical fish and then fall off after seven days or so. These parasites immediately drop into the substrate and begin to multiply. The new parasites are then released into the water and move around until they reinfect the fish in your aquarium. If the parasites can't find a living host within a period of two to three days, they die.

Treatment: Proprietary malachite green remedy. Add 1 tablespoon of aquarium salt for each 5 gallons of water.

Freshwater ich

Symptoms: The sudden appearance of small white spots, which look like little grains of table salt, on the body and fins. Fish infected with this disease continually scratch themselves on gravel and decorations during the advanced stages. (If your fish look like they're making love to the rocks in the tank, they probably have ich.)

Cause: *Ichthyopthirius* parasite. Adult parasites fall off of the host and multiply in the substrate. Soon after, new parasites search for another living host.

Treatment: Proprietary ich remedy (formalin or malachite green). Even if you remove the infected fish to a quarantine tank, you must still treat the aquarium water in the main tank with medication to kill off any remaining free-swimming parasites.

Wear gloves when using formalin.

Fungus

Symptoms: White growths on the body or fins that are fluffy in appearance and make your fish look like a cotton puff or marshmallow.

Cause: Fungus often attacks regions where the mucus or slime coating on the fish has worn off due to damage by injury or parasites. After the slime coat is damaged, the fish is more susceptible to all types of other disease.

Treatment: Spot treat with gentian violet, methylene blue, or use aquarium fungicide in extreme cases.

Gill parasites

Symptoms: Redness in the gill areas; labored respiration; scratching; excessive mucus coat; glazed eyes; inflamed gills; loss of motor control (your fish resemble slam dancers).

Cause: Flukes *(Dactylogyrus)*.

Treatment: Sterazin or other proprietary treatment such as Praziquantel. Formalin baths can be effective as well.

Hole in the head

Symptoms: Pus-filled holes on the head near the lateral line or the base of the tail. This disease is most common among cichlids.

Cause: *Hexamita* parasite.

Treatment: Flagyl. Recent findings show that Vitamin A and C supplements are effective in treating this disease (aquatic vitamins, not Flintstones Chewables).

Intestinal parasites

Symptoms: Worms sticking out through the vent; emaciation of the body.

Cause: Several different varieties of intestinal worms.

Treatment: Standard fungus cure or in advanced cases, such as API General Cure, and veterinarian-prescribed anthelminthic added to the daily diet. Add 1 tablespoon of aquarium salt for each 5 gallons of water to help your fish with normal body fluid functions. Remove any activated carbon during treatment. Change 15 percent of the water daily to keep environmental conditions optimal.

Large skin parasites

Symptoms: Scratching; visible parasites.

Cause: Fish lice (*Argulus foliaceus*) and anchor worms (*Lernaea cyprinacea*).

Treatment: Remove large parasites with tweezers. Apply an antiseptic solution to the injured site.

Mouth fungus

Symptoms: White cottonlike growths around the mouth area (your fish looks like Santa Claus having a bad hair day) or patchy white skin in the same region. In advanced stages, the jawbones begin to deteriorate badly.

Cause: Usually *Flexibacter*, which follows after other infections have begun.

Treatment: Proprietary fungus treatment or methylene blue in the early stages. If this treatment isn't effective and the fungus is out of control, consult your veterinarian about antibiotics immediately.

Pop-eye

Symptoms: Eyes inflamed and protruding from their sockets to the point where they almost pop out of the head. Often the fish's eyes develop a cloudy, whitish haze. Inflamed eye sockets are also common with this disease.

Cause: Parasites or poor water conditions.

The giant gourami is a bubble-nest builder and is the largest of all gourami species.

Koi grow very large and are great fish for coldwater ponds.

The cardinal tetra is one of the most popular aquarium fish due to its beautiful coloration and peaceful nature.

The bones and internal organs of the glass catfish can easily be seen inside its transparent body.

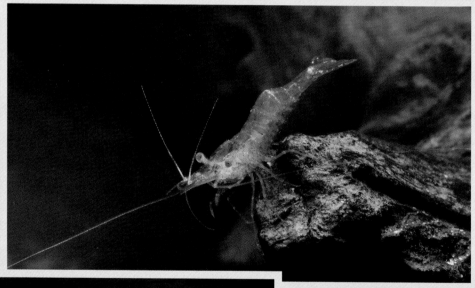

Ghost shrimp are freshwater invertebrates, not fish.

Orandas have a distinctive hoodshaped growth on their head that is also known as a "wen."

Danios are great fish for beginning hobbyists because they are very active and easy to see.

This bubble-eye actually has poor vision.

Siamese algae eaters help to keep algae in an aquarium under control by dining on it continuously.

The beautiful kuhli loach is a peaceful fish that does well in a community aquarium with other small, non-aggressive species.

When properly acclimated, sailfin mollies have been kept successfully in freshwater, brackish, and marine aquariums.

A pencilfish has horizontal stripes that make it resemble a standard school pencil.

Swordtails are colorful, hardy fish that are easy to breed.

The Mickey Mouse platy was named due to black markings near the tail that resemble Mickey Mouse ears.

The guppy is a good fish to consider if you want a species that breeds easily.

The angelfish is one of the few non-aggressive cichlid species

Oscars are very friendly, and many hobbyists compare them to other household pets.

The serpae tetra is an egglayer that can live more than ten years in captivity.

Pearl gouramis are generally timid fish that should be kept with other peaceful species.

Swordtails are good jumpers, so make sure you have a tight-fitting lid on your aquarium. This is a tux swordtail.

Balloon mollies may be very big eaters, but their temperament is peaceful.

The redtail shark is not a true shark; it is actually a cyprinid.

A plecostomus can attach itself to aquarium walls, rocks, plants, and other decorations using its mouth like a suction cup.

Comet goldfish have a metallic shiny appearance and were first bred in China over a thousand years ago.

Goldfish like this black moor will eat all types of live and dried foods.

Platys are colorful, friendly fish that are perfect for a community tank.

A community tank is a great place to keep several different varieties of fish who can live in harmony.

Treatment: There are no known commercially packaged medications to treat or cure this disease. The only thing you can do to help is to improve the aquarium's water conditions with frequent changes. Check and adjust all water conditions (pH, ammonia, nitrites, and nitrates) with test kits to make sure that they remain within proper ranges. It may also be beneficial to add 1 tablespoon of aquarium salt per 5 gallons of water to help with osmoregulation (the control of the levels of water and mineral salts in the blood).

Septicemia

Symptoms: Redness at the base of the fins followed by blood streaks that appear on the fins and body. Other symptoms include hemorrhage, loss of appetite, and listlessness. This disease usually follows fin rot or skin infections. Septicemia often results in major heart damage and blood vessel problems. These complications can in turn lead to fluid leakage in the abdomen, which in some cases causes dropsy.

Cause: *Pseudomonas* or *streptococcus* bacteria inflames body tissues made susceptible by a skin infection.

Treatment: Antibacterial Furan2 or Triple Sulfa. Change the water every 24 to 36 hours.

Skin flukes

Symptoms: Inflamed skin; excessive mucus coating (your fish looks like it was baptized in Vaseline); scratching.

Cause: *Gyrodactylus salaris.*

Treatment: Proprietary medication with labeling recommending for skin flukes such as Hakari PraziPro.

Slimy skin disease

Symptoms: Gray-colored slime on the body or fins; scratching; frayed fins; excessive mucus coat; shimmying like a politician during questioning.

Cause: *Costia, trichodina, cyclochaeta,* or *chilodonella* parasites.

Treatment: Proprietary remedy of malachite green and frequent water changes. Short-term (5-minute) formalin and salt baths can be effective. Check and correct any poor water conditions.

Swim bladder disease

Symptoms: Abnormal or irregular swimming patterns (your fish do the doggie paddle upside down) and complete loss of physical balance.

Cause: Bacterial infection, physical injury to the swim bladder from fighting, breeding, netting, transportation from the dealer, poor water quality.

Treatment: Treat with an antibiotic in a clean, shallow tank. (The water should be about 2 inches higher than the dorsal fin on the fish.) Carry out water changes as frequently as once a day if possible.

Tuberculosis (TB)

Symptoms: Fin deterioration; a paling of body color; clamped fins (fins are closed up or folded together); excessive weight loss; ulcers; and pop-eye.

Cause: A highly contagious bacterial disease caused by poor filtration or over-crowding in the aquarium.

WARNING

Many medical personnel believe that this disease can be transferred to humans through contact with the infected areas on the fish.

WARNING

Treatment: In my opinion, it isn't worth risking your own health or the health of your family, to try treating infected fish with this disease. Use strict care when handling these infected fish! Use plastic gloves when removing any fish infected with tuberculosis. Any tropical fish that has this disease should be euthanized immediately. Don't leave the TB-infected fish in the main aquarium because other tankmates will probably eat it and may develop the disease shortly thereafter.

Keeping an Eye Open for Frequent Causes of Disease

There are many causes of disease that aren't related to parasites and infection, such as carbon dioxide poisoning, poor water quality, metal poisoning, chemical poison, improper diet, overfeeding, and fright. Frequently monitor the following important physical and social conditions.

Carbon dioxide poisoning

Symptoms: Listlessness; increased or rapid respiration. Your fish may hang near the top of the water.

Cause: Lack of oxygen, too much carbon dioxide in the water.

Treatment: Add more aeration to improve gas exchange at the water surface; cut down on plant fertilization; check and correct any poor water conditions; and carry out frequent water changes.

Poor water quality

Symptoms: The first sign is that your tropical fish are gasping for air at the water surface of the tank and are generally inactive. Clamped or closed fins, overall bad health, and poor coloration are a few more symptoms of incorrect water quality.

Cause: Poor water quality due to infrequent water changes, poor filtration, and overuse of standard chemicals.

Treatment: Make daily water changes until any high ammonia, nitrite, or nitrate levels return to lower readings. Make sure the aquarium has enough aeration and add an extra airstone or more filtration if necessary. Make sure the pH of the water is within the proper range (a couple degrees of what is normal for the species).

Metal poisoning

Symptoms: Erratic behavior; paleness.

Cause: Metal objects coming into contact with the aquarium water.

Treatment: A complete water change. To avoid accidentally poisoning your tropical fish, never allow any metal to come in contact with the aquarium water. Old metal hoods and metal equipment clips are two common sources of poisoning. To keep this equipment from poisoning your fish, use plastic clips and make sure that the glass cover on your aquarium fits properly so that no water comes into direct contact with the hood and light fixture.

Chemical poisoning

Symptoms: Erratic behavior; gasping for air; fish lying on their sides; paleness; clamped fins; refusal to eat.

Cause: Other common sources of water poisoning in aquariums are cleaning, cosmetic, and insect-control products. Never use insecticides, hair sprays, or mist cleaners near your aquarium. Small drops of these airborne products can easily fall through the small equipment holes in the top of your tank and poison your fish. If you have to use one of these products near your aquarium, tightly cover your tank ahead of time with plastic sheets or large towels to protect your fish.

Treatment: Complete water and filter change.

Improper diet

Symptoms: General poor health; paleness of color; inactivity.

Cause: You. Poor nutrition.

Treatment: An unbalanced diet doesn't contain all the vitamins and minerals important to your fish's health. Begin feeding a wide variety of commercially packaged flakes, small servings of fresh lettuce, peas, and other green vegetables, and live foods (see Chapter 10 for more information on what foods are good for which species).

Overfeeding

Symptoms: Lethargic fish; excessive weight gain; and constipation.

Cause: Overfeeding your tropical fish on a regular basis.

Treatment: Fast your fish for two days. Improve poor or fouled water conditions caused by uneaten, rotting food before it leads to more disease problems. If your fish are beginning to resemble a blimp and are bobbing up and down in the water like corks, start measuring each serving of food so that you don't feed them too much at one time (again, see Chapter 10).

Frightened fish

Symptoms: Your fish dash for cover when the aquarium lights are first turned on; constant physical injuries from collisions with decorations.

Cause: Sudden changes in lighting, quick human movements, people rapping on the glass, and pets trying to get into the tank.

Treatment: Gradually increase room lighting by opening drapes and turning on lamps before you switch on the aquarium lights.

Relying on a Tried-and-True Home Remedy: Giving a Salt Bath

Here's a good home remedy that you can try to avoid giving your fish large doses of medications. This method works really well and can save you a lot of money.

A salt bath as a method of treating freshwater fish has been around since the aquarium hobby first began. Salt baths have proved effective over time to help cure problems such as fungus infestations, ich, and several other types of parasites such as gill flukes. Basically what happens is the parasites are submerged in the salt solution along with your fish and begin to take on water until they burst and fall off.

I've used this home-remedy method for more than 20 years and have found that it has a high rate of success in treating different types of diseases. (Don't try this in your home bathtub with your own sores, or you may end up peeling yourself off the ceiling — you've heard of salt in an open wound? Not good for non-fish.)

A salt bath is simple. Follow these steps:

1. **Add one teaspoon of table salt for each 5 gallons of water in your hospital tank.**

2. **Continue adding 1 teaspoon of salt twice a day for the first five or six days.**

3. **If the infected fish isn't completely well by the sixth day, continue to add one teaspoon of salt for another three days.**

WARNING

I'm not talking about adding salt to your main tank. When you hear that people have salt in their main freshwater tank, it's because they're keeping species such as the molly, which actually thrive better with a bit of salinity to their water. Don't confuse this concept with standard salt bath in a hospital tank.

Playing Detective: The Sherlock Holmes Method

Everyone wants to do a little bit of detective work at least once in his lifetime. If you're like me, you couldn't find more than one pair of matching socks in the dryer if your life depended on it. Fortunately, looking for clues that indicate the presence of a tropical fish disease is much easier to do than laundry. To get started, all you need to do is find one of those cool-looking detective hats, a long coat, and follow the clues I give you in this section.

I can't overemphasize the importance of checking the overall health of your fish very carefully every day. Shimmying, abnormal loss of appetite, weight loss, paling or darkening of colors, increased or labored respiration, and miniature For Sale signs on the aquarium's porcelain castles are a few of the warning signs that disease or environmental conditions are causing them discomfort.

Other telltale clues to look for include a bloated look, obvious visible damage to your fish's eyes, fins, or scale areas, and abnormal spots on the body. If your fish is hanging around the heater, continually scratching on tank decorations or substrate, or is normally active but is suddenly moving slowly, it may have a serious problem.

If you notice any of these problems, don't panic. Take the time to make careful observations on the efficiency of the equipment, condition of the water, and other disease-related factors. After you compile all the information you can, you're in a better position to make a sound judgment on the proper course of action. If you're unsure about what to do for a diseased fish, contact your local vet or fish dealer. The people there can give you good advice and help you with your fishy problems.

Using Quarantine Tanks

A *quarantine tank* is used to hold fish for a week that you have just brought home from dealer, so that you have time to see if any illness develops before you put them in your main tank. Both tanks are very important. Keep reading for more information.

Grasping the purpose and advantages of quarantining

All tropical fish go through a tremendous amount of stress being transported to your home aquarium. Think about it — if someone snagged you with a giant pair of panty hose and then stuck you in a large plastic bag, wouldn't you have a little bit of a problem with that?

Fish really aren't that much different from you and me when it comes to mental stress. A quarantine tank can be the perfect way to provide your fish with a suitable recovery area — it gives them time to regain their strength before moving into their brand-new home. This recovery period also gives you time to see whether any latent diseases or physical problems manifest themselves.

Knowing how much time to quarantine

When you bring your new acquisitions home (unless they are *starter fish*, the very first fish in a new aquarium), place them in a quarantine tank for two to four weeks. You don't quarantine starter fish because you need them to begin the nitrogen cycle. While your fish are in quarantine, check them daily for signs of disease and make sure they're eating normally.

Keeping good records: Writing it all down

TIP

A journal can help you keep track of your fish's quarantine and health record. You can check these records for information on previous treatments. Keep a separate page for each fish and include the fish's name, date of purchase, size, health record, length of quarantine, and any other information you feel may be important in future medical treatments. To look like a real pro, write something important looking like "Scientific Information" on the journal's cover. Your friends will be impressed.

Focusing on the tank

A 10- or 20-gallon tank is good for quarantining unless you plan on buying some very large fish. All the equipment you need to get your quarantine tank going is a good-quality power filter and a submersible heater. Make your new fish feel secure by adding a few floating artificial plants. The last thing you need is for your new pets to go into a bare tank where they can easily be frightened.

REMEMBER

Don't forget that a quarantine tank needs to be cycled just like your regular tank. A starter fish or two helps begin the biological cycle. When you go down to your local dealer to purchase starter fish for the main tank, pick up a couple of extras for the quarantine tank at the same time. The water conditions (pH, temperature) in your quarantine tank should be similar to those in your permanent aquarium to prevent stressing your fish further when you move them to the main aquarium.

Remember, it's much better to be patient and wait until your new fish complete their quarantine cycle than it is to place them immediately into a main tank where they can spread disease that could have been caught and treated. In the long run, treating disease can cost you quite a bit more money than setting up a simple and inexpensive quarantine tank.

Setting Up a Hospital Tank

A *hospital tank* helps you treat sick fish and is simply a small aquarium that acts as a hospital ward. You remove diseased fish from the main tank and place them in the hospital tank for chemical or other types of treatment. It's as simple as that. Unfortunately, there is no 911 number for your aquatic pets should they become ill. As a result, you need a hospital tank to help treat them when they become diseased. Hospital tanks are similar to quarantine tanks. The only difference is, hospital tanks are used to treat ill fish, whereas quarantine tanks are used to hold new acquisitions for observance. Treating diseased fish in a separate hospital tank is much more practical because many common medications affect different species in different ways. For example, a malachite green formula used to cure ich in most species has the potential to destroy any tetras in your aquarium.

Treating diseased fish in a hospital tank also lowers the risk of the disease spreading. Many antibiotic treatments destroy essential bacteria and cut down on the efficiency of a tank's biological filtration system, leading to even more health problems and new diseases. Using a hospital tank prevents these problems.

Setting up a hospital tank really doesn't take much money if you purchase a small aquarium (5- or 10-gallon) and a simple sponge filter to provide a good base for beneficial biological bacteria. Filtration systems that contain carbon don't work well in a hospital tank because the carbon often absorbs the medication. The frequent water changes you need to do when treating sick fish are much easier to handle in a small aquarium. A good submersible heater with an internal rheostat lets you monitor water temperature as needed. Diseases such as ich can be treated more quickly if you raise the standard temperature by a few degrees. Bacteria in a bottle can help your hospital tank quickly cycle if you find yourself needing to set one up without notice.

Remember that overly bright lighting reduces the effectiveness of many medications. Try to use a lower wattage bulb for your hospital tank setup. Add a few extra airstones to the hospital tank to increase the oxygen supply because many medications tend to reduce the oxygen supply in the aquarium.

Understanding Medications

A large number of medications are on the market, and many of them can treat a variety of diseases, so deciding which one you to use can be confusing. More often than not, the final choice of medication rests with you. Each case is unique, and many aquarists prefer one medication over another.

TIP

In time, you'll discover which medications work best on certain diseases and different species of fish. Until you reach that point, try to keep a wide variety of medications around so that your fish can be treated when problems occur, and your friends and family will be impressed to see that you have everything under control. Table 11-1 gives you an idea of how to use common medications and the pros and cons of each drug:

TABLE 11-1   ## Common Medications

Medication	Purpose	Pros	Cons
Acriflavine	Treats ich and fungus.	Works quickly.	May turn the water green.
Formalin	Treats parasites.	Colorless, won't change the water color.	Hard to get, expensive.
Malachite green	Treats velvet, fungus, and ick.	Very effective.	Toxic in large doses. Can't be used in tanks with baby fish or some species such as tetras.
Methylene blue	Treats velvet, fungus, and ick.	Inexpensive, works well.	Stains gravel and decorations blue sometimes permanently.
Penicillin	Treats bacterial infections.	Best thing there is for treating bacterial infections. Works fast.	Hard to get and is expensive.
Tetracycline	Great for treating bacterial infections on the fly.	Inexpensive, easy to find in any pet store. Nontoxic.	Turns water yellow and creates an unsightly foam on the surface.

3

The Background Players: Water, Chemicals, and Plants

Decide what type of water to use so that you can make the right choice from your local water supplies.

Buy chemicals that you really need to be prepared to keep your aquarium water conditions at their best.

Understand the nitrogen cycle so that your new system's water will have the beneficial bacteria it needs.

Take a look at different systems in case you want to try other setups after you've become comfortable with and understand the basics of aquarium keeping.

Purchase the right plants for your fish species to beautify your aquarium and to help them feel at home.

Know how to handle problems and pitfalls that arise so you're not left with an algae-ridden aquarium with dead fish from water problems.

Chapter **12**

All Water Isn't Created Equal

Adding the correct type of water to your aquarium is extremely important to the long-term health of your fish. You can obtain water from many sources, but only a few of these sources provide the correct requirements for your aquatic pets. Understanding the correct water parameters for your tank and choosing reliable water sources can help you become a successful hobbyist right off the bat. In this chapter, I take a closer look at water.

What you think may be safe water may not always be the case. For example, my college biology professor made my class look at pond water through a microscope, and I could barely believe my eyes. There must have been 800 billion creatures crawling in it. Remember that almost any natural source of water has some type of living organism in it. In the wild, fish aren't generally confined to a small amount of water, so the threat of illness is small. You need to find alternative sources of water if you want your fish to be healthy and happy.

Depending on where you live, your water supply can vary greatly. Some water sources have more metal content and debris than others. Never assume that your main water source is automatically safe for your fish, because it can contain contaminates such as rust. Have it tested if you're not sure. Contact your city's water department for information on tested metals in your tap water.

Comparing Different Water Types

You can get water from a variety of sources. Here I talk in depth about the pros and cons of tap water, rainwater, bottled water, natural lake/pond/river water, and well water.

Tap water

In order to protect the human population from being killed off by drinking water, water companies add chemicals such as chlorine or chloramine (ammonia bonded to chlorine) to wipe out small organisms that could make people sick. This treated tap water may be safe for humans, but the chlorine in it can be deadly to your aquatic pets.

WARNING

You have to get rid of the chlorine from any water source that you use to fill your aquariums. Chlorine kills all types of fish and invertebrates.

Dechlorinating with dechlorinator

You have a few options for removing chlorine and chloramines from tap water to make it perfectly safe to use in your aquarium. One option (and if you're like me, you'll opt for this method because it's the easiest) is to go down to your local fish store and purchase a bottle of *dechlorinator,* a product that instantly removes chlorine from your water. After adding dechlorinator, you can safely put your new starter fish in the aquarium water.

TIP

The best time to add dechlorinator is after your tank is filled and all equipment is up and running. You need to dechlorinate all the water you add to your aquarium — even the water you put in to replenish water lost to evaporation.

Dechlorinating the old-fashioned way

Your tanks are low, and you're out of dechlorinator because your local fish store has run out. If you want to be a practical hobbyist, you can simply dechlorinate water the old-fashioned way. (Don't panic; this method doesn't involve a lot of work.)

1. **Take a few plastic jugs (gallon milk containers work great) and rinse them thoroughly with clear water.**

TIP

Glass jars work fine, but they can break, so plastic is really your best bet for safety. Make sure you allow the water to run from the tap for a few seconds before rinsing to eliminate any water that has sat stagnant in the piping. Water can pick up trace amounts of metal if it sits unmoving in household pipes.

Never use soap or other chemicals to clean out containers for aquarium water! The soap leaves a residue that can be deadly to your fish.

2. **After rinsing, fill the plastic containers with tap water, allow them to sit with the lids off for 48 hours, and voilà, chlorine-free water!**

You can add an *airstone* (a small stone that splits an air supply from an aquarium pump into smaller bubbles) to each jug to cut your waiting time in half (to 24 hours) when adding water lost to evaporation. See Chapter 6 for more on airstones. Attach the airstone to a spare aquarium pump by tubing for 24 hours and then cover the hole in the container to keep contaminates out. If you keep three or four jugs like this sitting around, you always have a supply of safe water. Simply use a gang valve (again, refer to Chapter 6) so that you can use one pump to power several airstones at once for filling multiple jugs for larger tanks.

Floating dust particles, paint sprays, and so on can get into these water jugs. Keep the jugs in an area that doesn't have a lot of airborne debris. Placing a lid or small cloth over the top of each jug can help keep out unwanted particles. You can use food-safe containers and small buckets as well.

Guarding against metals

It's not just chlorine you have to worry about. Depending on your area, your tap water may also contain metal deposits, such as heavy amounts of copper or iron. Too much metal can be deadly for your fish. To be safe, buy water treatments from your pet dealer that safely remove the metals from water.

As mentioned previously, to be safe when using city water, let the water from your tap run down the sink for a minute before you start filling containers or filling with a Python device with water for your aquariums, just as you did when you rinsed them. (Refer to the "Using a Python" section later in this chapter.) This precaution allows water that's been in constant contact with metal sink pipes (and is slightly contaminated as a result) to flow through.

Seeding your new tank

The process of filling your new tank with some water from a healthy established aquarium is called *seeding*. The water is safe from chlorine and has a small number of good bacteria to help your tank jump-start the nitrogen cycle, which I discuss in detail in Chapter 14. A trusted friend or dealer may be able to help supply water, if she has quarantined her livestock. If you decide to go this route, make sure the tank is free from disease, algae, and debris.

Bringing water from an unestablished tank isn't a good idea because you aren't gaining anything by doing so except for the chlorine being gone. You're better off starting anew than going this route.

Rainwater

A few hobbyists collect rainwater for use in their aquariums. If you have an extremely large tank, this method isn't practical. The process is really more trouble than it's worth, unless you have a lot of spare time, small tanks, and energy on your hands, or you live in a region of the country that receives a tremendous amount of annual rainfall. If you live in the desert southwest, your fish will probably die from old age before you collect enough water to top off your tank, and it may not always rain when you need it to.

Collecting rainwater in large barrels attracts mosquitoes that your neighbors, family, and pets may not appreciate.

Another problem with rainwater (especially if you live in a large city) is that it may contain contaminants from factory emissions, smog, and other pollutants. To be honest, you may end up spending twice as much for chemicals to treat your rainwater than if you had just used your trusty old kitchen faucet.

If you decide to gather rainwater to help condition your fish for breeding, make sure that you use nonmetallic containers that are food grade for collection. In fact, never use metallic containers to collect water for any aquarium. Also keep in mind that rainwater tends to be *soft* (low in dissolved minerals) and may not be suitable for hard-water fish. Hard-water fish (such as red-tailed sharks, blindcave fish, and oscars, whose water has a high mineral content in the wild) that are forced to live in soft water conditions can't spawn properly or maintain good health.

You should always check the water parameters (specific water requirements) for your particular aquatic species before using rainwater.

Never collect rainwater from metal gutters. Over time, gutters rust and become filled with debris such as leaves, dirt, paper, and pieces of roofing shingle. No matter how often you clean your gutters, you're risking metallic and natural contamination by using metal gutters to funnel water for an aquarium supply.

You can buy test kits to test for iron and copper levels at most fish stores and on the Internet.

The advantages of bottled water (not Perrier)

Okay, when I mention bottled water, I'm talking about the kind you get in a machine outside of your local grocery store or the gallon jugs that you can purchase inside. Put it this way: If the water is really expensive, it's the wrong kind; if it's inexpensive, it's the right kind. Don't spend a fortune on expensive bottled water when the least expensive brand will do just fine.

TIP

Bottled water can be quite expensive if you're trying to fill a larger tank. Distilled water bought in bottles at the store needs to have necessary minerals added back to it to maintain normal levels.

Well water (don't count on it)

Take my word for it, deep well water can be truly one of life's great mysteries — all the filters and chemicals in the world won't be able to easily change the composition of this amazing liquid. The government doesn't test the quality of well water, unlike city water.

The water from an old well is guaranteed to turn every color of the rainbow within a period of 5 minutes during a shower, and your body will take on those glorious copper colors when you step out to dry off. Instead of buying an expensive Halloween costume, trick-or-treaters can save money by coming over to your house for a shower if you have a bad well. If you happen to live in a rural area with farms, take note that fertilizer, which is used for production, can contaminate ground water when it rains and seep into wells.

WARNING

The point is that well water generally isn't a good source to use for filling your aquariums because too many bad things can get into it, including sulfur, lead, and mud. Well water is usually lacking in good oxygen content and is high in dissolved nitrogen and carbon dioxide instead.

If you insist on using it anyway, take a small sample down to your local water company and ask for it to be tested. Water companies are pretty good about testing your water for little or no money, even if it's from your own well. If the test shows your well water isn't suitable, you can use bottled water or treated water from a friend's city water supply (dechlorinate it before using).

If your well water is free of metals and does test acceptable for human consumption, make sure you follow up with an aquarium test kit to check for tropical fish perimeters such as pH and nitrites. They may have to be adjusted using aquarium chemicals before you use it for your aquatic pets. The hardness of well water can vary greatly from state to state, so you may have to adjust the pH accordingly.

Collecting Water from Bodies of Water (Why You Want to Forget This Bad Idea)

If you're planning to set up a freshwater aquarium, someone has probably suggested that you can be a real nature lover and go down to your local river or pond to snag the water for it. You may be thinking that this isn't a half-bad idea — you can keep your fish closer to their natural environment. However, after your dream of a cameo on *National Geographic* fades a bit, you can go ahead and forget this idea entirely.

Why? Because most of the freshwater fish you purchase from the pet shop are raised in a hatchery and have never been near any river or pond. These fish are raised in standard aquarium water conditions. When you collect water from a pond or river, you take a great risk of introducing disease parasites, fungus, bad bacteria, and pollution into your tank. Another problem is that just the thought of hauling massive amounts of water long distances to fill or replenish a tank is enough to have anyone reaching for a bottle of aspirin.

TIP

If you don't want to worry about the shelf life of your test kits, purchase individual kits that have long shelf lives and have the advantage of allowing you to replace one part of the kit when needed without replacing the entire thing.

Adding Water to Your Aquarium

Filling an aquarium isn't a difficult job, but make sure that you're prepared in advance. Have a couple of towels ready just in case of accidental spills. Make sure that small children and pets are out of the way if you're using a hose to fill your tank and that you have time to complete the job. Don't turn on the equipment until the tank is filled.

Before you fill your aquarium, place your substrate, plants, decorations, and equipment. The following sections explain a couple of ways to fill your tank so that you don't disturb all the work you have already done.

Using a garden hose

If you have a very large aquarium to fill, you may want to consider purchasing a new garden hose and an adapter that allows you to hook it up to your kitchen or bathroom faucet. This setup allows you to fill your aquarium quickly. If you're using a hose type gadget, make sure you have it on slow or hold the end of the hose underwater at an angle against the glass so that the water cascades in slowly.

Using a Python

Don't panic — I'm not talking about a snake here. A *Python* is actually an aquarium vacuum sold at most pet stores that you can use to move water from your sink. It's a long, clear hose with one end that connects to your sink faucet. (Depending on your fixture, you may have to purchase an adapter.) The other end of the Python has a large plastic tube that suctions up water and gathers debris from around the *substrate* (gravel or other aquarium floor covering). The faucet end has a little gadget that you push up or down to direct the water to either go from the faucet to the end of the hose or to suck water from the other end so that water spills into the sink.

In other words, the Python works on the same principle as the garden hose, except it has all the attachments needed and allows you to easily control and reverse the flow of water with a simple switch for water changes that you will be doing on a weekly basis.

TIP

Pythons are usually available in many lengths. Get one long enough to hook one end up to the sink so that the other end reaches the tank.

To add water, follow these simple steps:

1. **Reverse the Python's plastic switch.**
2. **Put the other end in a clean bucket by your aquarium.**
3. **Fill it up.**

REMEMBER

Use this method if fish are in the tank because the water won't be dechlorinated straight out of the tap. Instead, after adding dechlorinator, pick up the bucket and slowly pour the water into your aquarium. This method is much easier than hauling water back and forth across your home. Make sure the water you're adding is the same temperature as the water in the tank by using a thermometer.

Moving water the old-fashioned way

Another option for moving water to your tank without a Python or similar device is to use a bucket. Carrying a bucket from the sink to the tank is the way I used to do it in the old days, but using a bucket can be tedious and hard on the back, especially if you're filling a larger tank or the aquarium is located a long distance from a water source. If you're filling your tank with buckets, place a small plastic or ceramic plate on top of the substrate and slowly pour the water on to it.

Chapter **13**

Considering Those Crazy Chemicals

H ave you ever been at the aquarium store and noticed shelf after shelf of mysterious-looking chemicals? Ever wonder whether you need a wizard's license or some type of magical scroll to decipher and use them properly? You really don't need to worry too much because the chemicals are actually fairly easy to understand and will become second nature as you progress through the hobby.

A wide variety of chemicals for your aquarium is available, so it's understandable that it can seem a bit confusing at first. But after you read this chapter and figure out the basics of some of the most popular and useful aquatic chemicals on the market, you can look at chemicals in a whole new way.

Right now I take a closer look at a few of these chemical products made for use in home aquariums and explain their purpose. Because such a multitude of aquarium chemicals are available, I can't possibly cover them all here. (In fact, I doubt I could cover them all in an entire book.) But by the time you finish reading this chapter, you'll be on the road to becoming a real chemical wizard.

Understanding Chemical Use

Just as there are guidelines to follow for using the chemicals you find around your home (especially in the laundry room and kitchen), there are rules for using aquarium chemicals as well. After all, you wouldn't even think of mixing ammonia and chlorine to help whiten your laundry unless you wanted to spend five days in an oxygen tent, right? Well, your fish don't cope well with excessive mixtures and overuse of chemicals either. My general rule for aquarium chemicals is to only use them when you absolutely need to.

Knowing when to use (and not use) chemicals

When you treat diseases, use chemicals as a last resort. Try one of the many more natural ways available (weekly water changes and keeping an eye on temperature and pH) to help your fish avoid illness (see Chapter 11).

If you're just starting an aquarium, you can use chemicals a little more frequently because you just need to dechlorinate your water and condition it, but you can avoid even doing that by using water that has been stored for 24–48 hours in a container. But you still don't want to overdo it even if you do go the chemical route. Too much of anything is usually bad in some way or other.

WARNING

Overdosing — adding too many chemicals at one time, or even adding too many chemicals over a long period of time — can affect the water conditions (pH and so on) in your aquarium. Dumping bottle after bottle of treatments into your tank also makes your fish look like they're swimming around in a swamp, and I guarantee that they'll end up hating you for it. The point is that you shouldn't just dump 15 bottles of chemicals into your aquarium hoping one of them will work. (If you have to step carefully while walking across your fish's room to avoid crushing discarded chemical bottles, you're probably overdosing.)

Following instructions to the letter

Always follow all the manufacturer's instructions on the label. Don't skip any steps and follow through on the entire recommended treatment or usage time.

WARNING

Chemicals are chemicals. I can't stress this point enough! *Any* chemical can be dangerous if it's mixed with the wrong substance. Although doing so isn't a common hazard with aquarium chemicals, certain mixtures and overdoses can be lethal to your fish. Before you use any type of chemical, read the bottle very carefully and follow the manufacturer's instructions to a T.

If you don't understand the instructions or the ingredients on a chemical's label (sometimes they seem to be written in some weird alien dialect), don't hesitate to contact the product's manufacturer and have someone there help clear up your questions. You will often find a 1-800 number right there on the label, and/or a company name you can look up online to contact them. If you're in a hurry, ask your local dealer for help.

Knowing Which Chemicals You Need to Start Your Aquarium

When you first set up a brand new aquarium, certain chemicals can help you out a great deal. You can purchase most of the chemicals in this section at your local pet shop, and the other ones you can most likely find at the supermarket, online, or even around your own house.

Glass cleaner

You can use a household glass cleaner to clean the outside of your aquarium and its frame. Standard window cleaning products work well. Make sure you cover the top of the tank with a towel so that mist from the cleaner doesn't get inside the tank. Cleaners that have a citrus base seem to work the best. They leave the glass clean and streak free and also help to keep fingerprints from reappearing on the glass, which is especially useful when you have small children in the house.

TIP

If you want to go more of a natural route, clean the outside of the glass with a 50/50 vinegar and water mixture and a soft cloth. Stick to just fresh water to clean the inside.

WARNING

Never use a household glass cleaner on the *inside* of your tank! Glass cleaner residue can kill your fish very quickly. The only liquid that should be used to clean out the inside of an empty aquarium is fresh water. Never use soaps or any other types of chemicals on the inside glass.

Dechlorinator

When you first add water to your aquarium, you have to remove the chlorine from it first. Chlorine kills your fish. *Dechlorinator* usually comes in liquid form and removes harmful chlorine instantly.

With most brands, you need to add only a few drops per gallon to do the job (read the label carefully, of course). Basically, the main purpose of dechlorinator is to make the aquarium water safe for your fish without your having to wait for the chlorine to dissipate naturally (which usually takes 24 to 48 hours).

Water conditioner

Water conditioners often combine a dechlorinator with other chemicals that instantly detoxify the heavy metals in tap water. You can use a water conditioner when you're setting up a new aquarium, changing water, or adding water. Many sources of water (old wells and the like) may contain harmful metals that a water conditioner can detoxify. Even if your water tests safe, you never know when its properties may change, so a water conditioner is always a good bet.

Cycling chemicals

Waiting around for an aquarium to complete the nitrogen cycle (see Chapter 14) can be difficult. Depending on the type of system you have — freshwater, saltwater, or brackish — and the overall size of your tank, the entire nitrogen cycle can take weeks or even months to complete. *Cycling chemicals* have been around for a long, long time.

During the nitrogen cycle, beneficial bacteria convert harmful ammonia (produced by fish waste) into less toxic nitrites. Following this conversion, another kind of beneficial bacteria convert the nitrites into even less harmful nitrates. The nitrates are only harmful to your fish after they begin to build up in large quantities. You can remove the nitrates from your aquarium water though water changes.

Some cycling products can start your nitrogen cycle and speed it up as well. The appealing idea behind this particular product is really simple. The faster your tank cycles, the faster you can add more new fish to your aquarium. And the sooner you have fish in your aquarium, the sooner you can impress others.

If these natural bacteria products speed up the cycling time and give your starter fish that extra edge, why not use them? The only danger that I can see is that of looking at cycling chemicals as a cure-all for a tank you overstocked. These products are an aid to the nitrogen cycle, not a substitute for it, and certainly not a license to put too many fish in your tank.

In other words, if you set up a 55-gallon freshwater aquarium and toss in a couple of tablespoons of cycling formula in an attempt to offset the 75 goldfish you started your tank with, you're in for some serious problems. These products have a specific purpose, so don't push them to the limit.

Bacteria in a bottle

Some products speed up your aquarium's cycling time because they contain massive amounts of various beneficial bacteria held in a dormant state. After you add the bacteria formula to your aquarium water, the bacteria become completely regenerated and rapidly consume ammonia and nitrites. These different types of microorganisms combine to create a powerful nitrifying team. Most of these products are nonpathogenic, meaning they won't harm any plants or fish in your aquarium. It's impossible to overdose your tank with bacteria in a bottle.

Bacteria on a medium

Some bacteria products come as a rapid-action biological filter medium. This type of medium is called *precolonized* (meaning it already has the bacteria attached) with a multitude of nitrifying bacteria which, in some cases, can cut your cycling time in half. The medium prevents clogging and helps maintain good water circulation in your filtration unit. A bacterial medium is designed to have a maximum surface area to encourage the largest supply of beneficial bacteria.

Maintaining Your Aquarium: Chemicals to Use

Here are some other useful chemicals that can come in handy after you start your aquarium system:

>> **Waste eliminator:** Organic waste eliminator rapidly reduces organic waste in aquariums and cleans filters, gravel, and the interior surfaces of the tank.

>> **Ammonia control granules:** Ammonia control chemicals have granules that trap ammonium ions on contact and therefore reduce ammonia concentrations

in the water. This chemical along with regular water changes keeps any potential ammonia problem at bay.

>> **Aquarium salt:** Aquarium salt adds electrolytes (sodium) and helps your fish breathe better by increasing their gill function when they're diseased. Use them in hospital tanks and for adding small amounts for species such as mollies who do better with a tiny amount of salt in the water.

>> **pH regulators:** pH regulators increase or decrease the pH of your aquarium water. You want to increase or decrease pH depending on which way you need to go (see Chapter 14 for more on pH) to achieve the proper pH for your particular species.

>> **Cichlid buffers:** A cichlid buffer is a mixture of trace elements, sulfates, sodium, calcium, magnesium, potassium, and carbonates that provide natural water chemistry for rift lake fishes. (See Chapter 8 for more on cichlids.)

Using the Right Chemicals for Your Plants

For hobbyists with or without green thumbs, you can use several of the chemicals in this section to help your living aquarium plants thrive to their full potential. (Don't try them on plastic plants, because they may turn funny colors or something.)

REMEMBER

The living plants in your aquarium system have special needs that you need to meet. Your plants deserve the best, just like your fish do.

Create your own rainforest

If you have plants in your aquarium that come from the Amazon region (Amazon swords, for example), you can purchase chemicals to help create a rainforest condition in your tank. Products such as Instant Amazon provide essential macronutrients (proteins, carbohydrates, and fiber), increase lush plant growth (without nitrates or phosphates), discourage algae and parasite growth, detoxify ammonia and nitrites, and help your plants create beneficial oxygen for your fish. They also give your plants a better chance of obtaining nutrients from the aquarium water and enhance biological filtration.

You can use these products for soft-water fish such as discus, angelfish, neons, barbs, and gouramis to create a yellow color to the water, simulating their natural environment. This type of product often contains trace elements, vitamins, bark, and wood.

Plant growth

This product enhances intracellular reactions in plants and provides them with better coloration and improved growth through vitamins and minerals. CO_2 boosters provide simple carbon compounds and slowly releases CO_2 that your plants will absorb from the aquarium water.

Root tabs

Root tabs supply aquarium plants with magnesium, potassium, iron, and sulfur. These tabs help new aquatic plants get a good start in your aquarium and keep already established plants flourishing.

Algae control

Algae-control products (`www.algone.com/algone_information.asp`) reduce and prevent algae blooms through the introduction of copper sulfate. This type of product generally isn't used in tanks with live plants or invertebrates because it can kill them.

PREVENTION AND CONTROL TREATMENTS

Several chemical treatments protect the *slime coat* (a natural coating that helps to protect it against disease) on your fish's body. These products (Stress Coat is a good example) also help relieve stress and deter the onset of disease. Slime coat products are important for your fish, especially ones that have just been transported or netted. Your fish's natural slime coat can easily be worn off and leave bare patches that are open to attack by various diseases.

Snail control products destroy snails in your freshwater aquarium and help you keep them from coming back. Most snails are brought into the aquarium system on live plants. Snails are very sneaky and crafty (kind of like my kids) and have the ability to slip by even the most experienced eye. Snails can multiply faster than your household bills and can ruin the appearance of an aquarium as they get out of control. Nip them in the bud. As soon as your aquarium is overrun with snails, they're almost impossible to get rid of, and they often carry diseases that can damage your fish's health.

Naming Chemicals Your Fish Need for Medication

No matter what you do, disease is going to strike. Even the most experienced fish-keepers must deal with aquatic health problems from time to time. The following list gives you a few examples of products you can use to fight back when all other methods have failed (Chapter 11 has more on diseases and keeping your fish healthy):

>> **Antibiotics** treat bacterial infections, fungus, ulcers, gill disease, popeye, and dropsy.

>> **Formalin** is used to treat fish that have contracted external parasites. A formalin bath helps alleviate problems such as skin flukes.

>> **Malachite green** is often used in the treatment of ich (*Ichthyophthirius multifilius*).

>> **Paragon** treats inflamed gills, anchor worms, copepods, open sores, hemorrhaging, and hole-in-the-head disease.

REMEMBER

Medications can be confusing. Many manufacturers combine medications to treat a variety of illnesses. The label of most medication bottles lists the types of illness the product treats. These label listings help you wade through the confusion and choose the right product for the job.

KEEPING A CLEAR HEAD

In order for your fish to keep a clear head, you have to do the same. If you get carried away and turn your aquarium water into a chemical nightmare, your fish are going to start acting funny, suffer health problems, and face the possibility of death from toxicity. Make sure you check that your water conditions are correct for your system (temperature, salinity, pH, and nitrate levels) before you add medications. It's also important to make sure filters, heaters, and other equipment are running properly.

The golden rule of chemicals states that an aquarist should always attempt to remedy aquarium water problems naturally before adding chemicals. Think about it. Why add something that your aquarium doesn't need? Proper aquarium maintenance helps keep your water in good condition so that you don't have to add chemicals to correct problems. Carrying out consistent water changes regularly will help ward off serious problems in the future.

Remember, many chemicals claim to cure just about any problem under the sun. Always take each product's claims with a grain of salt until you check them out yourself!

Chapter **14**

The Nitrogen Cycle and Water Testing

Water quality is an important element in maintaining a successful aquarium system, so it's important that you discover a few basics about water chemistry such as the nitrogen cycle, pH, and hardness. Excellent water conditions in your aquarium will allow your pets to live long and healthy lives. Poor water conditions can leave your fish in poor health or cause their demise. Fortunately, you can easily monitor and maintain proper water conditions for each species with a few simple test kits.

REMEMBER Take the time to monitor your water conditions on a weekly basis so that you can correct any problems with ease. Your fish have to live in their aquarium water 24 hours a day. Make sure that you provide them with the best conditions possible. This chapter helps you get started.

Eliminating Fish Waste

Your fish are going to look great swimming around in your new tank. The water and the decorations are going to look sparkling clean and will impress everyone. But it won't stay that way without proper biological, mechanical, and chemical filtration because your fish have to settle themselves with Mother Nature each and every day. The total number of fish in your tank can quickly add up to a whole lot of waste being excreted. This waste takes the form of *ammonia* (a combination of nitrogen and hydrogen), a dangerous chemical that in high amounts can be lethal to your fish, and carbon dioxide (CO_2). Don't worry; for every aquarium problem there is always a solution.

To solve the waste problem, your fish and you join forces to provide proper *biological filtration* (utilizing living bacteria that constantly remove waste) and *cycling* (building up bacteria at the beginning to convert ammonia to nitrites and then to less harmful nitrates). Plants through photosynthesis in the aquarium and airstones and filters running in the tank remove the CO_2.

Now for the good news: There is no problem getting these certain bacteria, which are present in the water to start with, to help take care of excess buildups. The word bacteria is usually associated with bad and scary things such as infections, but in an aquarium system, certain bacteria actually act as the good guys and save the day.

To understand all the weird and wonderful processes taking place in the water of your aquarium system, you need to know about ammonia, bacteria, cycling, and the other aspects of the *nitrogen cycle.* These ideas may seem a little complicated at first (only because they are!), but the tips and explanations in this chapter can help you cut a clear pathway through the darkness that plagues the topic of water conditions.

REMEMBER

A new system isn't as biologically stable as an old one (conditioned aquarium), but in time, a new system becomes old and stable.

Conditioning Your Tank

You need to *condition* (also known as accomplishing the nitrification process, start-up cycle, and biological cycle) your new tank to provide your fish with the best possible chance for good health and survival. Conditioning sets up a bacterial colony to get rid of the nasty waste products your fish excrete. You have to be patient during this conditioning cycle because it does take time.

WARNING

Rushing headlong through this vital conditioning process will undoubtedly lead to quite a bit of heartache as you lose your fish to *new tank syndrome* (see the section "Preventing new tank syndrome" later in this chapter).

The main danger in any new aquarium is the rapid buildup of ammonia in the water through excretion and the decay of nitrogen products such as fish food and waste. As your aquarium begins to age, beneficial bacteria begin breaking down the ammonia so that the levels don't become too high. Bacteria are always present, but not enough in the beginning to take care of the problem.

Generally, conditioning takes about four to six weeks, but the time needed depends on the temperature of the water, the type and number of filtration units, the size of your system, and the number of livestock (starter fish) doing the backstroke around your tank.

Starting the Nitrogen Cycle

The nitrogen cycle plays an important role in your aquarium system (see Figure 14-1). These sections break down the different stages of the nitrogen cycle.

Encouraging nitrosamonas (good bacteria number one)

During the first part of the nitrogen cycle, beneficial bacteria called *nitrosamonas* in the aquarium water increase to detoxify and remove the ammonia from your aquarium by converting lethal ammonia to nitrites. High levels of nitrites are still killers in large amounts. Nitrosamonas bacteria require a good oxygen supply (which can be provided through filtration and airstones) in order to multiply and grow correctly.

Three ways to lower the buildup of ammonia and then the resulting nitrites are as follows:

>> Don't overfeed your fish.

>> Don't overstock the tank.

>> Carry out regular water changes.

When uneaten food and fish waste are broken down, they're turned into either ionized ammonium (NH_4+, a pH lower than 7.0 will cause more ammonium) or non-ionized ammonia (NH_3, a pH higher than 7.0 will cause more ammonia). The ammonium isn't harmful to your aquarium unless it's found in high levels, but the ammonia needs to be taken care of immediately.

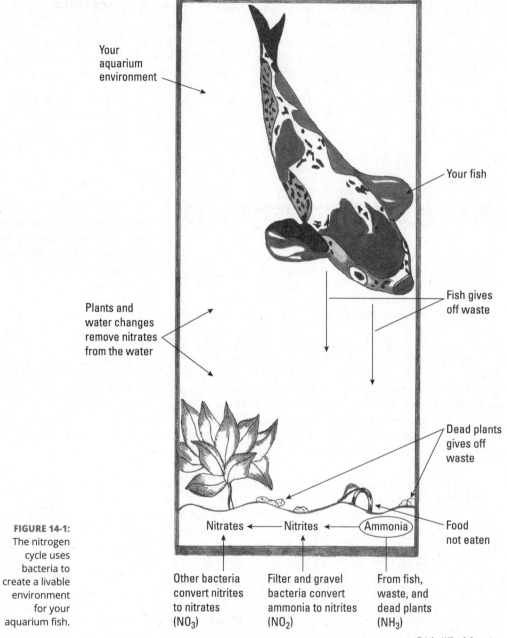

Your
aquarium
environment

Your fish

Fish gives
off waste

Plants and
water changes
remove nitrates
from the water

Dead plants
gives off
waste

FIGURE 14-1:
The nitrogen
cycle uses
bacteria to
create a livable
environment
for your
aquarium fish.

Nitrates ← Nitrites ← Ammonia

Food
not eaten

Other bacteria
convert nitrites
to nitrates
(NO_3)

Filter and gravel
bacteria convert
ammonia to nitrites
(NO_2)

From fish,
waste, and
dead plants
(NH_3)

© John Wiley & Sons, Inc.

Promoting nitrobacter (good bacteria number two)

When nitrite levels climb, a second type of bacteria known as *nitrobacter* converts them to less deadly nitrates during the second part of the cycle.

In this phase nitrate levels continue to increase slowly over time, but you can maintain them at proper levels through frequent water changes. If you don't change your water, the nitrates build up to the point where they're just as toxic as the ammonia you got rid of. Live plants will also help by using some of the nitrates for food. Ironically, if the plants ever die, they'll break down and produce ammonia.

About two weeks after you add starter fish to your aquarium, the ammonia buildup in your tank begins to peak. (You won't really have any ammonia in your aquarium until after you add your fish and they start excreting waste, or leaving food uneaten.) You're probably wondering what to do with the ammonia, right? Well, just sit back, because your friendly neighborhood bacteria take care of everything.

Monitoring through the conditioning period

During conditioning, you need to monitor pH, ammonia, nitrite, and nitrate levels using standard test kits (available at aquarium shops) so you can see how the cycle is progressing. Notice that the pH level decreases a little during the conditioning process, which is normal. Allowing the pH to decrease over a long period of time during the conditioning process keeps helpful bacteria from multiplying to its full potential. When nitrite and nitrate levels begin to overstep their limits, daily water changes help alleviate that problem.

Several types of bacteria multiply rapidly in order to remove toxic chemicals from the water during the weeks of the conditioning period. As the number of bacteria increases, the bacteria render larger amounts of waste product less toxic by converting them to less harmful substances in the nitrogen cycle.

WARNING

Don't use chemicals and medications in the main tank during the conditioning process, because they can potentially damage proper bacterial growth and, in turn, interfere with the nitrogen cycle.

When the conditioning process is complete, you can begin adding a few fish every week to allow the bacteria bed to increase at a normal rate. If you make the mistake of immediately overstocking your aquarium, ammonia levels (ammonia spikes) will gradually increase. To correct this situation, reduce the number of fish in the tank or add more filtration.

Speeding things up a bit

You can start up the nitrogen cycle by adding one or more of the following things to your tank:

>> **Starter fish:** Adding one or two fish is a good way to provide a minimum amount of waste to your tank so that essential bacteria can multiply at a normal rate. Using a couple of guppies or hardy danios to start the maturation process is one of the best ways to begin your nitrogen cycle. Don't get greedy and attempt to add a ton of fish all at once because not enough bacteria are in the tank to handle the load during the cycling process. As the tank cycles, you can slowly add fish later.

>> **Mature gravel:** Gravel from a mature (and disease-free) aquarium already has a large bacteria population on its surface and acts as an excellent starter culture.

>> **Food:** Adding a small amount of food to the tank each day can help begin the nitrogen cycle. The only problem with this method is that it's unreliable and can lead to water fouling if food isn't added in the correct amounts. The correct amount is a few pinches twice a day to start the ammonia production as the uneaten food begins to break down.

>> **Commercial additives:** You can purchase additives such as freeze-dried bacteria at your local pet store to help speed up the nitrogen cycle. Products such as *precolonized mediums* (you add them to your filter box or canister) can significantly increase cycling time.

TIP

The best way to begin the aquarium maturation cycle is to add a small amount of mature gravel and a few starter fish.

REMEMBER

Despite the fact that your starter fish begin the process of proper bacterial growth, it takes time to build up a well-established biological colony. Don't add too many fish right away because they can overload the biological filtration system and result in new tank syndrome (see next section).

Instead, simply wait a couple of weeks after the tank is cycled before adding a few small fish each week to the aquarium. This gradual increase in livestock keeps ammonia levels within an acceptable range for the bacteria present to do their job correctly.

TIP

During the cycling period, you may notice cloudiness in the water. Don't worry; it isn't a sign that all has gone wrong. The cloudiness is a beneficial bacterial bloom and is perfectly normal. If your aquarium has adequate filtration, the water should become clear again within a few days.

Preventing new tank syndrome

As time passes, waste builds up in your tank and needs to be eliminated. After a month or two, the significant amount of bacteria living in the substrate bed and filters (or any surface they can attach themselves to) take care of any fishy waste products.

New tank syndrome occurs when ammonia or nitrite is not properly converted to less harmful nitrates. *Overstocking* (putting too many fish in your aquarium) when you first set up your tank usually causes new tank syndrome.

WARNING

New tank syndrome is a silent killer, often striking without warning. It causes extreme physical ailments or even death. Your fish may look a little out of joint one day and be dead the next. You must discover how to recognize the symptoms of this problem. Fish suffering from new tank syndrome often

>> Lose some of their coloring

>> Hide in corners with clamped fins

>> Have trouble swimming

>> Hover near the bottom of the aquarium

If you notice any of these unusual behaviors, immediately test the ammonia and nitrite levels and carry out water changes as needed to reduce excess waste products.

Testing Ammonia, Nitrites, Nitrates, and pH

To *maintain* healthy water conditions at the beginning of the cycle and throughout the life of your aquarium system, you need to continue to test your water's ammonia, nitrite, and nitrate levels frequently. Keeping the following levels where they should be helps your fish stay much healthier overall.

Changing the water regularly

One of the best (and oldest) methods of keeping your ammonia and nitrate levels down is to change the water regularly. Water changes help remove unwanted waste and at the same time replace depleted trace elements. Besides, if you change your aquarium water on a regular schedule (yes, that means more than once a year!) your fish will love you for it.

TIP

Research shows that fish that live in aquariums where the water is changed often, display better coloration, live longer and healthier lives, and fight off disease with superhuman (I mean *superfishy*) strength. Water changes also help your filtration system function better.

You may wonder how much water you should change. I prefer to change about 15 percent of the water in my tanks every week. The figure varies depending on the hobbyist you talk to, but generally falls in the 10 to 20 percent a week range. I know that this may sound like a chore, but it really isn't. You can get a special kind of hose, called a Python (see Chapter 12), to help you. The Python can suck water out of the tank, and then be reversed to add water to a bucket near your tank so that you can dechlorinate it. You can also do it the old-fashioned way by using a bucket. Many local fish stores have maintenance crews that come to your home and test and change your water using a monthly service if you have the funds to go that route.

WARNING

Don't do lift heavy buckets of water if you have any health problems. Get someone to do it for you. One of your neighbors probably owes you a favor anyway.

If you don't keep changing the water in your aquariums every week, your nitrate level may rise to the point where it becomes lethal over time. There is really no practical way to get rid of excess nitrate levels without water changes.

As your aquarium system matures, the pH level drops due to acid buildup. Water changes help eliminate this problem as well.

Maintaining proper pH levels

The pH of your aquarium is simply a logarithmic scale that tells how alkaline or acidic your aquarium water is. The pH scale goes from 0 (highly acidic) to 14.0 (highly alkaline) with a value of 7.0 being considered neutral. Here you can find out which type of system you can use to test pH and why monitoring it on a regular basis is important.

Knowing which pH test systems are available

When you set up you new aquarium, you need a pH test kit, available at almost any pet store. Don't be afraid; they're really quite simple to use. Special test kits for freshwater aquariums test pH in the lower to neutral range to the higher ranges. Don't bother trying to use a home water testing kit because they're expensive and hard to find, and they' aren't made to test aquarium conditions. One type of aquarium water testing kit consists of a simple color card, plastic measuring tube, and chemicals that either lower or raise the pH. Usually, you fill the measuring tube with water from your aquarium and add a few drops of *regent* (a water color-changing chemical supplied with the test kit). Then you compare the resulting color to the color on the provided kit chart, which indicates the pH value of your aquarium water. This system is difficult if you have color vision problems like I do.

Some aquarium water testing kits have strips of litmus paper that, when you dip them into your aquarium, change color to indicate the pH level. With others, you read your pH level read electronically by inserting probes attached to a machine into the water.

The type of test kit you choose depends on how much mad money you have to blow when you find yourself picking up supplies. I like the probe type testers because they're the easiest to read due to their digital output.

Checking pH on a regular basis

Check the pH level of your aquarium water when you first set up your tank and at least once a week after the nitrogen cycle is complete. Many species of fish prefer to live in slightly alkaline, others like to hang out in acidic waters, and some like to remain in between (neutral). So the pH level you need for your particular system depends on what species of fish you have. See Chapter 8 for more information on correct pH for some common and popular species.

WARNING

The pH values in a freshwater system can fluctuate very rapidly. Even the smallest change in pH level can stress your fish and make them much more susceptible to various diseases. Make sure you keep an eye on the situation.

It's important to test and adjust the pH for your fish because if it's incorrect, your fish can become ill or die. Monitoring pH alerts you to excess ammonia or nitrate spikes that can change the pH of the water. These two terms are important when monitoring the pH level:

>> **Acidity:** If, after testing, you find that the pH level of your aquarium water is too low (that is, too acidic), you can raise it by adding sodium bicarbonate (also known as baking soda) from the test kit or through water changes, which also remove organic buildup. This organic buildup reduces pH. If your test kit doesn't have the chemicals, you can purchase them at your local pet store.

>> **Alkalinity:** If you find that the pH level of your water is too high (meaning too alkaline), you can lower it by adding the sodium biphosphate from the test kit or by adding de-mineralized water. Remember that pH-lowering chemicals are phosphate based and can encourage algae growth.

A pH of 5 is ten times more acidic than a pH of 6. So don't let the little numbers fool you — they can change your water chemistry drastically.

When you purchase your fish, make sure that your various species' pH requirements are compatible. Carefully research the pH of any species you purchase.

Remember that ammonia is more toxic in a system with a higher pH.

If there are any fish in your aquarium, change the pH level gradually. Changes of more than one range value per day (for example, from 6.5 to 7.5) can shock your fish and result in their death.

Testing Hardness (dH)

The degree of hardness (measured by a term called *degrees of hardness,* or dH) in water refers to the amount of dissolved mineral salts (mostly magnesium and calcium) in your water. The more minerals that are present, the harder the water. You don't have to worry about your water's degree of hardness unless you live in an area where the water is very hard (150+) or very soft (0–4). You can test for hardness by using a simple hardness test kit available at your local fish store.

Some fish like to live in slightly hard water, and others don't. Having a fish in *very* hard water that is supposed to live in soft water can lead to illness and death.

One way to dilute hardness is to add rain or distilled water to your tank. Another way is to boil the water and let it cool before adding it to your tank. Both methods lower the pH levels. Extreme hardness is found in alkaline (high pH) waters. *Reverse osmosis* units soften aquarium water, but these units tend to be expensive and use a lot of tap water in order to produce a small amount of mineral-free water.

You can also use a water softener or add peat moss to your filter (boil the peat first to remove any unwanted organisms). You can easily increase hardness by adding sodium bicarbonate in small amounts at a time (about a teaspoon per 55 gallons) and then monitoring the change.

Chapter **15**

Putting It All Together

If you're reading this chapter, you've probably purchased most of the equipment for your new aquarium. If you haven't, take a look at the first six chapters of this book, which cover equipment, substrate, and tanks. But I'm sure many of you are wondering in what order all those hoses, funny-looking pieces of tubing, and gadgets all fit into your system. That's what this chapter is for.

You're probably crossing your fingers in hopes that I talk about the type of system that you want to set up. Never fear! This chapter shows you how to set up a freshwater tropical system, a coldwater system, and an indoor pond system. You can't beat that with a stick!

The setups here are my own personal choices for a beginning hobbyist. You can find many other types of equipment, substrates, and so on that can be put on these systems, but I want to lead you through the simple steps of putting together a minimal setup that will work fine and not cost you mega bucks. Later on, you can add more equipment if you choose to do so. Part of the excitement of the hobby is discovering and trying new things, and I wouldn't want to take that opportunity away from you by giving you system setups that are set in stone. Begin with the basics, do your research, and then let your imagination lead you from there.

REMEMBER

Don't forget to read the directions on every piece of equipment that you purchase. There are a lot of good tips and advice that the manufacturers have printed out for your convenience. Take advantage of them. These instructions usually come with pictures and other good information about replacing broken parts, so don't be afraid to take a few minutes to scan the enclosed materials. If the piece of equipment has parts, do a dry run to make sure they all fit together before you place them in your aquarium. If you still have problems, your local fish store will be happy to help.

Whichever aquarium setup you choose, be bold and experiment with different combinations of equipment. Take time to research your fish and plants and add them slowly over time (a couple a month) so that your system remains stable. Remember not to overstock.

Setting Up Your Tropical Freshwater System

What follows are the basic steps to set up a tropical aquarium. For this example, I use a background, gravel, a power filter, a heater, and lighting.

1. **Find a good location.**

   Choose a place that has a solid floor and is away from windows, doors, and high-traffic areas. Make sure you have adequate electrical outlets and a handy water supply.

2. **Set up the stand.**

   Place the stand so that it is stable (that is, it doesn't rock). You can use a carpenter's level to accomplish this goal. Lay the level along the length of the stand to make sure that it's completely level. If not, use hardwood shims (available at hardware stores) to level the stand by placing them one at a time under the legs.

   Make sure you leave room behind the stand for hanging equipment and leave enough room for yourself to do cleaning and maintenance.

   REMEMBER
3. **Clean your tank.**

   Clean your aquarium with clear water and a soft sponge. Don't use soap or other chemicals! Make sure you dry the outside of the glass with paper towels to avoid streaks that may be hard to reach after the system is completely set up.

4. **Place the aquarium on the stand.**

   Make sure that the tank fits properly on the stand. Don't allow any of the tank's bottom edges to hang over. If you want, you can place a thin sheet of Styrofoam underneath the tank to cushion it and even out minor changes in level.

5. **Add a background.**

   If you want to add a background, tape it onto the back of the tank so that you don't have to work it around the equipment and cords later. Some backgrounds are self-adhesive. They usually cling to the glass, so you need to put them on slowly and smooth them out as you go along to avoid bubbles.

Another option is to paint the back glass on the *outside* with a roller. One method that works well is to apply a couple of thin layers of Krylon spray paint. Doing so hides any cords or other objects that you don't want to show behind the tank. Apply two coats of paint and make sure that it's completely dry before you continue. Be careful not to splash any paint into the tank's interior because it can be toxic. You can cover the top of the tank with a towel while painting. I like to use an ocean blue paint for the back of my tanks, because it allows the fish to show their true colors and helps reflect lighting. Midnight blue and black look great, too.

6. **Wash and add your substrate.**

TIP

Wash gravel with clear water. You can use a colander to rinse the gravel. Set the colander over a bucket and rinse the gravel under water until the overflow is clean. Doing so removes dirt, dust, and excess dye.

Put one and a half to two inches of gravel on the bottom. Slope the gravel so that it's about half an inch higher in the rear.

7. **Add a power filter.**

Add a power filter (see Chapter 6) to make the total filtration system complete. Place the filter on the tank by hanging it on the outside of the rear glass. The intake tube should hang inside of the aquarium. Rinse the filter pads under clear water and place them in the slots inside the filter. Don't plug the unit in yet!

8. **Fill the tank up two-thirds of the way with water.**

Doing so allows you to arrange the gravel if it has moved during filling and provide leeway to add decorations later without spilling water from the tank.

Pour the water into the aquarium by letting it splash on top of a small plate that is resting underwater on top of the gravel. Doing so makes sure that the water doesn't move the gravel and decorations around while you're filling the tank. Make sure the water is the correct temperature for your species.

9. **Install the heater.**

Install a submersible heater at an angle along the rear piece of glass. If you're using a nonsubmersible heater, attach it onto the rim of the tank.

Don't plug in the heater yet!

10. **Put the thermometer on the tank.**

Hang a hanging thermometer on the rim of the tank or stick a floating thermometer in one corner of the tank. If you have a stick-on thermometer, stick it on to the outside of the glass. I like to place these on the side of the tank in one corner so that they don't take away from the front view.

11. **Add decorations.**

    Add rocks, caves, driftwood, and other decorations such as artificial plants that you have chosen for your setup.

12. **Fill the aquarium.**

    Add water until the aquarium water is at the same level as the bottom edge of the aquarium frame that wraps around the top of the glass.

13. **Add dechlorinator to the water.**

    Follow the instructions on the product for the correct amount.

14. **Plug in all the equipment and set the heater to the correct temperature for the fish you're going to purchase.**

    Add water from the tank to the power filter to prime it if necessary.

15. **Check the pH.**

    Use a test kit to test the pH of the water. If it's okay, continue on. If not, adjust it until it's correct.

16. **Put the hood on top of the tank.**

17. **Add lighting if you have strip lighting separate from a hood or top glass.**

    Place the light on top of the tank and plug it in.

18. **Let the aquarium run for 24 to 48 hours.**

19. **Do a pH and temperature check and then adjust as needed.**

20. **Put in your starter fish.**

    Just a few small ones! Don't go overboard!

There you have it in a nutshell. Remember that you must monitor your water conditions *daily* (using test kits you buy at aquariums shops) to keep an eye on ammonia, nitrite, and nitrate levels until the tank has finished cycling. You can start to slowly add more fish after the chemical levels stabilize and check the conditions once a week thereafter. Be patient during this process.

Setting Up a Small Plant Tank

Some hobbyists like to have a tankful of plants and no fish. Here is how to set it up. Follow the instructions in the previous tropical freshwater section, just don't add the fish. Plants require carbon dioxide (CO_2) as part of photosynthesis to make food for themselves, generally 15 to 30 parts per million to thrive. Fish provide

CO_2, but because you're making a plant-only tank, you have to provide the CO_2 with a piece of equipment called a CO_2 diffuser. Follow the manufacturer's instructions on the diffuser for the best results.

I recommend LED full spectrum lighting for your plants in this setup. Remember to supplement your plants with aquarium plant food and monitor the pH so that you can keep it in the range needed for your species of flora.

Setting Up Your Coldwater System

Sure, tropical fish are great, but coldwater species are beautiful too. What follows are the basic steps to set up a coldwater aquarium. For this example, I use a bio-wheel and artificial plants. Follow Steps 1–6 in the previous "Setting Up Your Tropical Freshwater System" section and then proceed here:

1. **Add a biowheel filter.**

   Place the filter on the tank by hanging it on the outside of the rear glass. The intake tube should hang inside of the aquarium. Rinse the filter pads under clear water and place them in the slots inside the filter. Place the biowheels in their marked slots. Don't plug the unit in yet!

2. **Fill the tank up two-thirds of the way with water.**

   Doing so allows you to arrange the gravel if it has moved during filling and provide enough water to add decorations later.

   Pour the water into the aquarium by letting it splash on top of a small plate that is resting underwater on top of the gravel. Doing so makes sure that the water doesn't move the gravel and decorations around while you're filling the tank.

3. **Add decorations.**

   Add rocks, driftwood, plastic plants, and other decorations.

4. **Fill the aquarium.**

   Add water until the aquarium water is at the same level as the bottom edge of the aquarium frame that wraps around the top of the glass.

5. **Add dechlorinator to the water.**

   This step isn't always necessary with two-day wait time on fish, but it never hurts to add it anyway.

6. **Plug in all the equipment.**

7. **Add water to the biowheel unit if it isn't self-starting.**

8. Check the pH and adjust as needed.

9. Put the hood and lights on the tank.

10. Let the tank run for 24 to 48 hours and retest pH and adjust as needed.

11. Put in your starter coldwater fish.

Setting Up Your Simple Indoor Goldfish Pond

A good place for this pond is on an enclosed patio or in a finished basement. For this setup, I use a half whiskey barrel with a submersible pond filter:

1. **Place your half whiskey barrel in a level area that is free from windows and drafts.**

2. **Add the pond liner.**

   If it's a pre-fit barrel liner, just set it in place. If you have to make your own, use a flexible liner and fit it into the barrel, allowing the excess to hang over the edges.

3. **Fill the barrel with water, leaving about 6 inches at the top.**

4. **Add several inches of gravel or smooth river stones to the bottom and set your pond filter down into the barrel after attaching it to your pump.**

5. **Add dechlorinator and then trim off the excess liner.**

   You can tack the end of the liner 6 inches below the rim on the outside using a staple gun.

6. **Place your pond plants in the pond.**

   To start, add a few floaters. For stand-up plants, you can use overturned clean flowerpots as a base to raise the level of your plants.

7. **Plug in your pump and add a top.**

   There are several ways to add a top to the barrel, but my favorite way is to have a lumberyard cut a heavy board in the shape of a circle with a large donut hole in the middle. Simply set the board on top and you'll have a little rim around the opening to place decorations and small rocks. This also covers the overhanging liner.

8. **Let the pond run for 24 to 48 hours then add your starter goldfish.**

Chapter **16**

What You Need to Know: Live Plants for Aquariums

Live plants are one of the most overlooked but truly wonderful aspects of the aquarium hobby.

Plants come in a wide variety of sizes, shapes, colors, and densities. Living plants offer a unique and natural beauty that artificial plants can't achieve. All you need to enjoy live aquatic plants are proper water conditions, good lighting, plant food, and a little patience. Take time to bring your fish a step closer to their natural environment with live plants, and they'll love you for it!

Live plants are a lot of fun, look cool, and help boost your image as a serious hobbyist. What better reasons can you think of to keep them in your aquarium? Actually, there are a lot of other good reasons to keep live plants, as this chapter discusses. Unfortunately, many small fish shops don't carry live plants, and even if they do, they may have limited or poor stock. If your local dealer doesn't have the plants you're looking for, ask about special orders. Many aquatic shops have access to live plants but only order them on demand because of limited tank space.

Understanding What Live Plants Do for Your Aquarium

You can use live plants to enhance the natural look of your freshwater aquarium, and they can be beneficial and beautiful at the same time. Plants can produce a calming affect (both for you and your fish) and help maintain a natural, biological balance in your aquarium. Don't get me wrong. Many hobbyists aquascape their aquariums with artificial plants and are perfectly happy with the outcome. Then again, many hobbyists use plastic plants because they don't have the knowledge to maintain live aquatic plants successfully, have fish species that are detrimental to plants, or don't have the time to care for them.

WARNING

Certain species of fish destroy any live plants you may put into your tank, so in certain situations artificial plants are much more beneficial than the real McCoy. Artificial plants are only slightly less costly than live plants, so don't let cost alone affect your decision. If you really want live plants but are on a limited budget, just start out with a few and add them when you're able to grab a bit of aquatic mad money. (See Chapter 17 for a lot more on plant species.)

Live plants in an aquarium

>> Offer good shelter for pregnant females who want to escape from aggressive mates.

>> Supply shade and cooler temperatures during the warmer months.

>> Help protect small fish, fry, and shy fish from bullying tankmates.

>> Provide a safe refuge for all your delicate and long-finned fish that may otherwise end up on the aquatic lunch menu.

>> Absorb nitrates through the substrate and their leaves to help increase water quality.

>> Release oxygen into the water that is beneficial to your fish.

>> Condition the water in your tank by removing carbon dioxide (CO_2) and sulfur substances and by harboring bacteria to remove other wastes.

>> Inhibit algae growth by providing resource competition. Plants use the excess nutrients in the water to thrive. These are the same nutrients that algae need to survive. Plants help "starve" algae production by keeping them from having enough nutrients to flourish.

>> Create food for themselves within their own cells and release oxygen, which is extremely beneficial to your fish, during the process, as Figure 16-1 illustrates.

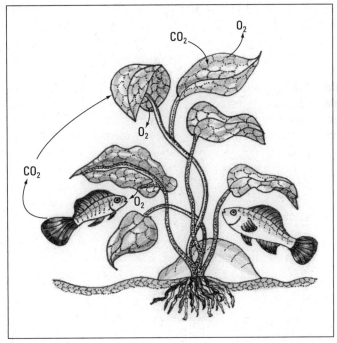

FIGURE 16-1: During daylight hours, plants absorb carbon dioxide and expel oxygen.

© John Wiley & Sons, Inc.

When you turn off your aquarium lights, plants start absorbing oxygen. They then release CO_2 in a process similar to your fish's respiration process.

REMEMBER

Living plants can also be a food source for fish that prefer a high amount of vegetation in their diet (of course you'll have to continually replace plants as they get munched). Your fish's color is much more intense in a naturally planted tank. And because plants provide security, your aquatic pets also act much more confident in a planted tank. (They won't have to spend the entire day trying to dig an escape tunnel.)

Identifying Different Plant Types

You can find three basic types of plants in an aquarium shop:

>> **Aquatic:** *Aquatic* plants can be entirely submerged beneath the water line of your tank and still survive. These plants die when they're removed from the water. Sagittaria (*Sagittaria natans*) and pygmy sword (*Echinodorus quadricostatus*) are two good examples of aquatic plants.

>> **Marginal:** *Marginal* plants spend only part of their time submerged beneath the water. These types of plants flower and seed out of water during the dry periods of the year. Examples of marginal plants include cryptocoryne (*Cryptocoryne balansae*). Marginal plants require special handling and should be left in the hands of expert hobbyists.

WARNING

>> **Terrestrial:** *Terrestrial* plants live on land and don't survive very long if they're completely submerged. I don't recommend them for use in the home aquarium.

Each type of plant is unique in its requirements for survival and growth, so you need to know exactly which species you can accommodate before you purchase any plants. Make sure each plant type is labeled correctly before you take it home. (Chapter 17 delves deeper and gives you good examples of live aquatic plants that you can enjoy in your home aquarium without having to worry about them too much.)

Just like animals are sorted into different general categories (reptiles, mammals, and so forth) plants have their own unique groupings based on physical attributes. Here are a few different categories that can help you understand the different types of plants you can add to your aquarium.

Ferns and mosses

These types of plants don't flower and will propagate using spores. Here is a bit more about the two:

>> Ferns propagate through spores that are collected in clusters beneath the leaves and rhizomes that produce roots. They have large compound leaves that are divided into many smaller leaves. Ferns grow much larger than mosses overall to attain interesting height transitions.

>> Mosses also reproduce spores and spread quickly. They have no true leaves, instead they just have green shoots. Mosses can be used to create seamless transitions between rocks and other decorations due to their soft carpetlike appearance.

Floating plants

Floating plants don't anchor themselves to the substrate. Instead, they drift around the top of your aquarium. Floating plants can grow extremely quickly, so you need to thin them out — or prune them — when they become too thick and bushy. If you don't, they may block out the light that enters your aquarium from the hood. The resulting loss of light can lower the temperature of your aquarium water, which has a devastating effect on the health of your fish and plants. If they become too thick, they can also block light from reaching lower plants. Floating plants reproduce easily by sprouting young daughter plants and propagating new plants from severed pieces. Use floating plants in spawning tanks to hide young fry.

Stem plants

Stem plants such as *Ludwigia* and *Cabomba* are often sold bunched together in groups of up to ten and are held together with a small weight and aquarium safe material to protect their roots. They're great starter plants because they can fill spaces quickly and are a great bang for the buck.

Rooted plants

Rooted plants anchor themselves in the substrate and draw part of their nourishment through their leaves and part through their roots. Rooted plants reproduce by creating *runners* (slender plant shoots) that branch off from the main stem. These runners eventually reroot and form new plants or sprout young shoots out of existing leaf surfaces. Many species of rooted plants can grow very large, so use caution when choosing the correct species for a small tank.

Potted plants come with a small receptacle around the roots and are often raised in humid nurseries. With this type of plant, you have the option of submerging the entire basket in the substrate or removing the basket and planting the roots directly. If you leave the basket intact, the plant's roots will grow through the basket's holes and then anchor themselves in the substrate.

TIP

I remove the baskets so that they don't show above the substrate level when rooting fishes begin digging around them. Unless you have 10 feet of gravel in your tank, these horrid baskets always seem to find a way to show off and emerge into the limelight.

Removing the basket often reveals several small plants combined into one tight group. Carefully separate each individual plant from the others around it. Plant each of these little cuttings in the substrate separately. Remember that these plants aren't full grown, so you need to allow ample space for them to spread out.

Cuttings

Many varieties of plants are sold in aquarium stores as cuttings. Cuttings often grow very rapidly because they gather nourishment through their leaves. A group of small cuttings (plants too small to stand alone) can be bunched up together with aquarium weights (which you can purchase from your local fish dealer) and planted until they begin to root on their own. After they begin to grow a bit, you can separate them from each other.

Maintaining Plant-Friendly Aquarium Conditions

To keep your plants healthy, you need to provide them with the proper temperature, nutritional food, proper substrate, good water conditions, and adequate lighting. Keep reading for specific advice.

Temperature requirements

Plants have temperature requirements just like your fish do. Check each species' temperature requirements before you purchase them so you know whether they're compatible with your fish's needs. A large majority of aquarium plants are tropical and need to be kept warm — they eventually die in cold water.

TIP

While you're checking out a shop's tropical plants, see whether they're being kept in warm tanks. If they're kept in cold water, they probably won't survive long after you place them in your home aquarium.

Substrate for rooting

TIP

Live plants prefer a 1- to 2-inch deep substrate that consists of fine gravel or coarse sand ($\frac{1}{16}$ inch to $\frac{1}{8}$ inch is great). This type of substrate allows water to move through plant roots so that they can gather nutrients. It also provides plants with the space they need for their roots to fork out as they grow. Chapter 5 discusses different types of substrates.

Filtration

Clean water is extremely important for successful plant growth in your aquarium. Dirt and debris settle on the surface of the leaves and clog the plant's pores. Keep plant leaves clean by gently brushing them with a soft toothbrush that you keep for plant aquarium use only. If your aquarium water gets too dirty, the amount of energy-giving light is drastically reduced. Water changes and vacuuming the water help correct the problem.

TIP

Try to use filtration that doesn't pump tons of air bubbles into the water, which drives out the CO_2 your plants need. A power filter or canister filter would be the best bets for a plant-heavy tank setup. If you're running bubble generators such as wands, having too many bubbles can also destroy the view. Fish don't want to feel like they're hanging on for their lives because the inside of your tank resembles an agitating washing machine either, so don't overdo the bubbles. Keep the combination of bubbles coming from the filter and generators to a couple slow streams.

Feeding

The tap water in your aquarium doesn't have the necessary trace elements and nutrients your plants need for proper growth. You can put tablets and liquid feeders (which provide nutrients, found at your local pet shop) in the gravel near the plant's roots for fertilization — best done after a water change. You can also place a single cutting in the center of a plug, which provides nutrition on a continual basis. You then bury the plug in the gravel.

WARNING

Don't use household plant fertilizers in your aquarium because they contain extremely high amounts of phosphates, which are bad for fish.

Lighting

Tropical plants require a constant source of light during the day in order to grow properly. Most tropical plants should receive at least 8 hours of light each day. Planted tanks require more intense lighting than fish-only aquariums, but your fish probably won't mind an opportunity to get a bit of an extra tan now and then.

On the other hand, some plants such as the Amazon sword and the Java fern prefer low lighting situations. Check the requirements of each species before you buy so you get plants that will survive under the same lighting conditions.

TIP

You can use a plant-growth light, which provides the proper light spectrum plants need. You can also control the amount of light your plants receive by using a simple timer on your aquarium light so that peak intensity remains the same each day.

TIP

One way to compensate for the different lighting requirements between plant species, if you choose to mix them, is to place taller plants so that they shade the shorter species that thrive in low-light levels.

Other supplements

One of the most important supplements for plants is iron because plants use it to produce chlorophyll, necessary for photosynthesis. Make sure you get an iron supplement for your plant tanks. You can find it on most aquatic Internet plant websites and in some fish stores.

Purchasing and Transporting Your Plants

If you're fortunate enough to live in an area where the local pet shops stock a wide variety of live plants, you need to know how to get them home safely. If possible, always purchase your plants from a dealer (in town or on the Internet). So, where do you get these aquarium plants from? Luckily you have several options available, including taking them from the wild, buying from local stores, and purchasing them on the Internet. If you have a computer, skip the first two options and buy them online because you'll get higher quality stock.

Taking from the wild

You *can* collect plants from small bodies of water, such as ponds, but take a few precautions if you choose to do this:

» Make sure the plants in your area match the water conditions that will be in your aquarium.

» Carefully clean any plants you take from the wild in clear, cool water with a toothbrush to avoid introducing disease and aquatic pests such as snails and parasites.

» Before you go yanking up any plants at your local stream, make sure that their removal won't have any detrimental effects on the natural environment.

» Check with local authorities about endangered species and other regulations to ensure that your liberation of the plants doesn't cause your own removal from home to jail.

Buying from a dealer

Before purchasing any live plants, you need to have a good idea of which types and sizes best suit your project. Write out a list that includes the total number of plants you need to reach the design effects that you desire. It's possible that your local fish shop won't have all the plants you're searching for. Include substitute species on your shopping list just in case the shop can't order them for you.

TIP

Start out by purchasing just a few of the plants on your list. Remember that plants usually grow quickly. If you buy too many in the beginning, your aquarium may end up looking like an Amazon rainforest in a couple of weeks. If your gardener has to come in and trim your aquarium plants back so you can open your front door, you may want to thin them out a bit. One general formula to obtain the total number of plants for your aquarium is to calculate one plant for every 6 square inches of gravel area. Simply multiply the length of the aquarium by the width (in inches) and divide by six to get the number of plants you need.

You also need to use a little common sense when you buy your plants. Some species are naturally "fuller" than others and take up quite a bit more space. After you become familiar with a particular plant species, you'll have a better idea of how much room the plants occupy when they are full grown.

Buying online

If you want high-quality plants at decent prices, order them on the Internet. Online dealers have an outstanding selection of high-quality plants available. Often these sites explain the conditions required to keep each species in optimal health and give good tips for grouping them with other plants. Online businesses carefully package and ship plants in a timely manner. I've never received a plant in poor health from an online dealer.

You can find an entire aquatic forest just by cruising the cyber highway for an hour or so. Many Internet plants from reputable companies can't be beat for price and quality. Here are a couple of websites to get you started:

>> www.aquariumplants.com

>> www.freshwateraquariumplants.com

If you don't have a computer, borrow your neighbor's for a while (tell her you're doing international biological research) or go the library.

TIP

How many plants can you put in your aquarium? I generally like to leave a minimum of 40 percent of the tank unplanted, but other hobbyists like planting more or less. Start with planting about 30 percent and see how it works for you.

Getting plants home in one piece

To maintain your plants' good health, you need to make sure that they don't dry out on the way home from the shop. Ask your dealer to bag your plants in water or carefully wrap each one in wet newspaper. If it's cold out, transport your new plants in a cooler so that the water remains warm.

Achieving acclimation

After you come home, remove any torn or browning leaves by pruning them with aquarium scissors and then placing your plants in a pan of water that contains a 10 percent solution of potassium permanganate. *Potassium permanganate* is a substance that kills unwanted germs and disinfects plant surfaces. If you can't find this solution in your local pet store, clean the plants under room-temperature water by gently brushing them with a soft toothbrush as I mention previously. Trim all cuttings to the correct height for your tank and remove any dead or wilted leaves that are still remaining with a sharp pair of scissors.

WARNING

Never pinch off or tear dead plant pieces with your fingers — you may damage the delicate tissues!

REMEMBER

Plants need time to acclimate to their new home. Don't expect them to flourish in a day. Some plants may lose leaves and struggle before taking a firm hold in their new environment, so give them a month or so to make themselves at home.

Noticing Potential Plant Problems

Even the best hobbyist's green thumb turns black once in a while. Hey, no one is perfect. Fortunately, plant diseases in aquariums are rare, so don't get too worked up at the thought of all your beautiful sword plants kicking the bucket at the same time. If your plants are growing at a normal pace and are developing new shoots and buds, they're probably in good health.

In order to keep your plants healthy and happy, you need to know what to look for when they're sick so you can fix the problem right away. You also need to know about medications that can harm your plants and the different types of algae that can interfere with plant growth if allowed to grow uncontrolled.

Recognizing signs of poor plant health and what to do about them

Knowing how to identify and cure foliage problems before they become too severe can help you avoid losing your new aquatic plants. Here are some warning signs to look for when carrying out your daily aquarium maintenance routine:

>> **Your plants have holes in them.** This problem is often caused by fish nibbling on the leaves. If your fish are vegetarians and you provided the plants as a food source, get used to losing plants. If your plants begin to fall apart after the holes appear, they may be suffering from rot, which is usually caused by excess nitrates in the aquarium. Water changes help correct this problem.

>> **Your plants' leaves are turning yellow.** They may be suffering from an iron deficiency. Aquatic plant fertilizer with iron solves this problem.

>> **The leaves have turned brown or black.** This indicates decay, probably caused by too much iron. Water changes help this problem.

>> **Some plants are dying, and some are surviving.** Hard-water plants are better able to extract CO_2 from the water, whereas soft-water plants have a harder time. Make sure you have enough in your aquarium water for each type.

If you want to keep different types of plants together, try adding CO_2 (through water change or CO_2 equipment available at pet shops) to the tank. Different areas of the country have different amounts of CO_2 in the tap water. Note that adding CO_2 to the tank lowers the pH so you'll need to test the pH after doing so (flip to Chapter 14 on how to test the pH).

Algae

No matter what you do, you always have some type of algae in your aquarium system. Algae is often introduced into your aquarium by fish and live food. But, if you keep healthy plants in your system, algae doesn't stand much of a chance.

If your algae gets out of control, though, look out! Algae comes in different colors, so keep the following in mind:

» **Blue-green algae:** Caused by poor water conditions, this type of algae can form a layer on all your decorations and substrate, and if your fish stop swimming for a few minutes, they start to resemble a moldy cupcake.

» **Red algae:** Caused by a lack of CO_2 in the water, this type is really nasty and hangs in threads all over your aquarium. Extra oxygen can be added to battle the red algae, but often a tank must be cleaned and restarted if it gets out of control.

» **Brown algae:** Caused by inadequate light, this type forms huge brown layers in your aquarium.

» **Green algae:** Caused by too much light, this type makes your aquarium water look like pea soup.

TIP

A good way to battle algae in your aquarium is to add algae-eating fish, such as the Siamese algae eater (*Crossocheilus siamensis*) or the bushy-nosed pleco (*Ancistrus sp.*). These fish help keep algae populations under control naturally. Don't depend on algae-eating fish to solve your problem alone, though. They couldn't eat that many algae in a million years.

WARNING

Algae grows quickly in a cycled tank, but eventually the plants declare war on it and remove the nutrients that it needs to survive. Don't change your water constantly when algae becomes very intense; doing so can lead to an even bigger problem. If your plants are in good condition, they'll eventually win the algae war. The combo of algae-eating fish and pristine water conditions will keep your tank looking great.

Medications

Aquarium salt, copper medications, some algae control medications, and metal-based treatments can be harmful to your plants. Make sure your new fish are quarantined so that you won't have to medicate them if they become ill after arriving home. If your fish do require medication, treat them in a separate hospital tank away from your live plants. (Chapter 11 discusses how to set up and use a hospital tank.)

Planting Techniques and Aquascaping

Putting live plants in your tank after you add the water is a whole lot easier. Arranging plants in a dry aquarium can be difficult. All they do is look limp and fall over. Lock your front door until all the decorating is complete. That way, you can work undisturbed and then look cool when all is said and done. A full aquarium allows you a better view of the plants after they spread out into the water.

Don't push a plant into the gravel below its *crown* (the area between the plant's stalk and the roots). Space plants far enough apart so that they have room to spread their roots and grow properly. The distance between them should be approximately equal to the span of one large leaf. A crowded tank causes the plants to wither and die.

TIP

One of the best strategies is to place all of your tall plants near the back of the tank. Fill the center of the aquarium with short or bushy plants. Use taller plants that spread out (such as elodea) to hide heaters, undergravel filter tubes, power filter tubes, and other unsightly equipment. Place small plants near the front of the glass. Try to arrange your plants so that they don't look too symmetrical (the same on both sides of the tank) because they normally don't grow that way in nature.

TIP

If you continually remove and replant the little shoots that grow out of a main stem, the parent plant grows faster. Chapter 5 gives you some more aquascaping tips.

Chapter **17**

Choosing Plant Species for Your Tank

C hapter 16 discusses the benefits live plants add to your aquarium, the aquarium conditions required for live plants, the methods to purchase plants and transport them, and ways to troubleshoot problems that may occur. This chapter covers specific types of plants that you can put in your tank and maintain as a beginner.

REMEMBER

Live plants add realism to your aquarium!

The species in this chapter are by no means all that are available. There are too many to name in one chapter, so I focus my attention on some of the really cool-looking ones that you can use to enhance your own special aquarium setup.

Don't be afraid to experiment with different types of plants to see what is most pleasing to your own eye. Purchase plants that you really like, but don't forget to make sure that they will work well with the aquarium conditions and habits of your aquarium fish.

WARNING

Don't overstock your tank with plants to the point that your fish have no swimming room. Overplanting causes stress and disease. If you want a good setup that looks natural, it should include a variety of plants and open spaces as well.

AQUARIUM LIGHTING LEVELS

So that you have a good idea what is meant by *low, medium, bright,* and *very bright* lighting, here is a guide:

- **Low:** 1 to 2 watts per gallon

- **Medium:** 2 to 3 watts per gallon

- **Bright:** 3 to 5 watts per gallon

- **Very bright:** 5 or more watts per gallon

Considering Foreground Plants

All aquariums look good with *foreground* plants, and by that I mean smaller plants placed toward the front and middle of your aquarium. The last thing you want to do is have your tank look like it's just lined all around the outside with live plants. You need shorter plants in the front and center of the tank to compliment taller ones toward the rear, provide easy viewing, and add variety to the aquascaped decor. Here are some great choices.

Baby tears (Micranthemum umbrosum)

Baby tears is an amazing plant that is fast growing and covers surfaces like a carpet. For this reason, it's recommended that you use it for larger tanks (more than 30 gallons). In good conditions, this plant spreads like wildfire, so you'll need to prune it back from time to time unless you want your aquarium to look like an uncut back lot or the front steps of a funeral home.

This plant also grows well if you allow it to float, and many species of fish just don't seem to like the taste of it, making it a good one to purchase if you have fish that like to nibble on foliage too much. Baby tears is also hardy and seems to be able to put up with beginner's mistakes.

This plant has delicate little clusters of slightly round leaves (shaped, not surprisingly, like a baby's tear) that are a beautiful light green color. Carbon dioxide (CO_2) addition is recommended for the best growth, but it will survive without added CO_2.

Level: Easy

Temperature: 70–80 degrees F

Light: Bright

pH : 5.5–7.5

Placement: Foreground

Brazilian micro sword (Lilaeopsis brasiliensis)

This South American plant is an interesting-looking species that resembles thick green grass. The thickness can be a problem, because it will encourage algae to grow all over it. Keep tank algae in check if you want this plant to thrive. The best thing to do is to thin the plant by pruning interior leaves (the thick leaves inside the outer leaves) so that light and water can reach all the plant's surfaces. After you've thinned the plant, carefully rinse it under room-temperature water to remove any excess debris before adding it to your aquarium.

TIP

To prevent this plant from becoming a big bound-up ball, keep it in areas of the tank that have high circulation (near airstones or filter return water). This slow-growing plant does really well in fine substrate such as sand. Eventually your aquarium will look like it has a lawn growing in it.

Level: Moderate

Temperature: 60–79 degrees F

Light: Very bright

pH : 6.0–8.0

Placement: Foreground

Cryptocoryne (Cryptocoryne wendetti)

This species is a beautiful plant that has long leaves resembling a garden trowel. The leaves are green with red-tinted areas. This plant is great for tanks that are cycled (see Chapter 14 for more on the nitrogen cycle). In the wild this plant grows on riverbanks and uses rhizomes for growth, so tie it off to driftwood or rocks with plastic gardening ties.

This plant requires a lot of nutrition. That's why placing it in an aged (cycled) tank will keep this species happy. Placing it in a new aquarium may cause it to die from lack of nutrition if you don't use any type of plant food supplement.

Don't be concerned if this plant looks like it's struggling a bit and loses leaves when you first add it to your aquarium. That's normal in many cases. This plant tends to grow rather slowly and is great for smaller tanks.

Level: Medium hard

Temperature: 70–80 degrees F

Light: Bright

pH: 6.5–7.5

Placement: Foreground to midrange

Dwarf anubias (Anubias nana)

This plant is wonderful for beginners because it seems to thrive even in less than perfect water conditions.

This slow-growing plant has broad green leaves that add a wonderful splash of color to any aquarium. It also uses rhizomes for nutrients and likes being tied to driftwood so that water can flow around it. It doesn't need to be embedded in gravel.

WARNING

Don't keep this plant in direct sunlight or under strong artificial lighting.

Level: Easy

Temperature: 59–79 degrees F

Light: Low

pH: 5.5–6.8

Placement: Foreground to midrange on driftwood and rocks

Dwarf four-leaf clover (Marsilia hirsute)

This plant has two sets of leaves that are combined to make a four-leaf clover design forming a thick carpet using its runners. This plant requires high lighting conditions. The dwarf version grows to about 2 inches in height, while the standard form grows to about 8 inches. You can separate the juvenile plants at the roots when they start to grow from the main plant and plant them separately.

Level: Easy

Temperature: 68–84 degrees F

Light: Low level lighting

pH: 6.2–7.5

Placement: Midlevel

Java moss (Taxiphyllum barbieri)

This plant attaches itself to rocks, driftwood, and roots. It doesn't need a ton of special attention and seems to grow readily in almost any water condition. This plant is clingy in nature and is often used to keep baby fry safe from pesky adults.

Level: Easy

Temperature: 60–86 degrees F

Light: low to high

pH: 5.0–8.0

Placement: Base layer over bottom

Madagascar lace (Aponogeton fenestralis)

This species (check out Figure 17-1) is dark green and has leaves that look like they're made out of a lace tablecloth. It's fascinating to watch this plant sway in a light water current. Because algae tends to gather in the latticework of the leaves, having algae eaters in your tank will be beneficial to this plant.

TIP

You can move it to the back of the tank after this plant gains height.

Level: Easy

Temperature: 60–75 degrees F

Light: Very bright

pH: 5.5–6.8

Placement: Foreground to midrange

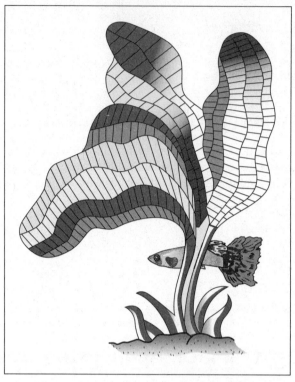

FIGURE 17-1:
Madagascar lace is a lattice leaf plant.

Pearl grass (Hemianthus micranthemoides)

Pearl grass is a graceful-looking plant that is great for the foreground of your aquarium. This species is light green and has half-elliptical shaped leaves. As this plant grows, you'll see it developing side shoots (in time you'll come to think of them as runners) in all directions. You can easily prune this plant so it continues to grow and fill in the gaps that you want it to cover up.

Level: Easy

Temperature: 68–82 degrees F

Light: Medium to bright

pH : 5.0–7.5

Placement: Foreground

Looking at Midwater Plants

Midwater plants are placed toward the center of the aquarium or mixed into the front of large background plants. Here are a few great starters.

Aquatic banana plant (Nymphoides aquatica)

The aquatic banana plant is easy to maintain and gets its name from its banana-shaped roots. This plant does well in almost any lighting and water conditions.

> Level: Easy to Medium
>
> Temperature: 70–82 degrees F
>
> Light: Moderate
>
> pH: 6.0–7.5
>
> Placement: Mid-level or floating

Coffeefolia (Anusbis barteri)

The coffeefolia has heavy thick leaves that are rippled in appearance. When the plant is young, it has reddish-brown leaves that change to green when it matures. This plant requires iron supplements and should be planted in rocklike gravel. This plant is good for a tank with fish nibblers because most species tend to leave this plant alone.

> Level: Medium
>
> Temperature: 68–86 degrees F
>
> Light: Medium
>
> pH: 5.5–9.0
>
> Placement: Middle of tank

Dwarf sagittaria (Sagittaria subulata)

This species has long slender leaves and is hardy. It needs iron supplements and moderate lighting to thrive. If it receives too much lighting, the leaves will develop a red tint to them. Propagation is achieved through runners, which will eventually provide a carpetlike appearance.

Level: Easy

Temperature: 72–82 degrees F

Light: Moderate to strong

pH: 6.5–7.5

Placement: Middle of the tank

Water wisteria (Hygrophila difformis)

This plant is native to India and Nepal. It greatly benefits from extra CO_2 being added to the aquarium. This plant often floats in nature so make sure to anchor it accordingly. Keep this with fish that don't nibble on plants, because it can easily be destroyed.

Level: Easy

Temperature: 75–82 degrees F

Light: Moderate to strong

pH: 6.5–7.5

Placement: Mid to rear of tank

Contemplating Background Plants

Background plants are important for rounding out an aquarium aquascape. These plants can also help cover up unsightly filter tubes, airline tubing, and heaters in the rear of the tank. A spreading background plant placed in the front corner of a tank can also add an interesting aspect to the scene.

Experiment with these examples and see what looks good to you.

Amazon sword (Echinodorus amazonicus)

This plant gets its name from the fact that it grows naturally in the Amazon, and the shape of its leaves resemble the blade of a sword. This amazing plant looks fantastic if you make it the centerpiece of your planted scheme. It will bloom, so if you can have the blooms above the water line, you'll be in for a really pretty treat.

This plant really should be provided with extra CO_2 and fertilizer if you want it to flourish. The plant's root system is quite large, so keep an eye on it to make sure it isn't choking out your other plants.

Level: Moderate

Temperature: 72–82 degrees F

Light: Medium to bright

pH: 6.4–7.2

Placement: Midrange to background

Carolina fanwort (Cambomba caroliniana)

This species is a beautiful light green plant that has a feathery or wispy appearance. It's another great plant for hiding background spots, and fish seem to love to nibble on it.

The problem is, the leaves come off very easily so if you have nibblers, you may find an annoying number of plucked leaves floating all over your tank. These leaves will tend to clog up your filters as well.

This fast-growing plant loves soft, acidic waters, and is stunning when planted in groups of three or more. Make sure you have enough gravel to keep it down because this plant seems to float up quite a bit.

Level: Moderate

Temperature: 75–82 degrees F

Light: Very bright

pH: 4.0–7.0

Placement: Background

Corkscrew val (Vallisneria spiralis)

Corkscrew val is a unique fast-growing Asian plant that resembles a corkscrew. No other plant seems to stimulate the imagination like this species does when it's gently swaying in water current. Corkscrew val can be a bit difficult to keep alive when it's very small, so try to obtain larger plants with well-established roots if possible.

Level: Moderate

Temperature: 59–86 degrees F

Light: Does well in any lighting condition

pH: 6.0–8.0

Placement: Background

Elodea (Egeria densa)

Elodea (as shown in Figure 17-2) is great for beginners because it grows very quickly. This plant also secretes substances that help to discourage algae. Elodea grows thick in bright light and is a good way to fill in the background. This plant can also float, removes large amounts of nitrates, has roots, and flowers under good condition.

Level: Easy

Temperature: 50–79 degrees F

Light: Bright

pH: 5.0–8.0

Placement: Background

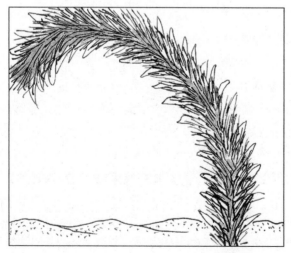

FIGURE 17-2:
Elodea is a great choice for your tank's background.

© John Wiley & Sons, Inc.

Giant anubias (Anubias barteri)

This slow-growing plant (refer to Figure 17-3) can grow up to 15 inches tall and makes a great background plant. It has extremely tough leaves and stems so it's a great species to use for cichlids and other plant-aggressive fish. The rhizome should be above gravel because it shoots down roots to grab nutrients from the substrate.

Level: Easy

Temperature: 59–79 degrees F

Light: Low

pH: 5.5–6.8

Placement: Background

FIGURE 17-3: Giant anubias is tough and grows tall.

© John Wiley & Sons, Inc.

Hornwort (Ceratophyllum demersum)

Hornwort (refer to Figure 17-4) is one of the most popular aquarium plants on the market. It doesn't have real roots but can be planted in gravel. This fast-growing, beautiful plant has green featherlike appendages that reach skyward like upside down umbrellas waiting to catch the rain.

FIGURE 17-4:
Hornwort is very
popular and
grows in gravel.

This plant consumes a lot of nutrients and is an enemy to algae because it secretes a substance that isn't good for its rival. It has bright green leaves that are stiff.

Level: Easy

Temperature: 50–80 degrees F

Light: Does well in any lighting condition

pH: 6.0–8.0

Placement: Background or as a floating plant

Oriental sword (Echinodorus oriental)

This slow-growing plant (see Figure 17-5) has broad red and green leaves that are shaped like the blade of a sword. When it produces newer leaves, they have a semi-transparent pinkish color that can add great variety to your aquarium. As the leaves begin to grow, they become reddish with green veins and eventually wavy deep green at maturity. These plants are great to put in places in your aquarium where you want a nice pop of color. This species is a real plant version of a chameleon.

Level: Easy

Temperature: 68–79 degrees F

Light: Bright

pH: 5.5–7.0

Placement: Midrange to background

FIGURE 17-5:
Oriental sword does best with a rich substrate.

Red ludwigia (Ludwigia mullertii)

This beautiful plant has green leaves, with a slight tinge of red, and red stems. As it matures, the red can spread to the leaf edges. Ludwigia grows very rapidly, so you'll soon have a large plant even if you started with a smaller one.

This plant also grows side shoots, so you may have to prune it back if it gets out of control. It has very tiny flowers that can be difficult to see.

Level: Easy

Temperature: 64–77 degrees F

Light: Very bright

pH: 4.0–7.0

Placement: Background

Red-stem milfoil (Myriophyllum matogrossensis)

In my opinion, this plant is one of the coolest you can buy. It looks like a winter tree that has lost it leaves, except that it's red and pinkish in color. It grows thickly and often resembles seaweed with its three to five feathering leaflets around the stem.

Red-stem milfoil can be anchored to gravel or left to float. It pretty much takes care of itself and is great for coldwater systems.

> Level: Easy
>
> Temperature: 60–75 degrees F
>
> Light: Medium
>
> pH: 6.4–7.2
>
> Placement: Background

Stargrass (Heteranthera zosterifolia)

This fast-growing plant has bright mint-green leaves that grow on thick and numerous stems. Due to the rapid growth and fullness, you'll have to prune it back periodically. The entire plant resembles an aquatic pine tree, and many aquatic species love to use it as a breeding ground.

> Level: Easy
>
> Temperature: 70–80 degrees F
>
> Light: Medium to bright
>
> pH: 6.2–7.0
>
> Placement: Background

Going with Floating Plants

Floating plants are important for aquariums that require dim lighting because they block the light from above. They also provide a lot of place for small fry to hide and provide privacy for mating. Even in setups that don't require dim lighting, one small floating plant can give a realistic river or pond look to your aquarium. Here are my recommendations.

Amazon frogbit (Limnobium laevigatum)

The frogbit plant grows into the shape of a rosette. It then produces shoots that form a tiny plant at the end. As soon as this end breaks off, it becomes a new plant on its own. The leaves are waxy green and tend to resemble a pond lily. Although it's a floating plant, you want to make sure that the leaves don't get too close to the aquarium lights because they're sensitive to burning.

Level: Moderate

Temperature: 64–82 degrees F

Light: Medium to bright

pH: 6.5–7.5

Placement: Floating

Duckweed (Lemna minor)

This fast-growing plant is wonderful for ponds because it blocks out a lot of harmful sunrays that can quickly overheat the water or produce algae. However, it multiplies so rapidly that your tank may look like the lights have burnt out permanently. Avoid buying duckweed unless you have time to prune it back constantly. This plant also provides shelter and is a great incentive for spawning among its numerous clusters of oval green leaves in an aquarium.

Coldwater and pond fish love to eat this plant, and it provides good nutrition because it's high in vitamins and minerals. Duckweed is also good for your pond's water because it helps to absorb excess nutrients and ammonia.

Level: Easy

Temperature: 64–79 degrees F

Light: Medium to bright

pH: 4.5–7.5

Placement: Floating

Envisioning Pond Plants

Pond plants are fun and add realism to any pond. The following are a few examples I recommend.

Water hyacinth (Eichhornia crassipes)

This plant grows very quickly and will become matted if not pruned.

The shiny green leaves are oval in shape. The plant stalk is thick and keeps the plant buoyant. It has beautiful purple flowers. This has a huge root system that fish will love to eat. Fortunately the roots grow faster than the fish can eat them.

> Level: Easy
>
> Temperature: 59–85 degrees F
>
> Light: Bright
>
> pH: 5.5–8.0
>
> Placement: Floating

Water lettuce (Pistia stratiotes)

Water lettuce (as shown in Figure 17-6) is a plant that has soft, light-green, ribbed leaves that are large and round.

FIGURE 17-6:
Water lettuce provides lots of hiding places for your fish.

© John Wiley & Sons, Inc.

The leaves form a rosette. The long, thick roots provide an excellent hiding place for fish that like to swim near the surface of the aquarium, but it has to be pruned periodically or it will take over your entire tank or pond. This plant is also useful for filtering your aquarium water.

Level: Easy

Temperature: 65–85 degrees F

Light: Bright

pH: 5.0–8.0

Placement: Floating

Starting with Some Easy Plants

Some plants are a little easier to grow and keep than others. If you're not quite sure where to start, don't worry. The following are suggestions on freshwater plants that are good for timid beginners (refer to the earlier sections in this chapter for more information about each species):

» Amazon sword (*Echinodorus grandiflorus*)

» Corkscrew val (*Vallisneria spiralis*)

» Dwarf swordplant (*Echinodorus tenellus*)

» Hornwart (*Ceratophyllum demersum*)

» Hairgrass (*Eleocharis acicularis*)

» Java fern (Microsorium pteropus)

WARNING

Avoid buying any plants that look deteriorated, have a huge amount of brown leaves (if not natural coloring), and/or look transparent, because these are signs of poor plant health.

PICKING PLANTS FOR A BRACKISH AQUARIUM

You may want to attempt a *brackish aquarium* (an aquarium where the salt content of the water falls between freshwater and marine). If so, be careful when choosing plants for a brackish tank became most freshwater plants have little tolerance for salt and will die or grow poorly in this type of system. Here are a few easy-to-keep brackish plants:

- **Green cabomba** (*Cabomba caroliniana*): A plant with soft leaves and foliage resembles feather wisps.

- **Mangrove** (*Brugiuera species*): Usually purchased in pots, this plant spreads out all over the tank.

- **Giant hygrophila** (*Nomaphila stricta*): A beautiful plant that produces a purple flower.

Chapter 23 explains more about starting a brackish aquarium.

4

Breeding and Other Fun Stuff

Use tried-and-true strategies to get your fish in the mood to breed.

Tackle any breeding problems you may encounter like a pro so your fish reproduce better than you'd ever expect.

Photograph your fish and share your impressive photos with your friends and family.

Record your fish to have a permanent record of their health and the success of breeding strategies that you choose.

Expand your hobby by taking trips to zoos and aquariums, writing, and setting up aquariums for others.

Discover new systems so that you understand the differences between freshwater, brackish, and saltwater systems.

IN THIS CHAPTER

» **Fixing fish problems**

» **Solving equipment problems**

» **Mending a broken tank**

» **Alleviating water problems**

Chapter **18**

Being Prepared When Trouble Strikes

E ven if you're the world's greatest fishkeeper, problems are going to occur.

No matter what you do, things will go wrong, and at the most inopportune times. Mother Nature doesn't always follow your timetable.

The best thing you can do when a problem happens is to have a solution at hand, which is what this chapter is for. Here you can find a list of the most common problems that can happen to or in an aquarium system. This handy little chapter should get you and your aquatic pets through thick and thin.

Even if you aren't having a problem, take the time to read through this chapter to get a good idea what to do if something goes wrong. I keep the solutions short and to the point so you don't have to wade through a bunch of text in a time of need.

REMEMBER

Problems have solutions, so don't sweat it. Things will go wrong from time to time, so remember to simply do your best to resolve the issue. Nobody can ask for more.

Tackling Physical Fish Problems

Most fish problems can be cured if you take time to check your fish on a daily basis in order to catch illness, aggression, equipment malfunctions, and feeding problems early. Here are some common problems and what to do. Check daily to see if your fish have

- >> Torn, clamped, or ragged fins
- >> Missing scales
- >> Cloudy eyes
- >> Unusual white spots or body fungus

Take immediate action if you notice any of these signs (see Chapter 11 for details on treating disease in freshwater fish).

TIP

Put the ill fish in a hospital tank for treatment. If you don't have chemicals on hand, keep the lights on the hospital tank off to reduce stress.

TIP

When you're ready to restore your tank, make sure your fish remain disease free for two weeks after treatment before returning them to the tank.

Here are some other potential issues that may pop up and what you can do.

Separating fighting fish

There's no way to guarantee 100 percent compatibility between two fish until they're placed together. Spats do break out from time to time. If they happen too often, immediately remove the most aggressive fish by adding food to the tank to lure it to the top so you can net it. Another option is to have a Plexiglas insert handy to separate the two fish into opposite sides of the tank until one can be netted.

Solving the aggression problem

As with people, some fish just can't seem to get along. Try these things:

- >> If possible, permanently move the aggressive fish to another tank.
- >> Rearrange aquarium decorations (rocks, plants, and other decorations) to break up established territories. Build caves from rocks and give all fish places to hide.
- >> Made sure your fish get plenty of food. Fish that are constantly hungry from lack of proper nutrition tend to fight more.

Aggression also can occur during mating. If possible, move the love birds to a small tank just for mating. Consider it their honeymoon suite.

Looking at the injured

Check for torn fins or other bodily injuries such as missing scales after a fight. If some fish are hurt, place them separately in a quiet hospital tank with a stress-relief formula and allow them time to heal. Check for disease that may develop from the damage.

Dealing with a stuck fish

If your fish become stuck on decorations, slowly pull the decoration away and let the fish swim on its own. If a fish becomes stuck in a suction tube, turn the equipment off so it can free itself.

Correcting Feeding Problems

Often fish won't eat due to being stressed out from the trip to your home or because of problems with other fish in the tank. These sections address some solutions for any feeding problems you face. (Sorry, they probably won't work for any picky toddlers you know.)

Getting your fish to eat

Fish can lose their appetites. Here are a couple ideas to help them get it back:

» Try giving them frozen brine shrimp or other appropriate aquatic treats to kick-start them into eating again. In the wild, fish eat a variety of foods.

» Rearrange the aquarium decorations to bust down territories that may be keeping some fish from getting their fair share.

Addressing a food hog

When one fish eats all the food, feed your fish in different areas of the aquarium at the same time and set up a routine to change food placement locations regularly.

Dislodging items eaten by your fish

Add 1 level teaspoon of Epsom salt for each 10 gallons of water in the aquarium.

Cleaning up the aftermath

Monitor your tank closely after problems occur and make note of them. After the problems are solved, try to go back to a regular routine.

Addressing Equipment Problems

If you want your aquarium to function the way it's supposed to, you need to ensure your equipment is running properly. Here are a few common equipment problems and their solutions.

Handling uneven stands and tanks

Level the stand using shims under the corners. Use a carpenter's level when setting up the stand for the first time to avoid this problem later.

Fixing a clogged filter

Having a clean filter is extremely important. Be sure to do these things to keep yours from getting clogged:

>> If your filter uses pads, rinse them under used tank water that you've removed from the tank and placed in a clean bucket.

>> If you're using an undergravel filter, vacuum the gravel.

>> Clean all tubes with a filter-cleaning brush. Make sure impellers (the little whirling blade thingy) on filters are cleaned as well.

Analyzing heater problems

Heaters have a way of conking out. Here are some ideas for fixing them:

>> If the tank isn't staying the proper temperature, make sure you have enough wattage for your aquarium to avoid the heater running constantly. (Quick general rule: 5 watts per gallon.)

>> If you have the correct wattage, make sure that plants or other decorations that could stop the flow of warm water throughout the tank aren't covering the heater.

>> If all else fails, replace the heater. Consider a temperature controller with a warning alarm to keep consistent water temperature and alert you to problems.

Lighting falling into the tank

You wouldn't believe how often this happens. Do this if it does:

1. **Put on a rubber kitchen glove (kept in your fish kit!) and unplug the lighting.**

    Chapter 24 discusses what to keep in your fish kit.

WARNING

2. **Remove the lighting from the tank and allow it to completely dry before plugging it back in.**

    Never remove a light that is underwater and plugged in!

Exploding light bulbs

Do the following if you have an older hood with bulbs:

1. **Unplug the lighting system.**

2. **Allow the bulb to cool down completely before removing it to avoid burning yourself.**

3. **Gently remove the remaining part of the bulb by wrapping a kitchen towel around your hand.**

    If you can't remove the bulb, push a small potato into the broken bulb socket (screw in bulbs) to grasp and remove the light.

Flickering lighting

If a light is constantly flickering, replace the starter unit if it has one. If the bulbs continue to flicker, remove the light to make sure the metal connections are dry and replace. If this doesn't work, replace the bulb. For newer LED systems call the manufacturer for repair advice or replacement.

Facing Tank and Decoration Problems

Nothing is worse than a leaking tank. Fortunately there are solutions to this problem. The important thing to remember is to act quickly. These sections can help.

Checking for leaks

Check for leaks on a daily basis. Doing so only takes a few moments to see if the tank itself is leaking or if a poorly placed piece of equipment is causing the leak. Hardware stores sell leak detectors that sound an alarm if your aquarium is leaking. They're similar to smoke detectors but for water.

>> Make sure the tank itself is leaking by doing an inspection. Sometimes what appears to be a tank leak is actually an airstone-driven decoration pushing water over the rim or a leaking power filter.

>> If the airstone is causing the leak, shift the decoration until the problem stops.

>> If a power filter is leaking from being cracked, replace it.

Getting your fish to safety

If the tank is leaking, immediately remove the fish to another tank. If you don't have an extra tank, a large plastic bowl or clean aquarium bucket works. Add gravel to the bottom of the bowl or bucket, put a few floating plants in, add an airstone connected to a pump, and cover it with a plate to keep the fish from jumping out.

Repairing a small crack

Sometimes buying a new tank will cost you less money if you find a crack, depending on the size of your tank and prices in your area. However, sometimes you may find it more economical to repair the leak instead. Follow these steps to repair a small crack:

1. Remove *everything* from the leaking tank: water, gravel, and equipment.

2. With a safety razor, remove the old silicone from the whole side where the leak is occurring.

3. Wipe the area dry with a clean cloth.

4. Apply new aquarium sealer to replace the old sealer you removed.

5. Allow the sealer to completely dry (drying time will be listed on the sealer tube) before adding water.

When an entire side of your aquarium breaks

If the entire side of an aquarium breaks, get your fish into a hospital tank or aquarium bucket as quickly as possible.

If the fish are out of water, use a clean paper towel to gently pick them up because the oil and other residue on your hands can damage their scales and fins.

TIP

Call a professional glass installer to have the side replaced. Replacing it yourself is dangerous and risks further leaking. You probably wouldn't replace broken glass in your home's picture window, and aquarium glass is even more of a challenge due to the water pressure that is constantly on it. Let the professional glass installers handle it. They know what they're doing. If the tank is small, it may be more economical to just replace the tank.

Uprooted plants and decorations

Keep aquascaping tools around to gently move or replace uprooted plants or decorations that have become dislodged from their normal position.

What to do when you lose power

Keep a battery-operated pump, tubing, and airstone on hand to generate water circulation until your power is restored. If the tank overheats due to a power failure, you can float ice in a bottle in the tank to slowly lower the temperature. (Refer to the section, "Cooling a tank that's too hot" later in this chapter for more advice.) If you have a large tank, you can use a mobile air-conditioning unit pointed at the tank to help lower the temperature. If the water is too cold, you can float a hot water bottle. Always keep a mechanical thermometer on hand to keep track of the temperature in case of a power failure. If your funds will allow, a generator is the best option.

Confronting Water Problems

Problems with your water can lead to stress, poor health, and death for your freshwater friends. Here are a few of the most common water problems and solutions to get your aquarium back on track.

TIP

Sometimes simply using your senses can help identify problems.

Solving green algae problems

Having too much light and dissolved waste in the water can result in green algae — that cloudy green gunk. Look for this problem on a daily basis. Here's what to do:

» Cut back on the light.

» Do 10 percent water changes daily until the algae clear up.

» Purchase algae-eating fish such as Siamese algae eaters or add tablets that are specifically manufactured to keep algae at bay.

Controlling chemical problems

If household chemicals are dumped or spilled into the tank by accident, you'll usually be able to see a change in the water clarity or smell an odor, so do this:

1. **Remove your fish immediately to a hospital tank.**

2. **Completely drain your main tank and clean the decorations, tank, and gravel with warm water before restarting your tank.**

3. **Replace any filter material with new material as you're setting up the tank, and add a tank starting chemical to encourage rapid bacterial growth.**

4. **Remember the tank will have to biologically cycle again, so keep an eye on the situation and add a couple fish for starters (hardy fish, such as guppies and swordfish) until it has established itself.**

Keep your other fish in a reserve tank until the chemical problems are resolved.

Cooling a tank that's too hot

Overheating is one of the main problems that happen due to equipment failure and power problems. If your tank gets too warm, follow these steps:

1. **Unplug the heater and allow it to remain in the tank and then remove the hood and replace it with a mesh top (like the ones sold for the tops of reptile tanks).**

   Don't remove the heater before it cools down or it can shatter. Don't remove the fish or you'll shock them.

REMEMBER

2. **If you don't have an aquarium chiller, put ice into a plastic bag and float it in the tank to *slowly* lower the temperature.**

   An *aquarium chiller* is a piece of equipment that can be added to your tank to keep the water cool. Never try to lower the temperature quickly because you'll do even more damage to your fish.

3. **Add an extra airstone to the tank to increase oxygen because the levels will have dropped with the higher water temperatures.**

4. **When the temperature is back to normal, reset your heater and monitor it closely to make sure it's functioning properly.**

   If it still isn't working correctly, replace it.

Warming a tank that's too cold

If your tank gets too warm, follow these steps:

1. **Put a hot water bottle in a plastic bag and float it in the tank to warm the tank until you solve the heating problem.**

   Don't remove the fish or you'll shock them.

2. **Make sure the heater is functioning and slowly raise the temperature back to normal.**

   A couple degrees per hour is best. You can cover the tank with a blanket to maintain some heat while doing this step.

Chapter **19**

Setting Up the Breeding Tank

The first thing you need to know about breeding your fish is that there is no perfect way to breed any single species of fish. Sure, a lot of techniques are known to be successful, and a lot of aquatic breeding methods are steadfast and true — but, what one hobbyist finds to be a successful method, others may have no luck with. Better methods are waiting to be discovered, and there is always room for improvement and new ideas when it comes to breeding fish.

Many hobbyists have bred fish accidentally, just by having the right combination in their aquariums. Whether it occurs by accident or on purpose, breeding is breeding. Don't let anyone tell you any differently. (If they do, tell them to come see me.) When you're breeding your fish, take the time to observe everything:

» What are the spawning pair (male and female that you want to mate) doing about the other fish around them?

» Are there any changes in the pecking order?

» Have feeding patterns changed since the courtship started? Are the fish eating more or have they stopped feeding normally?

By making pertinent observations of all your fish's activities, you can gain a better understanding of how aquatic relationships work.

TIP

Keep a logbook so that you have a permanent record of your spawners' ages, successes, diseases, and brood sizes. Furthermore, careful records can help you select positive physical traits for future brood.

It's a great idea to exchange information, such as by calling other hobbyists on the phone and bragging, or writing an article and bragging. Only by sharing information can breeding methods be refined and perfected. Never adopt complete secrecy: You may hold the key to solving a difficult puzzle for someone else. Also, by exchanging information or asking for advice, you can avoid breeding hazards and unwanted mutations (no one wants to produce piranhas the size of the Titanic).

Deciding to Breed Your Aquarium Fish

Aquarists, like everyone else, have goals for their hobby. One of your first goals as a fishkeeper is to maintain a healthy and successful aquarium. After you accomplish that, then what?

You may decide to try another type of system (such as brackish or marine) or investigate unfamiliar breeds. But when all is said and done as far as maintaining an aquarium is concerned, what does the future hold? (If you're like me, one answer is: a lot of bills at the local fish shop.) But it's all worth the expense in the long run. Selling fish you have bred can help to offset some of these expenses.

The following sections explain the reasons why fishkeepers breed. Knowing this information can help you determine if breeding your fish is a viable option.

Breaking new barriers

Breeding aquarium fish successfully is kind of like getting into a sport's Hall of Fame: There is no greater reward. So many species can be bred easily that you should have no problem getting into this fascinating and enjoyable aspect of the aquarium hobby. Many fish are out there that have never been bred, which leaves the door wide open for you to become a pioneer. Just imagine what it would be like if you were the first person on earth to successfully breed a species or provide personal knowledge and experience to help breed that particular species with ease. It can happen.

Gaining new knowledge and enjoyment

The satisfaction of accomplishing something new (and perhaps snagging a little fame and money while you're at it) is a good reason to start breeding fish. You can gain an overwhelming amount of wisdom, knowledge, and pleasure by partaking in this scientific aspect of the hobby. When you successfully breed a particular species, you also find out much more about that species than the average hobbyist learns in a lifetime.

And, above all, breeding fish is fun. Hey, if you think human courtship is a little odd at times, wait until you see your fish go a few rounds.

Conserving the environment

Probably the most important reason to breed fish is to contribute to the conservation (keeping species alive for future generations to enjoy) of the earth's aquatic species.

At one time, freshwater fish were shipped from many countries around the globe so that the average hobbyist could enjoy them. Today, thanks to massive freshwater breeding programs, most of these species are captive-bred. If anything ever happens to them in the wild, aquarium hobbyists will be there to pick up the ball. Already, many home aquarists and organizations such as the American Cichlid Association have saved many fish species from extinction by breeding them when their numbers reached alarmingly low rates in their native environments.

REMEMBER

You, too, can contribute to this aspect of aquarium fish breeding. Everyone has a responsibility to put back what he takes from the wild.

I think every aquarist should attempt to breed some species. Don't concern yourself with wondering whether it's already been done — just go out and do it.

Choosing Your Equipment for Breeding

Before you set up a spawning tank, decide whether you want to breed a few fish in your main aquarium (in which case you don't need a breeding room) or turn out fry faster than your local greasy spoon. (*Fry* is a technical term for baby fish, by the way.)

A large-scale breeding operation requires space. Easy-to-breed fish multiply very rapidly. You may end up living on the back porch permanently to make room for your new arrivals. To breed fish in a serious way — to develop new colors, sizes, and/or fin shapes — you need quite a *bit* of room. An extra bedroom or office offers the perfect solution. But if your house is the size of a small cabin, you may want to look into the possibility of a heated storage shed. Make *sure* you have plenty of room before you start, or you may end up hastily trying to bamboozle your local dealer into buying some fry off you. (When you sell fish to a dealer, don't look desperate or he may cut your profit margin because he thinks you need money.)

The following sections address equipment and aquascaping with a focus on breeding. Most of this equipment is the same as the equipment in Chapter 6.

The aquarium

A 10- or 20-gallon aquarium is a good starting size for a breeding tank for small species such as guppies and platys. You don't want to use a tank that is too large, because you might lose track of your spawners and their fry. In order to keep up with everything your fish are doing, you have to spy on them frequently. A smaller tank allows you to remain in control of the action at all times and is much easier to work with and clean. As with any aquarium, thoroughly rinse it with clear water before you use it.

Putting a lid on the whole thing

When your fish are ready to breed, they get a little excited. Excited fish tend to jump very high. High-jumping fish can end up as permanent decoration stuck on your room light or as an afternoon treat for the cat. A tight-fitting hood keeps your fish in the water where they belong, protects eggs and young fry from many unseen disasters, and minimizes heat loss. A good hood also prevents dirt and household chemicals (such as your daughter's hair spray) from entering the water.

Decorations

Plenty of places to hide, such as within and under rocks and plants, give your spawning pairs the opportunity to get used to being around each other before they start spawning. It's a fact of life; some couples just don't get along well. If your breeding tank has no hiding places, the male of many species may kill or maim his mate out of territoriality or frustration before any spawning has an opportunity to take place.

WARNING

Don't laugh, but many hobbyists mistakenly place two aggressive males together in a breeding tank (it's more difficult to determine sex in some species than in others), which leads to total disaster without places for them to hide. You can avoid the loss of fish in these cases by providing proper hiding places.

Furthermore, many species of fish like to breed on pieces of shale, rocks, flower-pots, or plant leaves. Chapter 5 gives you some aquascaping tips.

Substrate

Hobbyists disagree as to whether to use a gravel substrate in the breeding tank. I generally recommend using no substrate for several reasons:

>> A tank with gravel or sand is much more difficult to keep clean.

>> Most species are happy breeding in a tank that has no substrate and use rocks, plants, or flowerpots for protection and laying eggs if needed. Check the breeding requirements on your species, though, because some do require substrate for digging during breeding. (See Chapter 20 for more information.)

>> The newborn fry of *livebearers* (fish that bear live young) often sink down to the substrate after birth. I've seen many fry trapped by gravel too large for them to navigate around.

>> It's really difficult for you and the parents to see and keep track of the fry's health and growth with substrate in the breeding tank. For example, a betta male gathers eggs that fall from the surface and spits them back into the safety of his bubble nest. If the bottom of the tank is covered with gravel substrate, the eggs may fall between the individual stones and become unreachable.

Many hobbyists argue that a spawning tank isn't natural without substrate, but I've seen most species of fish bred without it. If you feel the need to use substrate for species that prefer to spawn on it (like some killifish), a thin layer of fine sand is okay.

Spawning grates

Once in a while, you run into a species that likes to eat its own young or eggs. To prevent this, lay a *spawning grate* (available at many pet shops) on the floor of the tank so that the young fry or eggs fall to the bottom through the holes. This allows you time to remove the parents before they can have their offspring for dinner. You can find woven lattice plastic mats that work well at most hobby or craft stores, and you can cut them to any shape you need.

Just place the lattice sheet on top of small stones, and you have a made-to-order spawning grate for very little expense. Another option is to buy a *breeding trap*, which allows newborn live fry to fall safely between a slot underneath the mother.

TIP

You know those green plastic containers that hold strawberries? (Remember you unsuccessfully tried to turn them into a Christmas ornament?) Laid side by side with the open side down, they work well as a spawning grate. Sometimes a little imagination goes a long way.

Turning up the heat

Use a good quality heater in the breeding tank to keep the water from chilling. This is especially important if your breeding room isn't insulated as well as the rest of your home. Besides, many fish require a small increase in temperature to prepare them for breeding. Although it's possible to control the water temperature with the heating system in your home, it doesn't work well because all home temperatures don't match species requirements, so this isn't a practical method. It's better to have a heater you can adjust as needed on each individual tank.

Filtration

Filters are important in breeding tanks, because they supply needed oxygen and produce the water movement that entices many species to mate. Filtration also keeps wastes that can destroy eggs and fry from building up. Here are a couple options that offer benefits for breeding:

>> **Sponge filter:** This filter is ideal for almost any breeding tank. This unit has a simple design and is easy to use. A sponge filter provides simple biological filtration without the risks of mechanical filters (such as youngsters being sucked up in the intake tubes). A sponge filter creates current, but it doesn't cause the excess turbulence often produced by larger power and undergravel filters. If your spawning fish are stuck together permanently due to excessive water waves, you may want to cut down on the current with a valve or a smaller filter. Heavy turbulence from an extra air supply (bubble disks or airstones) can damage delicate eggs or young fry.

TIP

If you use a sponge filter, you can always do water changes to remove any floating debris that is usually removed by a mechanical filter. If you decide to use a larger filter, make sure it runs slowly.

>> **Sochting Oxydator:** This oxydator slowly adds oxygen to your aquarium because it uses a catalyst to break down hydrogen peroxide into water and oxygen. This piece of equipment is quiet, produces no bubbles, and doesn't

use electricity, so it's good if the power goes out. The oxydator is good for breeding tanks and fry tanks because it helps clarify the water, keeps algae down, and gives the fish a good oxygen supply.

Plants for safety, spawning, and inspiration

Plants have a wide variety of uses in a spawning tank:

>> Plants look cool.

>> Plastic and live plants provide privacy and offer security.

>> Several species of fish use live plants in the construction of their nests.

>> Plastic and live plants serve as spawning sites for many species of fish.

>> Live plants remove carbon dioxide from the water and replace it with oxygen.

>> Live plants cut down on algae present in the water by competing for the same resources they require to survive.

>> Live plants are a natural food source.

>> A planted tank can make your fish think they're in a natural environment, which helps inspire and speed up their spawning plans.

>> Plants can provide protection and shelter when a spawning partner becomes aggressive (and many do). You're wise to always have several thick plants on hand just in case the lovemaking reaches Round 15.

If those aren't enough good reasons to use plants for spawning, I don't what is! Of course, if you have live plants that you want to keep healthy in the spawning tank, you'll need to add substrate for them if they aren't of the floating variety. I've found that most fish I've bred have no problem reproducing with artificial plants in the tank. Floating types and plants that stick to the aquarium walls with a suction cup work well.

WARNING

Thoroughly clean any plants with room-temperature water that you choose for your spawning tank before adding them to the tank. Plants often carry snails and small nematodes (worms) that can potentially harm eggs and fry. To be on the safe side, you can set up a separate tank to grow plants that can be used especially for spawning.

In case you're wondering what types of plants to use in your tank, Table 19-1 can help you get started. Remember that many freshwater plants have different pH and temperature requirements. So, check this list and match the plant to your individual aquarium setup accordingly. (See Chapters 16 and 17 for more on live plants and for explanations of the terms I use to describe these plants.) By the way, dH means degrees of hardness.

TABLE 19-1   **Plants for Spawning Tanks**

Name	Temperature Range (in degrees F)	pH Range	dH Range	Planting Method	Uses
Amazon swordplant (*Echinodorus bleheri*)	72–83	6.5–7.5	2–15	Planted or potted	For species that prefer to spawn on large plant leaves
Cryptocorn (*Cryptocoryne affinis*)	72–82	6.0–7.5	3–14	Planted or potted	For species that spawn on leaves
Hornwort (*Ceratophyllum demersum*)	60–84	6.0–7.5	5–14	Anchored or free-floating	For almost every free-floating type of freshwater fish
Java moss (*Vesicularia dubyana*)	68–85	5.8–7.5	3–15	Anchored	For free-spawning fish (fish who let their eggs scatter anywhere)
Ludwigia (*Ludwigia repens*)	62–82	5.8–7.5	3–14	Planted or free-floating	For fish that like to spawn on leaves
Sagittaria (*Sagittaria subulata*) dwellers	68–83	6.0–7.7	2–12	Anchored, planted, or free-floating	For many varieties of bottom
Spiral val (*Vallisneria spiralis*)	60–85	6.5–7.5	5–12	Planted or anchored	For species that spawn on leaves
Water hyacinth (*Eichhornia crassipes*)	72–82	6.0–7.8	2–14	Floating	For bubble nest builders
Water lettuce (*Pistia stratiotes*)	72–80	6.5–7.5	5–14	Floating	For bubble nest builders
Water sprite (*Ceratopteris thalictroides*)	68–84	6.5–7.5	2–12	Anchored or free-floating	For fish that build bubble nests, such as bettas

Getting the Water Right

The water in your spawning tank must suit the species of fish you're trying to breed. Take a look at Chapters 12 through 14 for more info on getting the water right. Here are a few water basics to get you going when breeding.

pH and dH control

You must keep the pH and dH levels of your water under control in a breeding situation. Changes in pH are very damaging to your fish, and the ill effects double in intensity during the breeding ritual. Eggs and young fry are especially susceptible to the smallest of fluctuations in pH level. A good pH test kit and a dH test kit allow you to monitor your water (as I discuss in Chapter 12). dH levels are important for breeding fish, such as the discus that have a less than 1dH in nature and don't breed successfully on a constant basis unless their water parameters are good. Check each species you plan on breeding to find the right dH and pH for breeding.

Water temperature

The water temperature is extremely important to keep an eye on, especially if you have *egglayers* (fish that don't bare live young, but lay eggs that hatch). Eggs can be severely damaged in temperatures above 85 degrees F. You may end up with poached eggs. Higher temperatures also cause eggs to develop too quickly, which can lead to weak, deformed, or weird-looking fry. Research each species that you want to breed carefully before starting out so that you know what their water requirements are.

Cleanliness

Young fry and eggs are much more susceptible than adults to problems resulting from too many nitrogen compounds (waste) in the water. Poor water conditions can destroy eggs or damage the growth cycle of newborns. Carefully change at least one quarter of the water each day in a spawning or growout tank and make sure you have some type of filtration.

TIP

To avoid fouling the water in a breeding tank, feed the fish small amounts of live foods instead of flake.

IN THIS CHAPTER

» **Getting the conditions right**

» **Figuring out what breeding type your fish are**

» **Protecting those newborns (and their parents)**

» **Caring for fry**

» **Selecting breeding traits**

» **Deciding which species to breed**

Chapter **20**

Ready, Set, Spawn

B reeding your fish is a great way to advance your fishkeeping skills. After you discover the basics and have successfully bred your first fish brood, there's no reason why you can't begin thinking about selling the excess offspring to a local dealer, trading them to friends, using them as feeder fish, or buying more tanks to house them. You may get lucky and find a dealer who needs a regular supply. This little bit of extra money can help offset some of the expense incurred with your hobby (and offset your spouse's financial wrath at the same time). This chapter spells out what you need to know to set the ambience and breed your fish.

Simply ask your local dealer if she would be willing to trade equipment or purchase your extra fish at a cost that will satisfy both of you. You can also run an ad online and sell your fry to other hobbyists.

Before you actually sell your new fish, decide which ones you want to keep for further breeding. For example, you may have a particular fish in the new brood that has a slightly different color or pattern that is pleasing to your eye. You usually have to wait for the fry to grow up a bit before they develop their colors and patterns because many fish look completely different as an adult. Make sure their markings are no longer changing before you make any final decisions.

REMEMBER

Some fish breed in your community or species tank without any help from you. For example, if you have a bunch of male and female guppies in a community tank, chances are they will breed on their own, as long as the aquarium is clean and has good water conditions, without any extra work on your part. Some species are simply more willing to breed in captivity than others.

But if you want stay in control of which fish breed and when, set up a spawning tank (a tank designated only for breeding and raising certain fish at a certain time). That way, you can adjust the water quality and feeding schedule as necessary, as well as cull the fry of each species you're raising. *Culling* is simply the process of separating the fish you want to keep from the fish you don't. This ensures being able to breed individuals with the characteristics you want.

A good spawning tank is just a miniaturized version of the main tank. Make sure it has proper filtration, good water conditions, gravel, and plants to give your fish that "feel at home" sensation. A spawning tank should be decorated to resemble the natural environment of your species for the best results. A 5- or 10-gallon-tank makes a great breeding tank. Many hobbyists remove a majority of the decorations in a breeding tank, but I like to keep it as natural as possible. The final choice is yours.

WARNING

Beginning a fish-breeding program brings with it some humane responsibility. Fish that you produce through breeding should, as they do in the wild, find their place in the biological ecosystem. Some species produce dozens or even hundreds of young. It's doubtful that you will want to keep every fish that your breeding pairs create. You should make every attempt to raise these fish, sell them, trade them, or give them away to good owners. If you think you cannot do these things, it may mean using excess fry to feed larger carnivore fish. Although this situation is found in nature, if you don't like the sound of you yourself doing it, then breeding is not for you.

Introducing the Bride and Groom

Many fish practically jump into the spawning tank from across the room in order to breed. Others, however, have a hard time adjusting to their new partners and your breeding goals. With most species, give the female plenty of time to become comfortable in the new tank (at least a day or two, until she is swimming normally and not hiding in her new surroundings).

Males are more aggressive, and putting the female in first allows her to establish a little bit of territory for herself. This rule does have a few exceptions, so check the breeding requirements and strategies for each individual species by talking with other hobbyists who breed that species, attending fish clubs, talking to your local dealer, and researching species on the Internet.

When she looks like she has become queen of the hill, place her behind a clear tank partition (usually made of professionally cut glass, plastic, or Plexiglas) before you introduce the male (see Figure 20-1). You can also use a breeding partition after you've introduced the male and female, and they're being stubborn about getting along. While separated, keep feeding them small bits of live food until they show signs of mating such as displaying brilliant colors or excessive contortions and body movement. This method works best when you only have one pair of fish in the spawning tank.

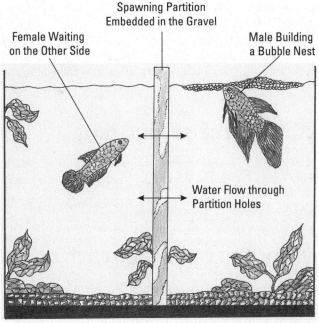

Spawning Partition
Embedded in the Gravel

Female Waiting
on the Other Side

Male Building
a Bubble Nest

Water Flow through
Partition Holes

FIGURE 20-1:
Use a breeding partition to make their hearts grow fonder.

© John Wiley & Sons, Inc.

You can purchase partitions at pet stores or make your own. This "prenuptial" separation lets the male get accustomed to the sight of his mate and gives him a chance to calm down a little bit before he actually meets her. Leave the partition up until the male seems like he's calm. You don't need to do this with all species, but it's usually the safest way to go.

This section gives you some die-hard methods that you can try to help introduce and *condition* (get your fish in the mood to spawn) your aquatic lovebirds. (Don't bother with Mozart and a little wine in the water, because it won't work.) No lovemaking tricks are completely foolproof, but several tried over the years have proven to be quite reliable and accurate.

Dealing with aggressive males

Some males are naturally more aggressive (actually *nasty* is the word I'm looking for) than others, and it's difficult to determine an individual's habits before you see him in action. I've had very peaceful males of one species, only to turn around and end up with one of the same species that was ready to take on Mike Tyson. The only way to tell how aggressive a male is going to be during breeding is to keep a close eye on him after you introduce him into the spawning tank.

WARNING

If your spawning tank is heavily planted and contains many safe areas where a female can hide, you may be able to introduce both partners at the same time. I personally don't use this method very often because I've seen too many females torn up by normally peaceful males that got a little too excited or are harassed to death before they have become comfortable in their new surroundings. Be safe and use a partition to allow them to get to know each other first.

Setting up the second date

If a spawning pair seems to get along well on the first date, it's probably safe to put them back into the same spawning tank at the same time. But fish in love can be very unpredictable, so don't bet the farm on their getting along again. It never hurts to use a partition more than once.

Yay, my fish really like each other!

If your fish are having a real romantic picnic, why spoil the fun? Let them continue to breed as long as they're in good health. If you don't want any more newborns, keep them in separate main tanks.

Darn, my fish hate each other!

If your fish are throwing gravel at each other, they probably won't be in the mood to mate. Don't force something that isn't meant to be. Give them a little time away from each other and then try again. If they still try to kill each other, forget it and work with a different set of partners. I've witnessed a couple of instances where one male would refuse to mate with only one particular female out of a group of ten identical-looking fish! Why they seem to turn on one individual is unknown. A bit of fin nipping during spawning is normal in many species such as the betta. Just make sure they aren't seriously injuring each other.

The following are a few reasons why fish won't spawn:

>> Their water looks like a sewer.

>> Their tank is too small.

>> They need more fish (for example, neons mate more often in schools).

>> One of the partners is cradle-robbing, or is older than dirt.

>> The fish haven't been fed live foods prior to spawning.

>> The fish may be sterile.

>> You have two females in the spawning tank (not good).

>> You have two males in the spawning tank (even worse).

>> They just don't feel like it.

Unfortunately, there are no fish psychologists to help you along, so if these tricks don't work you may as well forget it and try another pair. Read the following sections for some Fish Psychology 101.

The way to the heart is through the stomach

Everyone loves to eat, right? Fish are no different. You probably already picked up on that last time they jumped out of the water and into the open food can in your hand. So, you can turn the tables and take advantage of the fact that your fish are real gluttons most of the time.

TECHNICAL STUFF

One change that commonly occurs during the breeding season in a fish's natural environment is the sudden appearance and overabundance of live foods. When seasonal rainstorms sweep over ponds, lakes, and rivers, a large supply of live insects and fresh food drops onto the water surface. Offer your fish live foods such as brine shrimp and tubifex worms (okay, okay, so it's a bribe) to condition them for breeding purposes. Just remember to rinse all live food before feeding.

TIP

Fruit flies, mysis shrimp, and small earthworms also make great conditioning food.

The old fake rainstorm trick

Weekly water changes are extremely important to the health of your fish, and you can use them to aid in the conditioning process as well. In the wild, seasonal rains (you know, when you find your car has floated down the block) usually signal the start of the breeding system. It's not practical to run outside with your fish tank in your hands every time it rains in your neighborhood. The only other option is to create an artificial rainstorm.

TIP

In the home aquarium, you can duplicate a rainstorm to some degree by doing frequent water changes (about 20 percent per day in a breeding tank). Clean, demineralized water stimulates most species into entering their seasonal spawning cycle.

Another way to duplicate the rainy season is by showering the surface of the water in your spawning tank with drops of water. You can do this quite easily by using an inexpensive plastic watering can purchased at almost any garden shop. No, you don't have to stand there all day imitating a stone fountain. Just run one full can of conditioned water slowly over the surface a couple times a day. (Don't forget to remove some water first!) You can also try pouring water slowly through a plastic fine-holed colander or fine plastic mesh.

The barometric pressure advantage

In the wild, an increase in *atmospheric pressure* (the weight of air as measured by a barometer) often makes fish more lovable and loving. Many hobbyists report that their fish breed more actively right before or during a rain or snowstorm. Follow the local weather conditions and you may be able to introduce pairs to the breeding tank during a barometric pressure drop and have a successful spawning.

The old change-the-temperature ploy

If you go backpacking out to your species' natural environment, you soon find that they don't live in an area that remains the same temperature 24 hours per day. (If you don't believe me, pitch a tent for a night out there.) Try fluctuating the temperature of the breeding tank overnight. Slowly drop the temperature 3 degrees at night by adjusting the heater, and then slowly raise it back up in the morning. Now don't get carried away and start tossing ice cubes into the tank or anything. All temperature changes must be done slowly.

The new-guy-next-door approach

If you have a beautifully colored male that is being really stubborn and refusing to breed, you can always try introducing a second male (the meanest, ugliest one that you can find) in close proximity. This is kind of like sending your fish to a singles bar. Placing the rival male in a glass holding container near the spawning tank often inspires the stubborn spawner to breed when he suddenly realizes that there may be competition for his female.

Understanding Breeding Types

Fish reproduce in one of two basic ways. *Livebearers* bear live young. *Egglayers* lay eggs. Each type of breeder has special requirements.

Livebearers

Livebearers give birth to free-swimming young that are fully formed and resemble tiny adults. A female livebearer is internally fertilized by her partner and carries the fry internally for three to five weeks (called the *gestation period*) before birthing them. Immediately after entering this world, the young fry swim and search for food.

All livebearing fish are either *ovoviviparous* (the female produces eggs that contain yolk to feed the embryo) or *viviparous* (the young are nourished by the mother's circulatory system). Ovoviviparous females tend to lose their brood to miscarriage more often than viviparous ones.

How to tell male from female

A few well-known examples of livebearers include guppies, swordtails, mollies, and platys. Most livebearers are brightly colored and make great community fish. Determining the sex of most livebearers is easy because the female is usually larger and more full-bodied than the male. Most males have a rodlike organ (developed from the anal fin) called a *gonopodium*. This unique organ internally fertilizes a female. After a single fertilization, a female can produce multiple broods (batches of fry) month after month without a male being present.

Except when they're in drag

In some livebearers, females can develop secondary male sexual characteristics. Where not enough males are present to ensure survival of the species, the female's anal fin may change into a gonopodium, and that fish will then carry on male duties!

The egglayers

Egglayers lay eggs (which usually range in size from 1.4 to 3 millimeters) that eventually hatch into newborn fry. The fry of egglayers aren't as hardy and fully formed as those produced by livebearers. The babies of egglayers take much more time to mature. Popular egglayers include angelfish, cichlids, goldfish, and bettas.

When breeding egglayers, be aware of the following dangers to eggs:

- **Lack of oxygen:** The lack of oxygen in the water can seriously damage the eggs in your breeding tank. Without oxygen, their normal rate of cell division decreases. But you don't want heavy turbulence in the tank either. Hook up a small airstone or bubble disk (which splits the air into smaller bubbles) to a gang valve (which splits up an air supply to supply several pieces of equipment) so that you can adjust the oxygen flow. This setup provides beneficial aeration for the eggs without blowing the eggs into the next county.

- **Poor water conditions:** Dirty water can cause eggs to deteriorate. Make sure your water is clean and has the proper temperature and pH for your species.

- **Lack of vitamins:** Eggs can also be damaged if the mother lacks the essential vitamins needed to help them grow correctly. Diseased females can produce bad eggs. If the eggs from an unhealthy mother hatch, the young are usually defective and will produce deformed babies or none at all. Make sure that your spawning female is in good health before you attempt to breed her.

- **Intense lighting:** Light that's too bright can also damage fish eggs. Minimize lighting in your breeding tank.

Bubble-nest builders

Bubble-nest builders lay and incubate their eggs in a nest of bubbles that usually floats at the surface or is attached to plants. Bettas and gouramis are the most famous of these bubble-nest builders. A male betta builds a floating nest that he carefully constructs from mucus-coated air bubbles he blows out of his mouth. Males often use plant debris as a glue to help keep the bubbles together. In some species, the entire nest has a foamy appearance.

Nests are built in different shapes and sizes, depending on the individual male. Some males complete a nest in a few hours, whereas others take their time and end up working several days to accomplish the same task. If excess circulation or other factors damage the nest, the male constantly repairs it as needed. Often males build more than one nest to impress a female and entice her into breeding.

The female should be removed immediately after spawning. If the fish don't spawn, she should still be removed so the male doesn't attack her. The betta male cares for the eggs after they're laid and keeps them clean using chemicals in his mouth. Don't panic if he picks up eggs in his mouth and spits them back into the nest, because this is normal. After a few days the egg case will dissolve and the fry will emerge. This betta example is only one of the amazing things that you will see while breeding your fish.

Egg scatterers

Egg scatterers must hide their eggs because they don't take care of them after birth. These species scatter their eggs around decorations, rocks, plants, and gravel. During the courtship of these species, the male actively chases his mate and fertilizes her eggs as they fall freely into the water. They do this for large numbers of eggs at one time, ensuring that some survive by sheer numbers alone. A few common examples of egg scatterers are danios, barbs, rasboras, and tetras.

Substrate spawners

Substrate spawners lay their eggs in such a manner that the eggs attach to *one particular area* of rocks, driftwood, plants, or substrate. The male of the species fertilizes the eggs while the female expels them. Common examples of substrate spawners include some cichlids, catfish, and killifish.

Mouthbrooders

Mouthbrooders are unique, because they incubate their eggs in their mouth until it's time for them to hatch. As the eggs are laid, the male fertilizes them. The parents (either the male or female) gather them up in their mouths for protection and incubation. Examples of mouthbrooders are some labyrinth fish and some cichlids.

Saving Everyone from Everyone Else

After spawning is complete and the fry are produced, there may be a few problems between Mom and Dad, Mom and the kids, or Dad and the kids. As a result, it's crucial that you keep an eye on everyone after breeding — this is when the third world war may break out among aggressive species. These sections can help you.

Saving Mom and Dad from Mom and Dad

Just because your fish had a great night out on the town doesn't mean that they like each other *now*. In fact, there's a really good chance that they want to tear each other fin from fin. No one seems to know why they get like that. Perhaps they're just really tired after spawning or are suffering from PASS (post aquatic spawning syndrome). Whatever the reason, many fish have to be separated after they spawn.

If you have a pretty decent-sized fish room, move the female to her own holding tank (as small as 4 gallons, depending on the size of the fish) and then move the male to his own quarters. It isn't a good idea to move spawners back to a main aquarium immediately with other fish. The male may still be aggressive because his hormones are as high as a kite on a windy day. He may look for his next victim in your community or species tank. The female may be torn up or worn out, and you should allow her to rest in a tank of her own for at least 48 hours to recover properly.

TIP

The slime coat (coating on the body that helps to protect fish from disease) on a mating pair can be easily damaged during breeding. After you move the male and female to their own quarters for recuperation, add a little Stress Coat to the water to guard against bacterial infections.

Saving the kids from Mom and Dad

Many fish (such as cichlids) normally make good parents and perform tasks such as caring for their brood and defending their nesting spot. However, should this pair suddenly be upset by outsiders, they can turn from Ward and June into Bonnie and Clyde in a heartbeat. Unfortunately, the young fry or eggs suffer the most from their parents' newfound wrath.

TIP

One way to avoid this problem with aggressive species is to use a large tank equipped with many hiding places. Try to keep their breeding tank in a quiet, low-traffic area so that the fish aren't irritated by people walking by and making noise. You can also use a *spawning grate* (a plastic sheet with holes that allows the eggs to fall though) for protection (see Chapter 19 for more on spawning grates).

Livebearers (such as guppies) often eat their young. To prevent this, you can purchase a *breeding trap* to separate the young after birth. Breeding traps come in a few different designs. A net breeder, shown in Figure 20-2, is a simple rectangular device that floats in your aquarium, kind of a net shaped like a box. Put the female inside the net, so that her young are protected from other fish in a community tank. Unfortunately, the net trap doesn't protect the young from Mom. The advantage of the net breeder is that the net allows free water flow from the aquarium.

You can also put the expectant mother in a plastic breeding tank and float it in your larger aquarium until she gives birth. One advantage of this type of breeder is that after the fry are born, they drop through a small slit and are separated from their mother and future tankmates. Unfortunately, the plastic breeder doesn't allow water flow to keep the interior clean and can foul rather quickly if birth is delayed.

REMEMBER

Most breeding traps are too small to accommodate a pregnant female for any length of time. While under prolonged restraint, she may struggle to escape and damage herself or her unborn fry. Pregnant females should only be placed in breeding traps when they're ready to deliver. By becoming familiar with the species you're breeding, you can recognize when your fish is ready to give birth. This can vary from species to species, but it usually includes the mother looking complete bloated, constantly moving toward the bottom of the tank, or looking for cover.

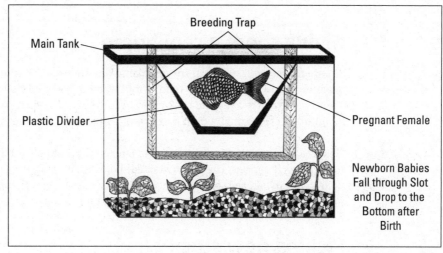

Breeding Trap

Main Tank

Plastic Divider

Pregnant Female

Newborn Babies Fall through Slot and Drop to the Bottom after Birth

FIGURE 20-2: A net breeder is a simple box shape made out of fine mesh netting.

Saving the kids from each other

Fry eventually reach a stage where they're sexually mature. If you have a bunch of juveniles in a *growout* tank (a separate tank for the young fish so they won't be attacked by other larger tankmates), you should separate the males from the females as soon as you can determine their genders. If you don't, you may end up with a lot of unwanted spawning that interferes with your breeding plan. As the fry grow, you need to start culling.

WARNING

A problem with growing fry is that the larger ones (the males usually grow quicker) start eating the smaller ones. This is very common, even if they're fed properly.

Raising the Fry

After the fry are born and the parents have been moved to a resting tank, you can begin feeding the babies. The fry (depending on the species) are usually very small and should be fed liquid foods or infusoria cultures through an eyedropper (to measure and add the food to the tank). Microworms are another good food choice.

Stepping up to brine shrimp

After a few weeks, you can begin feeding the fry baby brine shrimp — live foods help them gain maximum growth. Brine shrimp is a great choice because of the relatively low odds of introducing disease into the tank.

Giving them a real home

Be sure to feed your newborn fry small amounts three to five times a day to ensure maximum growth. Baby foods tend to foul water quickly, so change the water frequently in order to keep the tank clean. A well-planted aquarium allows your fry to mature more normally than a bare tank with no decorations does.

TIP

Check each species' specifications (see later in this chapter for a few examples of species specifications to get you started) before removing the parents. Some fry, such as discus, depend on their parents' slime coat for nourishment and may not survive if their parents are removed from the tank.

Picking new stock

When selecting future breeding stock from your own bred stock and new purchases, choose the most colorful, vigorous fish in the group and move all the females to one tank and the males to another tank. You don't want to rely upon chance sexual encounters or you may never be able to develop the strain you're seeking.

Understanding Genetics

A while back, a bored young monk named Gregor Mendel did a few experiments with peas in a quiet monastery garden. He selectively bred pea plants for certain characteristics and kept track of those characteristics. He was surprised to see traits (physical signs) not seen in either parent plant appear in their offspring. Everyone thought he was weird, but he learned a lot of cool stuff — such as, what you see isn't necessarily what you get (he had discovered recessive genes). *Selective breeding* allows you to choose fish that have the characteristics you're searching for and breed them until that characteristic remains stable from generation to generation. And, like Mendel, you may end up with a few surprises to boot.

Choosing the best

To breed selectively, you need to choose a male that possesses characteristics you want to develop into a pure strain, so that generation after generation of fish display the same certain colors, fin types, and whatever other factors you isolate. Selecting a good female may be a little more difficult, because they usually don't carry as much color as the males in many species. Just try to pick a full-bodied female in good health.

Obtaining variation the good way

Few *strains* (an entire breeding family tree) produce identical fish from generation to generation. If they do, it can take a long time to develop fish that are identical in color and shape consistently by interbreeding them with each other. Because genetics are so varied, it's possible that you may end up with a brand new characteristic (not seen in the parents) within a few years. This occurs because of *recessive genes* (genes that are present but that aren't "turned on" and thus don't show their traits in the physical makeup), which make an appearance periodically.

Obtaining variation through mutation

Another way you can obtain variation is when a mutation occurs. A *mutation* is a more radical change from one generation to the next and doesn't occur in increments. Mutations aren't very common. The main disadvantage of a mutation is that many mutants are sterile or, if they're fertile, they may carry deformed genes that aren't passed along to future generations. The odds of carrying a mutation long enough to make it pure are staggeringly long, to say the least.

Creating strains through inbreeding

The breeding process used to produce a "pure" strain of fish is known as *inbreeding.* After the first brood is born and raised, pick a healthy male and breed him back to his mother. From the next generation, select the best quality grandson (who displays the characteristics you want) and breed him with his grandmother. Keep repeating this process for successive generations. Doing so helps solidify the characteristics you want by keeping unwanted traits from other fish out of the picture. This is perfectly normal as far as fish are concerned, because they would breed with each other anyway, and you're just pairing them up for the best traits.

TIP

As each new brood is born, check for males born with unique characteristics that you want to continue on with. If the females that you started with die, select a healthy daughter and continue on. This method of inbreeding is more effective than *line* breeding, which involves mating half-brothers and sisters.

Inbreeding in mammals causes genetic defects, and many people find it a distasteful topic generally. However, in the fish world it happens all the time. Sometimes survival depends on it. In my opinion, don't think of inbreeding in fish in the same light as it is for higher animals. However, it's possible that no amount of evidence or argument can get you over that hurdle. If that's the case, then inbreeding to produce new strains of fish isn't for you.

Choosing the Right Species for You

When you've decided to breed, start out with a few of the easier-to-breed species so that you can find out the ins and outs. The following examples give you basic information on a few species that are relatively easy to breed so that you can get started on this fascinating adventure without encountering a lot of difficult problems off the bat.

Breeding livebearers

Livebearers are some of the easiest species to breed. Guppies, swordtails, and other livebearers are prolific, are tolerant of changing water conditions, and spawn constantly.

Guppy (Poecilia reticulata)

The guppy is probably the easiest aquarium fish to breed. Guppies would breed in a puddle of water if given half a chance. Combine several males with a few females in a species tank, and within a year you'll have to purchase a new aquarium to house all your new fish. Guppies readily breed in a community aquarium, species tank, or spawning tank. Males have a gonopodium and are more brightly colored than the larger-bodied females. The young fry are born fully formed and ready to eat food. Standard water temperature for breeding is between 74 and 78 degrees F; dH 12; pH 7.

Mollies (Poecilia sphenops)

Mollies are also easy to breed. The male with the boldest color and best-looking fins is usually the one who wins the breeding contest. It's best to have one male with several females. Remove the female as soon as she is pregnant because the male will often cause her stress by continuing to chase her around. Female mollies have been known to eat their own young, so remove her after the fry are born. The newborn fry will be able to feed and take care of themselves if no larger fish are around to make a midnight snack out of them.

TIP

The water should have a little salt for breeding, about a half a teaspoon of salt per gallon to reach a salinity level of 1.005 to 1.008. Keep the water in the range of 78 to 82 degrees F; dH 15–30; pH 7.5–8.2.

Platies (Xiphophorus maculatus)

Your choices of breeding platies are endless because Many new and different colors and patterns are available. When breeding platies, have one male to several females. When they become pregnant, a dark gravid spot will appear near the anal fin like in other livebearers. This spot is caused by the eyes of the unborn fry pushing against the mother's scales. Remove the female as soon as the fry are born because platies are cannibalistic. In order to breed the beautiful platy species, keep the water temperature between 70 and 77 degrees F; dH 10–28; pH 6.8–8.0.

Swordtails (Xiphophorus helleri)

The male of the species develops a long sword-shaped tale, and the female doesn't. Like other livebearing species, the male is often smaller than the female. Swordtails generally breed better in a larger aquarium with plenty of space. Live foods like brine shrimp help them get ready to for breeding. They can produce more than 100 fry in a single breeding, so be prepared! Remove the female as soon as the fry are born. Keep the temperature between 72 to 79 degrees F; dH 12–30; pH 7–8.4.

Other fun fish to breed

There are many other popular aquarium fish that are not difficult to breed. By starting with the easiest species, you'll have a higher chance of success right off the bat. Here are a few species that you can breed without a whole lot of effort:

Convict cichlid (Archocentrus nigrofasciatus)

Breeding convicts is extremely easy. Because convicts who are breeding can be aggressive toward their tankmates, put them in their own spawning tank with a few plants and rocks or a flowerpot turned on its side. The female is larger and shows much more color than the male. She also exhibits black and red bars during the breeding cycle. Water for breeding is between 69 and 79 degrees F; dH 8; pH 7.2.

Convict spawning occurs very rapidly. They lay their eggs in a rock cave or in a flowerpot. Both parents help take good care of the young — unless they begin to quarrel. If the parents fight, remove the losing partner. The young eat readily and flee to the parents when they feel threatened.

Angelfish (Pterophyllum scalare)

Angelfish breed steadily when you provide the proper conditions. Angle a piece of slate (about 45 degrees), 2–3 inches wide, against the glass of the tank for your angelfish to lay their eggs on. The spawning pair will clean off the slate before using it. When the housework is done, the female lays her eggs on the slate, which the male then fertilizes. Angelfish often pair up, so the easiest way to start matching them with a spawning partner is to pay attention to who hangs out with whom. Male angelfish have a bump (common among cichlids) on the front of their heads. The genital area is round in the female, and pointed in the male.

After the eggs are fertilized, both parents use their fins to gently fan them with water and remove any infertile or damaged eggs. The eggs hatch within 48 hours, and the fry absorb their yolk sacs before searching for food. Some angelfish are carnivorous and eat their own eggs. (Angelfish also help their young emerge from the eggs by removing the case, so make sure you know what you're seeing before you do anything about it.) If the angelfish are eating their eggs, remove the piece of slate with the eggs on it and place it in another tank with an airstone. Water temperature for breeding is between 75 and 78 degrees F; dH 7–16; pH 6.7–7.5.

Killifish (Fundulus diaphanous)

Live aquarium plants, such as java moss, help killifish feel right at home when breeding. The breeding tank should be dimly lit and have a sponge filter, shallow substrate or no substrate, and a heater. Another useful addition is called a spawning mop. A *spawning mop* can be made out of thick cork and dark colored acrylic yarn. Take numerous strands of yarn and tie them to the cork, which allows the whole thing to float for easy access by the killifish. The eggs can be left to mature on the mop. Parents are known to eat the eggs, so feed them well before breeding and remove them after spawning. The ideal temperature is between 72 and 80 degrees F; dH 3–10; pH 6–6.5.

Cory catfish (Corydoras metae)

Determining the gender of cories is difficult. The males are generally more streamlined, and the females are more compressed and thicker near the abdomen. Make sure the tank is well aerated and has a soft substrate and plenty of air flow using airstones and a sponge filter. Have groups of six for breeding and lower the temperature 2 degrees to induce spawning. This temperature change mimics the rain in their natural environment. The right temperature is between 72 and 79 degrees F; dH 10; pH 5.8–7.

As soon as the female lays the eggs, return the water temperature to normal and place an airstone near them to maintain good water floor and to keep bacteria away. The adults won't bother the eggs or fry after born. Feed the young fry liquid fry food and switch to baby brine shrimp after a few weeks.

Zebra danios (Danio rerio)

This species scatters non-adhesive eggs on plants and decorations in an aquarium. They breed extremely easily in captivity. The male is usually slimmer than the female and has more vibrant colors. There should be two males for each female. You can't use a regular filter system for breeding, because it will suck up the eggs. Use an airstone attached to a pump instead. The water temperature should be between 78 and 82 degrees F; pH of 6.5–7; dH of 5–12.

Danios can be placed in a breeder net and will usually breed within a 24-hour period. The eggs will fall through the net to the bottom of the tank. After they've spawned, remove the breeder net and the adults. The fry will hatch from the eggs within a couple of days and will become free swimming a few days later. The fry should be fed powdered egg layer fish food after they become free swimming.

Rainbowfish (Melanotaenia fluviatilis)

Determining the sex of rainbowfish is easy; the males have much brighter colors and are slenderer. Breed them in a tank with a lot of plants with several males and several females. Place a spawning mop near the bottom of the tank because rainbowfish like to breed in this area. Rainbowfish tend to breed in the morning hours and will eat their own eggs, so remove the parents after spawning. The fry will eat their own yolk sacks after birth and can then be fed liquid food. The fry are very small, so keep the aeration lower after birth. The temperature should be between 68 and 75 degrees F; dH 4–8; pH: a slightly lowered pH from the normal 7–8.

Chapter **21**

Recording Data and Photographing Fish

One great way to enhance your fishkeeping hobby is by keeping a written log and taking pictures of your prize aquatic pets. Photos and logs are good tools for discovering more interesting tidbits about your fish, their breeding habits, environmental quirks, and natural social interactions. Photography is also a fun way to enhance your social standing by impressing your friends with your great pictures. Most of the equipment you need for fish photography and written logs are fairly inexpensive and can be easily obtained. If you're interested in photographing your fish, this chapter gives you the lowdown.

Keeping a Logbook

Tracking your fish's individual health, breeding schedule, and food preferences can be quite a difficult job, especially if you have a large variety of species or more aquariums than the National Aquarium in Baltimore.

One good way to keep tabs on your aquarium fish is to use a written logbook. A complete record of each fish in your aquarium lets you monitor your pet's history, social habits, growth, water conditions, feeding habits, and spawning successes.

If you keep track of each new fish as you purchase it, you gain a better understanding of each species' needs, which can be beneficial in decisions regarding purchases of future tankmates. For example, the "calm" oversized molly you bought a couple of months ago cleverly turns your community tank into a wrestling battle royal, and you note its bizarre behavior carefully on your written log. On your next trip to the fish shop, this individual fish's rap sheet will remind you to run at warp speed past the giant molly section toward calmer waters.

Beginning a log is kind of like starting your first diary except you don't have to make up stuff. Keep a separate page for each fish. Your log doesn't have to be fancy or win a Pulitzer prize, just record the basics. I suggest encasing each page in a plastic slip-folder and placing the individual sheets in a three-ring binder to protect the logs from water and moisture. The following list details the information I usually record in my aquatic logs:

>> Date and place of purchase of each fish

>> Number and type of tankmates

>> Monthly growth record

>> Common and scientific names

>> Sex, size, and color

>> Preferred temperature, dH, pH, and lighting requirements

>> Type of feeder and preferred diet

>> Environmental distribution (for example, "found in Guatemala and Mexico")

>> Social behavior (whether it gets along with other species or needs its own tank) and what type of tankmates it tolerates

>> Spawning date and number of fry

>> A disease record that includes the type of disease, date contracted, treatment, and how long the treatment took to work

>> Date and cause of death if known

>> Any personal comments that can help you with future purchases

Making Your Fish the Stars They Were Meant to Be

You may want to photograph your fish for a plethora of reasons, including any of the following:

>> **You want to capture the beauty of your aquarium and share the photos of your aquatic treasures with your family, friends, and colleagues.** Nothing compares to the pride you feel when others openly admire your aquatic and photographic creativity.

>> **You want to turn good-quality fish photos into extra spending money if you catch the right scene, interaction, or pose on film.** Many aquarium magazines, stock photo houses, and publishers purchase photos to use in their articles. It takes time to build up a photo business, so don't quit your day job until you're established, or you can just sell them as a side business.

>> **You want to do your part in preservation.** All types of fish photos are important resources for historical preservation. In today's world where once-abundant species are slipping into extinction at an alarming rate, photographs may become the only reminder to future generations that a particular species of fish once existed and is now extinct due to human carelessness.

>> **You like new challenges.** Many hobbyists try their hands at selective breeding at one time or another. Have you finally succeeded in breeding the perfectly colored platy and now feel an overwhelming need to capture and preserve that beauty? Have you had a fish for a long time that has become very dear to you? Fish photography also can offer a new challenge for you.

>> **You want to get to know your fish better.** Photographing your fish gives you a closer look at their personalities and habits. Photographs are a great record to track your tankmates' health and happiness.

REMEMBER

After all is said and done, the most important rule of fish photography is *have fun!*

Knowing Where to Take Pictures

You don't have to always travel to fancy or expensive places to take pictures of aquarium fish. Opportunities often present themselves unexpectedly so keep your camera ready when traveling. You can photograph fish at the following places:

>> **At home:** One of the best places to take photos of fish is in your own home aquariums. You can use the photos to document your fishkeeping progress, sell them for profit, share information with other hobbyists, or just have fun.

>> **Aquarium stores:** In my experience, most aquarium stores don't mind customers taking photos of the aquatic stock. Taking photos at stores is a nice way to focus on fish you want to purchase in the future.

- » **Fish shows and other locations:** Take your camera or phone when you go to local fish shows because you can take photos of top-quality stock and converse with experts at the same time.

- » **Museums, public aquariums, and zoos:** They also often have great photo opportunities. Many zoos have small water areas with koi and other outdoor fish, and some even have indoor displays.

Check online for local opportunities to try out your photography skills.

Photographing Your Fish with Digital Photography

Digital photography has replaced many film-based cameras. Digital images are made up of small squares called pixels, which resemble a bunch of very tiny tiles laid out to make the image. Digital cameras are judged by their pixel count, which is represented in millions and abbreviated by MP (megapixels). So, a 16MP camera has 16 million pixels, or megapixels. Digital cameras store the pictures on small memory cards instead of film. You then transfer the images from the card to your computer or a printer.

You have a multitude of options when shooting digital photos. Most cellphones and tablets have cameras that typically offer large megapixel advantages. Generally, the higher the MP, the more expensive the camera.

You can also get top-down shots using a digital phone camera by floating a small acrylic tray at the top of the tank that houses the phone while you take pictures.

Using a digital camera has several advantages, including the following:

- » Most have a liquid-crystal display (LCD) screen, which allows you to see what the captured image will look like before you take the photo and also let you preview it after you take the photo to see if it's worth keeping.

- » You can take hundreds of photos and only keep the very best. You don't have to waste money on the cost of film.

- » If you want to purchase a digital camera other than your cellphone, it won't weigh much so will be easier to carry.

>> You can easily alter and improve your digital photos, using different varieties of image-manipulation software, such as Adobe Photoshop (expensive) and Paint Shop Pro (not so expensive) and Snapspeed to add filters (free). Many digital cameras come with basic software for this purpose as well.

>> You can easily store on your phone or on the cloud and share your fish photos with your family and friends. You can also easily post on Instagram and Pinterest to showcase your fish.

Recording fish

Recording your fish is a great way to show your aquarium system in action to friends, family, and other hobbyists without them ever having to come to your home or business. You can share videos on social media or via instant messaging apps like SnapChat or WhatsApp.

Recordings can be made in a variety of ways including standard handheld video cameras, laptops, tablets, and small security cameras. Most smartphones nowadays come with video capabilities that you can also edit, but you can download apps from places like Google Play Store that offer even more features. Smartphones allow you the freedom to capture fish video on the go at aquariums and zoos without having to carry bulky equipment. You can mount security cams to your aquarium or other household furniture to take video that you can edit together with computer software.

Outdoor lighting can create beautiful mood shots of ponds and outdoor displays if you use the sun to your advantage. Determine which angle creates the best clarity and complimentary shadows by walking around and filming a test video first. If you're inside, lighting isn't a huge problem due to free editing software that can fix pretty much any bad video and turn it into a prize-winning documentary. LED aquarium lighting on your tank or as a separate lighting unit can help to produce some well-lit videos.

Printing your work

You can print your fish photos right from your computer using a photo printer. If you don't have a photo printer, you can take your smartphone or camera to many photo stores, megastores, and drugstores to print the photos. Many stores have self-serve machines.

AQUARIUM WEBCAMS

Many inexpensive point-of-view webcams are now available at most electronics stores. This option is great for capturing an entire aquarium of fish swimming happily in their aquatic home. You could even make a website so that friends and family (and you) can see your fish from anywhere that has an Internet connection. The 1080P cameras allow hobbyists to watch their aquariums with their smartphones so they can know when a problem arises even if they aren't at home.

Sharing your work online

People love to share their hobbies with their friends, family, and in today's world, the Internet-viewing audience. Hey, looking cool is important, right? What better way to accomplish that than to share your beautiful fish photos online? I can't think of a better way. Most sites are free, so why not give it a whirl?

You can share your photos in plenty of great places. Uploading digital photos to social media sites such as Facebook, YouTube, Twitter, Instagram, Snapchat, WhatsApp, and Reddit is super easy. Each site usually has instructions on how to best upload your fishy photos. If not, just ask your 10-year-old kids. Many sites even have tools to edit your photos, create albums to share, add captions, or just improve the overall aesthetic of each photo.

Photographing Your Fish the Old-Fashioned Way

Okay, just admit it, buried deep within your creative depths is a shutterbug itching to get the old, dusty, 35mm (millimeter) camera out of the attic and snap a few quick photos. Or maybe you're just an enthusiastic hobbyist like me, continually searching for new and exciting ways to enhance your aquarium-keeping records. Yes, digital photography is the standard now, but there is a beauty to be found in film shots. If this type of photography interests you, then keep reading.

Film cameras

Almost any camera works well for fish photography. Despite the great advantages of modern cameras, older film cameras are fun to use and create beautiful photos if used properly. A *single-lens reflex* (SLR) camera has several options that other cameras lack:

>> The picture you see through the camera lens on an SLR is basically the image that you see in the finished and developed photo.

>> You can easily equip most SLRs with auxiliary wide angle, telephoto, macro, and zoom lenses.

>> SLRs are capable of taking synchronized electronic flash pictures, which can help you capture the action of fast-moving pets.

>> You can purchase a wide variety of cool attachments such as filters to help you make interesting shots and create different types of scenes.

>> A 35mm SLR makes you look like a pro if you get a cool camera strap and have a bunch of accessories crammed into a stylish bag.

However, the most important thing is to get the shot. Start with a camera that is equipped with automatic exposure so you don't miss shots fumbling with numerous settings. Many SLRs have a fully automatic feature, but some cameras are so complex that by the time you set up everything for your shot, your fishy subject has spawned several times and is about to collect Social Security. (If someone is watching as you, simply wipe imaginary sweat off your forehead, fiddle with all the camera buttons, and look relieved when the shot is over.)

Another good reason to begin with an SLR is that you can start with a 35 mm camera body and a standard 50 mm lens and then gradually add to the unit as your interests and experience expand. Inexpensive instamatic cameras usually have a fixed lens, and the quality of the picture compared to that of an SLR is the difference between a Rembrandt and my son's attempt at fingerpainting his bedroom walls.

TIP

Mount your camera on a sturdy tripod to help eliminate blurred pictures caused by camera shake. You can find cheap tabletop plastic tripods at camera shops that will work fine. You can also find nice tripods at decent prices online. If you don't have a tripod, support the camera on a table or firm surface.

The film

If you want good-quality photos, you must purchase the highest quality film on the market. In my opinion, Kodak is the best film made and produces the truest color.

Cutting costs with inexpensive or low-grade film costs you much more in the long run (buying tons of film to get a good-looking shot on bad film) than if you had just spent a few extra pennies on a better quality roll. Ask any professional photographer, and he'll tell you the same thing. When you're first starting, you can save money by purchasing rolls of film with more exposures (36 instead of 12 exposures).

REMEMBER

Always choose the slowest-speed film possible to avoid the grainy pictures produced by faster films. Film speed is measured in numbers such as 100, 200, 400, and 800, and the lower the number, the slower the film speed and the higher the level of detail, but the more light you'll need to get good pictures (see later in this chapter for more on lighting). A slow, fine-grained film such as ASA 100 produces higher quality images that can also be enlarged with better results than does a faster film such as ASA 400, which often makes your pictures look as if they were taken during a desert windstorm. Increase the lighting before you attempt to increase film speed. Begin with a 100 speed film and work from there.

Make sure to have plenty of extra film on hand, because it may take several rolls to get the one perfect shot you're seeking. After you achieve lighting proficiency and mastery of the camera and lenses, consider using *slide* film (very slow film that offers bright, realistic color saturation,) which gives you the ultimate in color saturation and picture quality.

Don't overlook black-and-white film, either, which can be a simple yet exciting medium that adds artistic impact to shots of fish, such as a convict cichlid, and can show the delicate shades and fin details of a veiltail angel. Black-and-white photography is an art form in itself, and you can get even more creative with it if you decide to develop your own film in a darkroom.

Lenses

A standard 50 mm lens works great on fish longer than 5 inches. But when working with smaller fish, use a zoom, telephoto, or macro lens to help eliminate background material. A macro lens is designed for taking close-ups and offers a 1:1 ratio, which results in a large center-of-attention subject in the finished photo. A 105 mm macro lens works great for small fish such as a pencilfish. However, macro filters can result in decreased sharpness and depth of field.

A zoom lens allows you to change the focal length of your lens to capture different sizes of fish. A 100–200 mm zoom lens is a good lens to use for most smaller fish.

Telephoto lenses enlarge images that are far away and provide you with the freedom to work at a distance from the aquarium. Taking photos from a healthy distance helps avoid the possibility of your fish going into cardiac arrest from fright during photo sessions.

The three disadvantages of telephoto and zoom lenses are as follows:

>> Camera shake due to the larger size and heavier weight of the lens if you don't use a tripod.

>> A shallower depth of field (zone of sharp focus), which tends to blur out any background.

>> A slight loss of quality in the finished prints.

TIP

Take time to experiment with different lenses to become aware of the advantages and disadvantages of each type. Look through photo magazines and books to gain new ideas on the various uses of each lens length. Talk to other photographers about their experiences using different lenses.

Considering Lighting

When taking photos of your fish and aquarium, you can make everything shine with the proper lighting. These sections identify your lighting options, what to keep in mind with the different lighting, and which techniques are best.

Relying on lighting

When lighting your aquariums and fish, your two best options are direct sunlight or strobe lights. These sections examine those two choices and point out which lighting to avoid.

Going with the sun

Ideally, place your photography tank (see the later section, "Shooting the Tank" for more information) in natural sunlight, which far exceeds artificial lighting in terms of color, shadow, and mood. The disadvantage of natural lighting is that the direct sunlight can quickly heat up the water in a small tank to lethal levels and turn your fish into a broiled entree. Take great care to ensure that the water remains cool until you're ready to start the photography session and that you don't leave fish in direct sunlight for too long. A large, thick towel to cover the entire tank and block out the heavy sunlight is a great tool to have handy if you need to take a short break.

WARNING

Avoid the sunlight 2 hours after sunrise and 2 hours before sunset because it's generally discolored. Photos taken in natural sunlight during these times tend to have a yellowish cast unless you use special filters. Instead, take photos in natural sunlight during the late morning or early afternoon hours when the sun is high in the sky.

Going strobe

A strobe light is also an awesome way to light your photography shoot. If you're using one strobe light, direct it at the tank from a 45-degree angle near the top of the aquarium. If you use two strobe lights, place them at the same angle on opposite sides of the tank.

The 45-degree angle offers these advantages:

>> Shadows appear below the fish and give your photos a natural look. These shadows also possess a softer tone than those in photos using straight-on lighting and are more appealing to the eye.

>> You avoid flash reflection off the glass, which can ruin an otherwise good shot. Another method to avoid excess reflection is to wrap a black-cardboard tube around the lens on your camera. This tube is known as a *mask*.

Strobe lights generally have a flash duration of $\frac{1}{1500}$ of a second and are extremely effective in stopping action if you're photographing a fast-swimming fish in a large tank that isn't equipped with restraining glass. (A *restraining glass* is an inserted piece of glass that is used in small photo tanks, usually 2–5 gallons, to gently pin the fish against the aquarium glass so that it won't move while its picture is being taken.) Strobe lights are usually powered either by electricity or rechargeable cadmium batteries.

Avoiding these lights

Here are some lighting options to stay away from when taking photos of your fish and aquarium:

>> **Floodlights:** Large floodlights have become quite popular in fish photography. Be careful when using these lights because they have the potential to quickly heat water. Always check the heat intensity of these floodlights before using them.

>> **Fluorescent lamps:** If your tank has them, you may end up with a green cast on your finished pictures.

>> **Hood lights:** The main hood lights on an aquarium usually don't provide sufficient lighting to take good photos.

>> **Tungsten lamps:** If you use them, an orange cast may appear.

Making your fish shine

Here are some techniques you can use when taking photos of your fish. Consider these tips ways to bring your fish to life in photos:

>> If you're shooting a very dark fish, move the lighting closer to the tank to compensate. On the other hand, if the fish is white or of a very light complexion, move the lighting back from the subject. LED lights give you a good basic lighting in most cases.

>> If your pictures are too dark or too light, try adjusting the lighting before messing with the lens settings. For optimal results, take a series of pictures as you slowly adjust your lighting from near to far. You'll be rewarded with at least one picture with the best lighting possible.

A series of photos can be valuable to your future shots, too. You can sit down and review different lighting angles and distances to see what worked. If you're using a digital camera or smartphone camera, you can get a good idea of how the lighting is going to work by using the LCD screen. Another option is to use the built-in color changing options in your smartphone or download apps to change the lighting.

>> You can avoid *red-eye* (also known as vampire syndrome), the common name for reflections caused by lighting placed very close to the subject, by adjusting your lighting. For digital shots, you can use image-manipulation software to remove most red-eye problems.

>> Aim your flash or strobes up at a mirror or white card suspended above the tank. The light reflects off the mirror or card and bounces back onto the subject, creating a softer look. This method is popular for delicate-looking species, such as angelfish and other long-finned tropicals. Make sure that the mirror and cards you use are clean and free of streaks.

>> If you're a fairly serious photographer, you can purchase a photographic umbrella to diffuse light. The manager of your local photo shop can make sure you get the proper piece of equipment for the job. Remember that a bounced flash loses up to half of its original intensity, so adjust your calculated exposure accordingly.

Focusing Your Camera

The aperture, or opening, of the lens, which decreases as the size of the image increases, determines the focus of a camera. The aperture itself is a hole in the lens that regulates the amount of light striking the film. The aperture is adjusted by a diaphragm inside the lens and is calculated in steps called *f-stops*. You can see the f-stops available on an SLR camera on the ring on the outside of the lens. The smaller the f-stop number, the less light required and the smaller the depth of field, or zone of focus. With fish photography, you're usually working close up and with limited ability to provide a lot of light, meaning smaller f-stops.

TIP

To get a large amount of the background in focus, you need a larger f-stop — or more light. The lens manufacturer usually supplies a table to help you determine the aperture you need for the magnification you want. Or set your camera to semi-automatic mode, if it has one, meaning you can set the shutter speed to, say 1/60 of a second, and the camera chooses the correct aperture automatically.

If your calculations point to an f-stop of 11, take one photo at f 8, one at f 11, and another at f 16. This *bracketing* technique reduces your margin of error, maximizing the probability of a useable shot. If you're using a digital camera or a smartphone camera, keep a log of each shot so that you know which built-in filter, aperture, or other techniques you used to get the perfect shot.

Larger lens openings (f 2, f 1.4) have a narrower depth of field (how much area behind or in front of the subject will be in focus), which means you have to focus more carefully. Smaller lens openings (f 16, f 22) have a larger depth of field and require less focusing to get the correct image. Depth of field increases with distance. The farther your camera is from your subject, the greater the depth of field. Macro photos (extreme close-ups of small objects) have little depth of field because the lens is so close to the subject.

You can crop your picture, which entails cutting out parts of the picture that don't appeal to you. Another option if you aren't using a digital camera is to scan the image into the computer using a scanner and then adjust it in your software. What's left is usually the shot that you were trying to get in the first place.

Understanding Composition Techniques

You need to organize all the visual elements into a balanced and appealing scene in order to take good fish photos. All photos require a center of interest (which is usually the most important image in the picture).

Obviously, most of the fish that you take pictures of are of some interest, but your aquatic pets can accent other subjects in the aquarium. For example, a piece of driftwood with an unusual shape or a beautiful plant can provide a center of interest that you can highlight by capturing a small school of fish swimming nearby.

Using the rule of thirds

One general rule of composition that always produces a pleasing balance is to place the subject at the intersection of imaginary lines dividing the entire scene into thirds, horizontally and vertically, as shown in Figure 21-1. This simple but effective placement of subjects, known as the *rule of thirds*, often gives excellent results. If there are other lines in the picture, try to arrange them in such a way that something about them leads the viewer's eye toward the main subject.

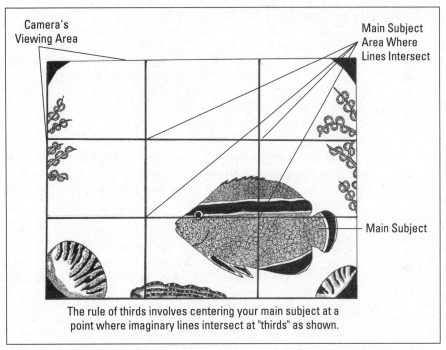

FIGURE 21-1: The rule of thirds is a time-honored way of achieving attractive composition in photography.

The rule of thirds involves centering your main subject at a point where imaginary lines intersect at "thirds" as shown.

Panning the scene

To obtain unique photos that stand out from the rest, try taking pictures of interesting moments, such as mating rituals or feeding sessions. Another fun thing to experiment with is a specialized effect such as *panning* — following a fish with the camera as the fish swims: You simply continue moving the camera in the direction the fish is swimming as you depress the shutter. The effect is a fish that's mostly in focus but with a blurred afterimage and background that can be quite interesting as it captures motion over time. To get the most realistic photo, keep the camera on the same horizontal plane as the fish. (If you suddenly look down and can see the back of your knees, you probably tilted too far down.)

Setting up for close-ups

For good close-ups, make sure your subject fills at least 75 percent of the frame — this keeps the background from overrunning or cluttering the shot. Focus on the best aspects of the fish (a beautiful flowing fin, for example).

Shooting the Tank

Fish can be a difficult subject to photograph, so you need to do everything possible to improve your odds of getting quality photos. If you plan to photograph your fish in your main tank, you must take a few important factors into consideration to insure good quality photographs. If you're taking photos from your main tank, do the following to get the best shots:

>> **Clear up the water.** Avoid glare (reflected light) by making sure that the aquarium's water is as clear as possible. Any debris or suspended particles (your toddler's uneaten lima beans from dinner) may reflect light and produce spots in your finished photos.

Add extra mechanical filtration to the tank a few days before you take the pictures. Another effective process is to filter all the main tank water through standard floss (the same type you put in many filters and can be bought at your local pet store). The only drawback to this procedure is that it is quite time consuming and can take anywhere from two days to five years, depending on the size of your tank.

>> **Clean the tank itself and the decorations.** Remove all unsightly algae from the glass of the aquarium; otherwise, your photos may end up resembling a bad still-life of chunky pea soup. Clean all plastic plants, rocks, and other artificial decorations before your photo session begins. The gravel in the tank should be vacuumed prior to shooting — a photographic lens does not miss nearly as much intricate detail as the human eye does.

>> **Check the aquarium glass or acrylic surface for scratches.** The surface must be scratch-free to obtain the best photos. Several commercial scratch-removal kits on the market remove imperfections from acrylic walls.

>> **Clean the lighting.** Make sure that the cover glass is clean so that it allows maximum light to enter and that the outer glass covering each light remains translucent and clean.

REMEMBER

Shut off all tank lights at least 30 minutes before you clean for safety purposes. (Photo lighting can be extremely hot and can cause serious burns if touched or electrocution if accidentally knocked into the tank while cleaning.)

Building your own photography tank

One of the easiest and most practical methods to ensure great photos of your fish is to construct a miniature aquarium to use exclusively for photo sessions. This technique was founded by Dr. Herbert Axelrod and is an important part of the famous Axelrod technique of photographing fish. The Axelrod technique involves using a small aquarium tank with an interior restraining glass embedded in fine sand and angled from the bottom front to the back top of the tank. The angled glass restricts fish movement when the restraining glass is gently leaned forward.

A photography tank is much smaller than any standard aquarium and offers several unique advantages over a larger tank:

>> Keeping the water in a mini-tank clean and clear for your pictures is easier in a small tank.

>> Arranging plants, rocks, and other decorations is simple.

>> Water changes are a snap for good photos.

Building a photography tank (if you don't choose to purchase a small aquarium) is something even a beginning hobbyist can do. It doesn't require much time, knowledge, or lessons from a home contractor to complete a simple tank 7 inches high by 7 inches long and 2 inches wide. You can build tanks of other sizes to accommodate the size of the fish you're photographing and the materials at hand. The glass you use to construct your mini-tank should be thinner than standard aquarium glass to help promote good photos.

The four sides and the bottom glass of the new tank can be easily positioned using clamps and then sealed with aquarium sealer or aquatic-safe cement to obtain a small rectangle. No frame or supports are really necessary if the glass you used in construction is thin. The newly siliconed sides should be allowed to dry for

48 hours before you add water or move the tank (unless you plan on checking out your new galoshes). Doing so ensures that the seal is tight and waterproof. Cut a sixth piece of glass to size so that it fits into the tank like a partition. The glass should slide in easily without scraping the sides of the tank. The safest way to do this is to go to a glasscutter and have it done for you, because glass cutting can be very dangerous unless you know what you're doing.

Gently place the fish you're photographing between the front glass on the photo tank and the restraining glass — which works like a cover slip on a microscope slide. (If your fish's eyes start popping out like Marty Feldman's, you might want to back off on the pressure a little bit.) Another advantage to this restraining technique is that you, the photographer, have the freedom to place the fish in creative arrangements that aren't possible in a larger tank. This glass restricts movement of faster swimming fish and keeps them safe during the photo shoot.

Using different backgrounds

Because flying off to the Cayman Islands or Cancun every time you feel the urge to photograph fish isn't financially practical, you can use simple nondistracting backgrounds to allow the natural attributes and colors of your fish to capture center stage. Many materials found around the home — a towel, solid-color wrapping paper, and thick construction paper — make excellent backdrops.

When choosing a background, take into consideration the color of your subject. A darker background is appropriate for a light-colored fish, such as a glass catfish. On the other hand, you're better off using a light background for a dark-colored fish, such as a tiger oscar.

Avoid cluttering the tank or the glass with too many objects (three plastic divers, a shipwreck, and Donald Duck on a life raft is too many) — they may take away from the natural beauty of your fishy subject. Keep all decorations, such as gravel, plants, and rocks to a minimum, especially in a smaller photo tank. But these decisions are a matter of personal preference and ultimately rest with the individual photographer. Some of the best fish photos come about as a result of the trial-and-error method of artistic arrangement.

IN THIS CHAPTER

» Knowing what fish shows are all about

» Joining aquarium clubs and volunteering

» Becoming an author

» Setting up tanks for a cause

» Teaching others about the hobby

Chapter **22**

Expanding Your Hobby in Fun Ways

After you have taken the plunge and set up your first aquarium, you may start to wonder if there are other ways to expand your new hobby. Fortunately, numerous options are available so you can enjoy fishkeeping in different venues. Fish shows are great way to discover things you didn't know about fish, interact with other hobbyists, and take a look at the best-looking fish around. You should also consider joining a local aquarium club so that you can share information and interact with others who have similar interests in fishkeeping.

If you have the time, you may want to consider volunteering at an aquarium or zoo so that you can find out more about fish and their natural habitats. The options are endless; this chapter examines a few options to help jump-start your creativity.

Entering a Fish Show

Participating in a local, regional, or national fish show can be a great way to expand your fishkeeping hobby; win a bunch of cool prizes such as trophies, ribbons, equipment, and money; and display your aquarium-keeping and breeding skills.

Fish shows also offer quite a few other personal attractions worth checking out. For example, you often find people dressed up as fish, aquariums, and equipment at these shows because they're either promoting a product or attempting to get a little extra mileage out of their Halloween costumes. Either way, a full-grown adult trying to win a five-pound bag of gravel by walking around with a glass fish bowl on her head can be a real scream. You can also glance at new products.

Many other cool things go on at fish shows — like door prizes and special drawings. Just by showing up, you may have a chance to win fishkeeping supplies, such as heaters and filters. You also find many experts in the aquarium field waiting to answer any questions you may have concerning your hobby. These pros can be representatives of manufacturing companies or hobbyists who have become experts in their individual fields.

If you finally decide to get involved in a little bit of friendly competition, your aquarium-keeping skills will steadily improve. After all, in order to display only top-quality fish at every competition, you'll need to do research on nutrition, water conditions, and other factors that influence proper growth, good coloring, and vibrant health.

Only through research and improving your aquarium-keeping skills can you consistently produce high-quality show fish. Sure you can get lucky and purchase a guppy for a couple of bucks at a local fish store and have it grow into championship material. But that's the exception rather than the rule, so you need to do your homework.

Participating in fish shows keeps your aquatic pets from becoming totally bored with their lives. (If you had nothing to do but swim back and forth in your bathtub all day, you'd probably be looking for a way out, too.) Fish are a lot like humans in that they need a little mental stimulation every once in a while.

In the wild, competing for food, avoiding larger predators that want to have them over for lunch (literally), and other factors such as unpredictable weather keep a fish's senses alert and stimulate it into constant action. After sitting in a home aquarium month after month, most fish appreciate a change of pace, even if that means being carted off to a weird place where strange-looking people with large, distorted faces walk by and stare into the tank.

Despite the fact that most freshwater species are bred for the industry, their natural instincts and desires remain intact.

Getting to Know the Types of Shows

Aquarium societies organize the great majority of aquatic competitions. These aquatic societies can be international in scope, as is the International Betta Congress (IBC), or can be local groups in large towns and cities.

Participating in exhibitions

One of the largest shows you can enter is known as an *exhibition*, or *aquatic convention*. International societies and tropical fish magazines put together these shows. Exhibitions are massive affairs, generally held in huge auditoriums and fancy hotels. Aquarium manufacturers are usually present to demonstrate their newest lines of tanks, food, chemicals, and equipment to people they consider prospective buyers. (If you don't want to spend the day listening to sales pitches, wear old clothes and look poor.)

Exhibitions are exciting and extremely important because they help to keep hobbyists informed on major new trends in the hobby. If you go to one of these shows, you'll probably find a lot of excellent information on new equipment and fish-keeping procedures, not to mention the tons of new ideas you'll get from other hobbyists.

Understanding competition classes

You need to understand a little bit about how fish shows operate so that you know what to expect when you enter your very first serious competition. True, fish shows have more rules than cribbage, but you can still go to a competition, have a great time, and pick up some important aquarium-keeping skills.

To make sure that the competition between individual fish is fair, you have to enter your contestant in a specific class. Classes are usually grouped by similar species. For example, if you have an oscar (*Astronotus ocellatus*), you don't want to place it in a livebearer class normally intended for guppies (*Lebistes reticulatus*) and mollies (*Mollienesia sphenops*). Your fish would be instantly disqualified simply because it was in the wrong class. Trying to convince a judge that your 11-inch oscar is really a champion guppy that has eaten too much usually goes over like a lead balloon.

Classes can also be divided into smaller subcategories. For example, a guppy class may be divided into fantails, lyretails, and spadetails. So, before you enter your fish in any competition, check with the show's sponsors to make sure that you're placing it in the correct category. It would be a shame if your potential best of show was disqualified from the competition just because you mistakenly placed it in the wrong class.

Preparing Your Fish for the Show

At competitions, you want your fish to make the best overall impression it possibly can. If your entry bolts for the corner of the tank when the judge comes up for her first look, she probably won't receive high marks because the judge didn't have the opportunity to look her over properly. Make sure to bring flawless stock.

The tank setup and water conditions are vital to showing your fish in their best light. A good holding tank is important to avoid damage to your entry. The display tank and water conditions need to be pristine so that the judges focus their main attention on the beauty of your fish and not the surrounding environment. The following sections discuss how to prepare your fish for their big reveal.

The holding tank

When you spend a great deal of time, effort, and expense raising a show-quality fish, you want to make sure it doesn't encounter any physical problems prior to a competition. For example, if you were a professional model, you probably wouldn't begin taking lessons a week before a photo shoot — the results could be disastrous.

A small holding tank is a great (and inexpensive) way to keep your show fish healthy and free from physical harm in the month or two preceding its competition. A holding tank negates the possibility of other fish damaging your prize entry's fins or scales by not allowing physical contact, which in turn prevents untimely fighting or breeding.

Your holding tank should be free from large decorations (such as sharp rocks) with the potential to damage your show fish. A few floating plants and a couple of rooted specimens give your entry the security it needs. A smaller tank also allows you to carefully monitor your fish's progress and makes cleaning and frequent water changes a snap.

The smaller environment of a holding tank allows you to check for any disease that may manifest during this waiting period. Physical ailments can be treated quickly and easily in a smaller tank. Solitary confinement also keeps your entry calm until it's time to enter competition and really show off. Being alone in a semi-bare tank prepares your pet for the same conditions it faces during an exhibition.

Water conditions

Bring water with you to the show so that your fish can remain in familiar conditions during the competition. Water supplies provided at the show may be quite different from yours at home. Discontinue feeding your fish the night before the competition to avoid water fouling (remember, it's good for fish to fast one day a week) and change the water frequently to keep your show tank looking crystal clear. If possible, use water that is a couple degrees warmer than what your fish is accustomed to — this generally helps fish show better. Make sure to provide an airstone, if possible, to keep the water well-oxygenated.

Tank considerations

Placing your show fish in a tank that correctly matches its size is important. For example, a single guppy in a 10-gallon tank is dwarfed by the sheer water volume and tends to look rather miniscule. Show this type of fish in a 5-gallon container. On the other hand, an 8-inch plecostomus doesn't look very good in a 2-gallon container. It doesn't have the room to display all its fins or the other attributes that may make it a winner. If you have to use a shoehorn to cram your entry into its show tank, then the aquarium is probably too small, and if you need a telescope to spot your fish in its show tank, then the aquarium is probably too large.

REMEMBER

To set up an exhibition tank properly, read the competition's rules. For example, some categories and competitions allow gravel and decorations, whereas others don't. If you use gravel, make sure it complements the fish you're showing. If you have a dark-colored fish, lighter gravel will show off its colors much more naturally than a darker-toned substrate. However, make sure you use the same color gravel you choose for the show in the fish's home tank for at least two weeks before a competition so that it feels safe and secure with that color.

TIP

Here are a few more tips for competitors:

» If the competition allows tank backgrounds, choose a solid-colored sheet over one with a pattern that takes away from the natural beauty of your show fish.

» When using plants for decorations, in such categories as community or species tanks, always use fauna native to the region of the fish you're showing. Take my word for it, judges do know the difference. A natural setup always scores higher points than a mishmash of plants from completely different geographic regions. Use live plants if possible for a more natural look that most artificial plants can't match.

>> The tank or container you use to display your entry should be immaculate. The glass walls should be clean inside and out. Vacuum any dirt or debris off the bottom of the tank right before the competition begins. (Or avoid this problem by bringing extra water with you.)

>> Make sure your show tank is well covered because you don't want your fish jumping out during all the excitement. A lid also prevents people's hands and foreign objects from getting into the water.

After you get everything set up, step back for a moment and look at the overall picture. Does the entire tank look clean and well kept? Is the water crystal clear? Are the decorations in the tank placed so that your fish has the best chance to show itself in front of the judge? Does the tank look natural? Does your fish look calm and happy? Does your entry seem to be adjusting to its surroundings well? If you can answer yes to all these questions, your fish is ready for competition.

Knowing what the judges are looking for

Each competition's evaluation system varies slightly, but most show fish are judged on a point system. A certain number of points are allotted for different physical traits, such as size, color, and fins. The fish with the most total points after the judging is complete is considered the winner.

Size

One of the main physical traits that consistently inspire judges to give a fish high marks is its overall size. Judges generally look for a fish that has reached its full stage of adulthood and is the maximum size for that particular species. In other words, the bigger the better. So an oscar, which should be 10 or 11 inches long, probably won't win if it resembles a minnow with anorexia. If you're able to raise a fish to achieve its full physical potential, a judge may feel that you're a responsible aquarium keeper who takes pride in her hobby.

Your fish's body is judged on several different criteria:

>> To begin with, your entry should have all of its body parts intact.

>> Your fish shouldn't have any unusual growths, such as humps on the head (except in the case of some cichlids, where a hump is consider normal in the males of the species) or large unnatural bends in the back, which is considered a sign of old age in most aquatic species.

>> The body is free from deformities and is in correct proportions for its species.

Color

A fish's body color is produced by pigmentation and reflected light. In the wild, fish use these colors for defensive and mating purposes. In competition, fish must meet the coloration standards expected of an aquarium-bred species. Especially in show species such as the discus (which is bred artificially to produce amazing colors like tangerine and numerous cobalt variations), color can be a major factor in determining points.

Fish have the ability to darken and lighten their colors or even change them completely, depending on their surroundings and the time of day. Moods such as fright, stress, and excitement, and other factors, such as illness, can change a fish's color quickly. Take all these variables into consideration while monitoring your candidate's color. (If your fish glows in the dark, it probably has sufficient color to sweep any competition.)

The color on your entry should be evenly disbursed, and it shouldn't look faded or patchy unless typical for the species. The color itself should be very dense, not superficial, and your fish shouldn't look as if it's been run through a chlorine cycle in your washer. The area where two colors meet should be distinct and well defined, not blurred or run together so that the fish resembles a tie-dyed shirt.

Recently, a few unscrupulous breeders started using enhancing devices to increase the coloration of their fish. As far as hobbyists are concerned, this practice is immoral. The artificial color fades in time and generally doesn't look natural at all. An artificially colored fish is similar to a studio's colorized version of an old movie. If you saw Humphrey Bogart running around in a shocking pink hat and purple trousers, you'd know that *Casablanca* had been colorized. The same type of color errors show up on your fish, and the judges immediately notice when you use color-intensifying foods (such as spirulina) or hormones to artificially enhance your fish's appearance.

WARNING

Never attempt to dye your fish to increase their color for showing, or purchase artificially colored fish for showing. This practice consists of injecting colored pigments into a fish's body and is unethical. Some species such as the glassfish develop a disease known as lymphocystis that causes growths on their fins, so never put a fish's health at risk by partaking in cruel practices.

Fins

Fins are judged very strictly in a competition. Your entry should have all the fins that are standard for its species. If your fish should have one dorsal fin, one anal fin, two pectoral fins, one caudal fin, and two pelvic fins — then it had better have all seven fins. Some species of fish have an extra adipose fin. If your fish falls into this category, make sure it has one. If it doesn't, don't enter it. If your fish is missing its tail or dorsal fin, wait until the next competition, because this physical problem doesn't go over well with judges.

All the fins on your entry should be in good condition. Make sure there are no frayed or ragged fins to detract from your fish's natural beauty. The fins should be erect and of good color, not clamped or folded. To keep a show fish's fins in top-quality condition, keep the fish by itself prior to the competition so that more aggressive fish don't get a chance to tear or damage its fins.

Other causes of poor-quality fins include inadequate water conditions, netting, genetic problems, disease, and breeding spats. Make sure the water conditions in your show fish's tank always remain optimal so that the fish doesn't contract a fungal disease that can easily damage its fins.

TIP

To avoid having your entry's fins destroyed by netting, always use a plastic bag or cup to capture your fish.

Genetic problems are permanent, and the only thing you can do when you come across a deformity is to weed out that particular fish from your list of candidates for fish show competitions. Often, certain species of fish damage their pectoral fins when they fan eggs during breeding. For that very reason, don't breed your show fish before competition.

Fins are no different from any other physical attribute and are judged against an accepted norm. Many species of betta (*Betta splendens*) are bred for long-flowing fins, and judges expect fin lengths and sizes in the proper proportion to the fish's body size. All fins should have a symmetrical (even) look pleasing to the judge's eye. If one pectoral fin is quite a bit shorter than the other, your entry probably will lose some points for this deformity right off the bat.

Transporting Fish to and from a Show

Safe transportation to and from a show is important for your fish's overall health. You want to avoid stressing out or physically damaging your entry on the way to the show so that it has the best chance of remaining happy and healthy and can display its beautiful physical attributes to the best of its ability.

REMEMBER

Keep the following transportation considerations in mind:

>> **Look at the distance between your home and the show area on a map.** Give yourself plenty of time so that you don't have to rush to the show and hastily try to set up your entry tank at the last minute. Always allow plenty of time in case something should go wrong. Any unforeseen delay can become disastrous if you're forced to rush your entry in right before the judging begins.

>> **Drive your route to the competition ahead of time so that you know how long the route is and what the road conditions are like.** Do your test drive at the same time that you'll be driving to the show. For example, if the show is on a Saturday morning, make sure to do your test drive on a Saturday morning (and not during Friday evening rush hour). If the roads are rough, plan on adding a little more cushioning to your packing box. Check the predicted weather for the day of the competition, so that you're prepared in the event of heavy rain, extreme heat, frigid cold, or snow. These factors are especially crucial on longer trips.

>> **Transport your fish in a proper carrying case or tank to make sure that its journey is as comfortable as possible.** It really doesn't matter if you plan to show one fish or several fish as far as transportation containers are concerned. A good transportation tank can be a small plastic or acrylic aquarium that is insulated by a Styrofoam container. Or you can use a 5-gallon bucket with a tight-fitting lid.

>> **Place your transportation tank in something that insulates it and absorbs shocks while you're carrying it in your car.** A homemade wooden case that you place in the back seat or hatchback of your vehicle works well.

Avoid carrying your fish in the trunk or other uninsulated areas that can quickly overheat or chill the water during the trip.

WARNING

>> **Cover your containers with dark cloth to help calm your entry during transportation.** You should always use a battery-operated air pump to keep the water aerated.

Remembering to Have Fun

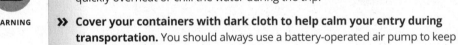

When you go to a fish show, have fun. Chat with fellow hobbyists so that you can make new friends, learn important aspects of fishkeeping from others, and catch up on the newest trends in the fishkeeping hobby.

If you win at a show . . . congratulations! If not, there is always the next show to look forward to. Enjoy the moment either way.

Joining an Aquarium Club

Joining an aquarium club allows you to meet hobbyists with a similar passion and share important information on a variety of topics such as equipment, fish care, tank setups, shows, and breeding. By participating in an aquarium club, you'll also be able to gain valuable information about new trends in the hobby.

Many fish clubs also put on their own fish shows for the local public or just for the members. Going to a club fish show is a great way to dive into that aspect of the hobby locally and gain a bit of experience and knowledge before attempting to show your aquatic pets at a large venue. You may also find other hobbyists who are willing to sell or trade good stock that you want.

You can find information on joining an aquarium club in several places, such as the following:

>> Look for fliers if your local pet shops has a bulletin board, or ask the staff about any groups.

>> Check with your local aquarium and zoo.

>> Search online. Here are a few sites to get you started:

- www.aquariumcoop.com/pages/local-aquarium-clubs

- www.aquariumdomain.com/adSocial/index.php/groups/category/31/united-states-clubs/

- http://fins.actwin.com/dir/clubs.php

Volunteering at an Aquarium or Zoo

Numerous studies have shown the many benefits to volunteering, which include living a longer life, gaining a good sense of purpose, and helping others. When you volunteer, you'll gain professional insight into how these organizations are helping to improve the health and wellbeing of fish and the environment. You can volunteer your time at a local aquarium or zoo. Many zoos have excellent aquarium sections. Check with aquarium clubs to see what other local places that feature volunteer opportunities.

REMEMBER

Volunteers are often hands-on with aquatic animals. Many are taught how to prepare food and feed the aquatic livestock. You may even get a chance to help with important aquatic research. Aquariums may carry the species of fish that you have in your home aquarium, so volunteering or visiting may help you gain valuable tips and tricks on how to best care for your aquatic pets.

If you don't have time to volunteer, you can always take the family and go visit a local aquarium. No matter the size, these places have a lot to offer. Who knows? You may find many interesting places along the way. I remember taking a trip to a small aquarium in New Mexico many years ago and ended up finding an amazing fish shop along the way.

Writing an Article

You may have a creative side. You don't even need a degree in journalism or English to write an article to share valuable information with other hobbyists. If you want to see yourself in print and make a little money on the side, then writing articles for fish publications may be just what you're looking for.

Read all the fish magazines you can to get a good idea of how the articles are written. Visit the magazines' websites for their submission standards like word length, type of file submission, and subject matter. Some magazines pay by word length, whereas others pay a flat fee. You can also get paid extra for submitting quality fish photos that the magazine can use to accompany your article.

After you know the submission rules, pick a subject. I learned a long time ago that it's best to write what you know about. Don't choose a species or system that you're unfamiliar with. Instead, write about the fish that you know and your personal experiences or pen an article on the basics of setting up a tank. The possibilities are endless.

Getting published in magazines isn't as difficult as it sounds. Most pet magazines are happy to take articles from unpublished authors as long as your article is written well and covers a subject that the magazine is interested in or hasn't recently published.

REMEMBER

When writing a manuscript, make sure you edit, edit, and edit. Make sure what you've written is accurate and polished. Ask a friend to proofread it before you email it to the magazine's submission email.

If you still feel you need a bit of help getting started, consider taking a basic writing class at your local community college. This type of class is often offered during the summer.

Setting Up a Tank for a Worthy Cause

You can start a new aquarium for a wide number of worthy causes. Doing so can benefit others and maybe even inspire a future hobbyist. Some organizations will be willing to help you pay for part or all of the cost of setting up an aquarium for them. Other organizations may not have the funds to pitch in, so be prepared to spend your own money. You can always talk to local pet shops that are often willing to donate or reduce the price of equipment for a worthy cause.

Here are a few places you may be able to set up a tank:

>> **At a school:** What better legacy to leave kids than the gift of your hobby? A great way is set up an aquarium in a school. Often a school will find room for an aquarium in a hallway or even in a classroom. While you're there, you can arrange to have a class watch and help you. My own interest in the hobby began to really solidify after I spent months watching fish swimming happily around in an aquarium that was set up at the main entrance of my elementary school. Contact the principal of your local school and see what you can arrange.

>> **At a local senior center:** What better way to liven up a senior center and making seniors smile more than having a nice aquarium to admire. Many senior centers would love to have a tankful of fish that their residents could enjoy year-round. Volunteer to set one up with big species of fish that everyone can see and enjoy. You even can agree to maintain the tank on a monthly basis. Contact the manager to see what you can set up.

>> **At a local library:** Many children still love to get their hands on a good book. Setting up an aquarium at a local library is a great way to share the hobby with youngsters who are itching to learn. Talk to the head librarian or library board to put forth your proposal.

Sharing Your Love of Aquariums and Science with Others

As hobbyists, it's important we plant the seeds for future generations to carry on fishkeeping. By taking the time to get others involved in the hobby, it ensures that fishkeeping remains an important part of the pet–keeping industry.

Everyone can benefit from an aquarium. Improved health and relaxation are important to everyone's wellbeing. Here are a few ways you can share your love of fishkeeping:

» **Take your children or grandchildren to local aquariums, zoos, lakes, and rivers and see what aquatic life they can discover.** The more they learn about aquarium keeping and fish in their natural environment, the more willing they'll become to pass on their newfound information to others.

» **If you own a business, set up an aquarium in the waiting area.** An aquarium can help bolster the happiness of your customers and bring in new clients. I used to go out of my way to eat lunch at a restaurant that had a big aquarium in the dining room simply because I needed to relax on my lunch break.

» **Volunteer at a school or library and teach kids simple science ideas such chemistry, biology, math, and geography.** Water temperature, minerals, and pH can help a child learn simple chemistry. Biology can show kids how fish swim and cope while gaining oxygen from a watery environment. Get out a ruler and measure your tank and help them figure out how many fish can live in a specific area safely if you want them to do a little math. Help children with geography by finding the country of origin for each new species of fish they identify. Every element of a home aquarium can be a shared learning experience.

» **Include a child when you're setting up an aquarium and talk about every aspect of what you're doing.** Use simple terms and tell how a small aquarium system's components all must work together to provide a proper environment. Explain how good bacteria help to stabilize the water and how the plants and fish all interact and effect their environment.

» **Teach children responsibility.** What better way to teach kids about responsibility than by allowing them to own an aquarium? Let your children or grandchildren help you set up a tank in their home or yours and teach them how to maintain it. A basic aquarium tends to be a bit more forgiving of mistakes than a dog or cat, so give them a simple-and-easy-to-maintain system like a freshwater aquarium.

Chapter **23**

Advancing Your Hobby: Other Types of Aquarium Systems

After you get the hang of keeping freshwater tropical fish, you may begin to wonder what else is out there. Not all water is equal, and some aquatic bodies are *brackish* (slightly salty) or fully saltwater. Different fish, plants, and invertebrates live in these waters. Brackish systems are easy to set up once you have mastered the basics. Marine systems are a little more difficult.

This chapter looks at a brackish system and some common marine setups and explains how to start them. Although I recommend these particular setups, they aren't your only options. I just give you the basics to help you get started.

Trying a Brackish Aquarium Setup

The water in a *brackish aquarium* lies somewhere between fresh and marine in salt content. Natural brackish systems fluctuate from season to season due to rains and evaporation, and brackish fish are well adapted to surviving. Here are steps to starting a simple brackish river setup:

1. Clean out your tank with fresh water.

2. Install a heater and a canister filter.

3. Add small gravel to the bottom of the tank and slope it higher on one side.

4. Take large rocks and built a couple of rock caves.

5. Add water and a dechlorinator to the tank.

6. Add 1 to 2 tablespoons of marine salt per gallon and monitor it with a hydrometer or a refractometer.

TIP

   Keep adding it until the salinity reaches 1.005 to 1.010.

7. Start the heater and filter and set the temperature to 80 to 84 degrees Fahrenheit.

8. Add the lighting and then let the tank run for a day and then add anubius and hairgrass.

9. Add a few bumblebee gobies and/or glassfish.

The equipment for a brackish system is similar to that for a freshwater setup, but only specific plants can tolerate a brackish system. The salt content in brackish systems can be achieved easily using synthetic marine mix in a ratio of 1 gallon of saltwater to every 2 gallons of freshwater. Your tank will basically end up being one-third saltwater and two-thirds freshwater.

You don't have as many choices with brackish fish as you do for other systems because few species in the wild can survive in an environment that is constantly changing. The good news is that brackish fish are very hardy and easy to feed, and many are very exciting to watch due to their high activity levels. Several plants work well in the brackish tank, including hornwort (*Ceratophyllum demersum*), eelgrass (*Vallisneria gigantea*), and corkscrew val (*Vallisneria asiatica*).

Considering a Marine Aquarium System

Marine or *saltwater systems,* not surprisingly, require saltwater. You see marine fish on scuba and underwater television programs. The most popular of these fish includes the coral reef species often found living in close proximity to various *invertebrates* (animals without backbones). Saltwater fish are often very colorful and beautiful. They can also be extremely expensive.

REMEMBER

You obtain the saltwater in a marine system by mixing fresh water with a manufactured salt mix available at fish shops. A good filtration system is important in marine tanks to keep oxygen levels high and ammonia levels low. Marine fish have lower tolerance to ammonia than freshwater species do, and an inadequate filter soon leads to disaster in a saltwater tank.

Identifying the types of marine systems

There are three main types of marine aquariums:

>> **Coldwater marine:** Many tanks of this type house animals such as lobsters and rockfish that are native to colder ocean areas.

>> **Tropical marine:** These heated tanks generally contain fish native to coral reef areas, such as tangs, clownfish, and damsels.

>> **Reef tank:** Some reef tanks contain only invertebrates, such as anemones, scallops, and organisms growing on live rock. *Live rock* is rock that has live beneficial organisms attached to it that provide food sources for your fish and help keep the water clean.

You can set up a saltwater system in a variety of ways (see Figure 23-1 for one example). Invertebrates are a little more difficult to care for, so if you do set up a saltwater system, you may want to start with a fish-only tank.

Gaining some experience with a freshwater system is a great way to prepare yourself to enter the marine side. A beginner *can* maintain a successful marine tank, but the lessons are expensive. I see many new hobbyists become disheartened because they start out with a marine setup that's too much to handle. If you have a friend experienced in marine systems, ask him for advice — he may be able to get you started successfully.

Many marine fish are social time bombs waiting to explode all over the other fish in your tank. In fact, saltwater fish can be downright rude. Most community freshwater fish have reached a state of enlightenment or something like that and are pretty cool with each other.

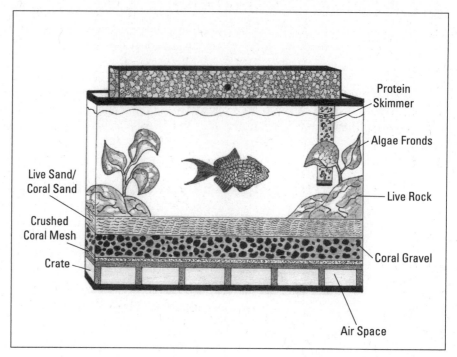

FIGURE 23-1:
A plenum marine system is a typical saltwater aquarium setup.

Protein Skimmer

Algae Fronds

Live Sand/Coral Sand

Live Rock

Crushed Coral Mesh

Crate

Coral Gravel

Air Space

© John Wiley & Sons, Inc.

Setting up a simple marine aquarium

Here are some steps to set up a basic saltwater aquarium. Check out the updated version of *Saltwater Aquariums for Dummies* by Gregory Skomal (John Wiley & Sons, Inc.) that walks you through the entire marine aquarium process in more detail.

1. **Rinse the tank with clean water.**

   I recommend a minimum 55-gallon tank for a beginning aquarium.

2. **Add a good canister filter, heater, and a protein skimmer to remove organic waste.**

3. **Add aragonite or dolomite to the bottom of the tank as a substrate.**

   It helps to maintain the pH around 8.3.

4. **Add shells and other marine rock.**

5. **Fill the tank and follow the directions on the package by adding marine salt and monitoring it with a refractometer.**

   Keep adding it until the salinity reaches 1.020 to 1.024 for a fish-only tank.

REMEMBER

6. Start the equipment and set the heater so the water reaches a temperature between 75 and 82 degrees Fahrenheit.

7. Add marine LED or halogen lighting.

8. Include a small group of yellowtail blue damsels.

9. After the tank is cycled, add more damsels and green chromis.

Setting up a coldwater fish-only marine system

A coldwater marine system is one that operates successfully at below-normal room temperatures. This type of system often houses deep-water species or those found in rocky shore environments where the temperature and light fluctuate constantly. These creatures are well suited to a changing environment. Here is an easy way to start your coldwater marine system:

1. Set up a 55-gallon tank and stand.

   I recommend an acrylic aquarium for this system because it keeps the tank cooler than glass. Make sure that the tank and stand is set up away from direct sunlight that can cause the tank to overheat.

2. Add aragonite aquarium sand mixed with small rocks to the bottom of the tank.

3. Place some dry reef rocks in clumps and around the tank to make an interesting design.

4. Add an aquarium chiller to keep the temperature cool.

   Generally, this system should stay between 50 and 65 degrees Fahrenheit.

5. Put a hang-on-tank protein skimmer on the aquarium that removes dissolved organic compounds before they add to the overall bioload of the tank.

6. Add a canister filter to the aquarium.

7. Add cool water and check the salinity and pH.

   Adjust it with marine salt until it has a specific gravity between 1.024 and 1.026. Adjust the pH to between 8.1 and 8.4.

8. Start all your equipment.

9. **Put a hood with LED full spectrum lighting on the tank.**

10. **Add bottled live nitrifying bacteria to the water.**

   Follow the manufacturer's instructions.

11. **Let the aquarium run for a few days until the water is in the range of what the chiller was set to.**

   I suggest the fish be a mix of zebra gobies and peaceful blue damsels.

Comparing Freshwater and Saltwater Systems

Consider the following pros and cons to marine and freshwater aquariums. Many hobbyists are happy keeping only freshwater systems, whereas others plunge into the brackish and marine worlds. You can find plenty of information in books, periodicals, pet stores, and on the Internet.

Adaptability

Freshwater aquarium fish originally came from rivers and lakes that are constantly in motion and affected by changing temperatures and conditions.

A large majority of freshwater aquatic pets are bred for the fishkeeping industry, but they're still naturally resistant to fluctuations in their environment due to genetic adaptation. This doesn't mean you should keep freshwater fish in less than excellent aquarium conditions, but freshwater fish will generally be a bit more forgiving of mistakes than marine species.

Marine species are much more sensitive to even the slightest fluctuations in their aquarium conditions. This doesn't mean that they'll automatically die the second your water temperature drops one degree. However, if the marine species tank doesn't remain consistent in temperature and *salinity* (amount of salt in the water), you could easily lose an entire tankful of fish. If possible, try to purchase tank-bred fish because they're less stressed due to not having long shipping times and excessive distribution chain handling.

Availability

Finding live plants for a freshwater aquarium is generally much easier than finding invertebrates for a marine tank in local stores. (Refer to the nearby sidebar "Considering marine invertebrates" for more information.) However, you can easily purchase marine invertebrates on the Internet. You may have to wait for certain species of marine invertebrates and fish to become available as divers bring them in. Thankfully, more hobbyists and aquarium industry folks are beginning to find ways to breed more species of marine fish such as dottybacks, damsels, clownfish, and gobies.

Cost

On average, marine fish are much more expensive than freshwater species. Compare a two-dollar guppy to a queen triggerfish costing several hundred dollars. A large marine tank could be *extremely* expensive to stock, and your wallet takes a huge hit if anything goes wrong. However, most aquarium hobbyists think marine species are well worth the extra money.

Beauty and friendliness

Marine fish are generally more colorful and larger than freshwater species. If you really like eye-popping colors in your aquarium, the marine side of the hobby will really dazzle you with brilliant yellow tangs, vibrant parrotfish, and many other spectacular species of saltwater fish. You generally can't keep as many marine fish in the same space as freshwater fish because the marine fish are larger and generally require more room to move around. Marine fish tend to be more aggressive than freshwater fish.

Equipment

Substrate and equipment are a bit more expensive for the marine aquarium. Freshwater gravel is less expensive than marine dolomite, and freshwater lighting costs less than the full-spectrum lighting of a marine reef system.

5

The Part of Tens

Look at cool aquarium tools that help you take care of your aquatic fishy friends and plants.

Buy the good digital stuff to monitor your aquarium system with ease.

Avoid common pitfalls and problems to make sure your fish remain healthy and the envy of all your other fishkeeping friends.

Understand weird aquarium science so that you know what to watch out for.

Jot down a few useful aquatic New Year's resolutions that help you maintain the perfect system and avoid serious pitfalls.

Chapter **24**

Ten Cool Aquarium Gadgets

E veryone loves to play with gadgets, right? Aquariums have useful gadgets that you can use to make your hobby easier. Most gadgets are inexpensive and are available in most pet stores and on the Internet. Here are a few examples of what you can use on your aquarium keeping adventure.

Aquarium Claws (Those Handy Picker-Upper Doodads) to Move Decor

An aquarium claw really isn't as menacing as its name might imply. This little plastic claw (such as aquatic tongs) is a handy tool to use in the home aquarium. It makes moving tank decorations as simple as spending mega bucks at the fish store. A button on the end of the handle closes the claw around an object as you depress it. After moving the item, simply release the button to release the grip.

The long handle on this device allows you to reach almost any area of a standard-sized aquarium without getting your hands wet. Keeping your hands (which may be covered in germs, dirt, or household chemicals) out of the tank whenever possible is always a good idea. Other good uses for this tool include inserting plants into substrate, grabbing unwanted objects from the tank (marbles, plant debris, and so on), and removing dead fish. At an average cost of less than 20 dollars, you really can't go wrong with this marvelous little gadget.

WARNING

Never use a claw to retrieve live fish from your aquarium because it can frighten them, injure them, and ruin their slime coat.

Algae Cleaners to Keep Dry

One simple way to remove excess *algae* (the green, alien-looking glop that is blocking your view) from the aquarium glass is to use an algae scraper. Several types are available, including the following:

>> **Two-way magnet system:** Magnetic scrapers are more practical, can easily reach more difficult areas, and are also more suitable for larger aquariums. A magnet attached to a scrubber goes on the inside of the tank and an exterior handle with a magnet draws it along the aquarium wall as you slowly move it. Just remember that any magnetic scraper that you buy will have a maximum glass thickness rating.

>> **Long stick with attached scrub pad/sponge:** You simply slide up and down the interior glass.

>> **A glove type:** It fits over your entire hand.

Stick and glove scrapers are good for small tanks, but they can disturb decorations, can be difficult to use, and can frighten fish to the point of having a stroke and going belly up.

REMEMBER

Know the thickness of your aquarium walls so that you can purchase the correct scraper for your system if you use the magnet system.

Sponge and stick cleaners can be used on any type of tank. Algae gloves can be used on both as well. When it comes to blade and magnetic scrapers, not all products can be used on acrylic and/or glass so check the directions carefully if it uses blades. For example, the Flipper algae scraper has one blade for glass and one for acrylic that can be switched out depending on what type of tank you own. This product is also good for removing hard algae.

Although algae can be beneficial as a natural food source, an overgrowth can quickly turn your crystal-clear water into mushy pea soup. Allowing a small amount of green algae to remain on rocks and decorations is okay, but a tank that is excessively overrun with "the green terror" is unsightly at best.

Extendable Fish Nets, the Long and Short of It

Fish come in a wide variety of different shapes and sizes. Therefore, aquarium manufacturers were kind enough to create nets to match the individual physical characteristics of whatever uncooperative aquatic friend you happen to be chasing around the tank.

If you buy one of those complete aquarium kits in a box, it will probably come with a small net. After enjoying your aquarium for a few months, you may begin to get the idea that one net just isn't going to cut it. Owning one net is kind of like a fisherman who expects to catch everything with one size of hook. Aquarium nets aren't expensive, so make sure to buy several sizes to suit the full-grown fish and baby fish (fry) in your system.

Extendable fish nets have a telescopic handle that allow you to reach different depths with the same net. This benefit keeps you from plunging your hands into taller tanks and gives you the option of easily catching fish in a variety of different sized tanks. I always try to buy lightweight nylon nets to avoid pulling on fish scales and models that have a hook or loop on the end so they can hang out to dry like the laundry I forgot about last week.

A Tool Box for Storing Stuff

If you're like me, your fish supplies are probably pretty well spread out along the entire length of the house, garage, and backyard. When your family starts complaining because they found fish food in the flour bin and air-line tubing in their underwear drawers, then it's probably time to purchase a storage box.

A plastic tool container or tackle box works wonders for keeping aquarium equipment, fish food, chemicals, test kits, nets, and other supplies all in one neat little place. And you can carry it from tank to tank if you happen to have more than one aquarium. I prefer to buy waterproof plastic boxes that have removable trays on top. These trays can hold small items like thermometers and medications while I store the bulkier items underneath.

Depending on the supplies you have on hand, you may need to purchase more than one box. I like to have an extra box just to keep a variety of fish foods clean and dry.

Most retail chain and sporting goods stores have a good selection in stock.

Light Timers for the Win

To keep your fish from feeling like the sun has suddenly decided to crash into the earth every morning when you turn on the lights, an automatic timer is a good item to control the lighting in your aquarium system. Light timers can provide a natural day and night cycle for your aquarium fish and can save you money if you forget to turn the tank lights off like me every once in a while.

These units can be set to turn on and off at specific times of the day and can even be programmed to be off on certain days if you want. Many units store your settings in case of a power failure that may occur when you turn your microwave and 30 other appliances on at the same time.

Another cool feature of many light timers is the ability to dim the lights in your tank to set the right ambience for spawning and to control algae.

Aquarium Sealer (Flood Insurance)

If you wake up one morning and find that your living room floor resembles a kiddy pool, then chances are one of your aquariums may be leaking. No hobbyist should be without a tube of aquarium-safe silicone sealer in case this catastrophe strikes. Besides, aquarium sealer is cool and squishy and fun to apply.

Unfortunately, in order to repair a leak, you must first drain and dry the tank to allow the sealer to set properly. But in the long run, it's also better to spend a couple of dollars on a tube of sealer instead of several hundred dollars on a new tank. Once in a while, factory sealer will fail due to age, weather conditions, and high or uneven water pressure. So make sure that you're always prepared. (Or buy extra flood insurance.)

REMEMBER

Every product has its limits, and a huge crack in a tank wall won't hold long under water pressure, even with the use of aquarium sealer. Only use sealer to repair pin leaks or to replace small spots of factory sealer that have been damaged or worn away.

Aquascaping Tools to Make You a Star

Aquascaping (also referred to *gardenscaping*) is a fun way to maintain a healthy aquarium system using live plants, rocks, and wood to create little aquatic worlds to escape to when your boss or annoying family members decide to come over and hang around. Aquascaping has few rules, and each tank can be decorated to suit individual tastes from natural landscapes to exotic temples. Aquarium plants can help to reduce algae, provide sanctuary and a natural habitat for your fish, and improve chemical filtration. See Chapters 5 and 16 for more good information on aquascaping.

In order to aquascape properly, these tools can help you get started:

>> **Long planting tweezers:** For adding and removing plants, wood, and small rocks from a tank, doing small grooming jobs, and removing unwanted debris.

>> **Curved aquarium scissors:** For pruning dead plant leaves and for trimming low grass type plants.

>> **A substrate spatula:** It has a flat wedge on the end of a handle and is a great tool to gently move substrate back into place after your fish have decided to spit it all into one giant mountain in the middle of the tank.

TIP

I like to purchase stainless steels tools to avoid rusting. Make sure that you rinse your tools off and dry them before putting them away, and they'll last a lifetime.

Digital Water Testing Makes It Easy

Keeping track of the pH in your aquarium is an important aspect of maintaining healthy fish and plants. Aquarium species come from a large variety of different habits in the wild so they have different pH requirements to mimic their natural environment and to help keep them from becoming sickly.

Digital units to test pH come in an assortment of styles including compact designs that fit right into your pocket. Other units come in large-screen tablet form that can sit on an aquarium stand or hang on the wall. These units make it easy to monitor your water conditions on a daily basis.

WARNING

Remember to never use your aquarium tools for other household chores because residual cleaning chemicals left in the bucket can kill your fish.

Automatic Gravel Cleaners Do the Job

Many aquariums need electrical outlet space for one or two heater plugs, one or two light plugs, one to three air pump plugs, power filter or powerhead plugs, and more, depending on your setup. As you can see, an electrical setup can quickly outnumber your available wall plugs. A good multi-outlet plug or bar with a built-in circuit breaker can take care of this problem.

Aquarium gravel cleaners are a great way to keep the substrate in your aquarium clean. These cleaners pick up dirt and uneaten food in your tank (that can destroy your aquarium system balance as they start to decompose), and can reduce the strain on your aquarium filter at the same time. Keeping the environment clean helps to maintain consistent water chemistry by removing unwanted agents so that your fish aren't swimming around in something that resembles the inside of a garbage disposal.

Suction tubes that you have to self prime can be a bit of a hassle, so automatic cleaners can make the job easier for you. Electric and battery-operated vacuums are a cinch to start, can remove debris by trapping it in a filter without disturbing the substrate, and can also remove and replace tank water. I recommend vacuuming the substrate to remove debris at least once a week.

Aquarium Smart Controllers (Spy on Your Fish)

Controllers can take care of almost every aquarium need so that you can spend more quality time spying on your fish instead of constantly monkeying around with equipment until your hair becomes frazzled and your fish think that you're the most annoying owner on the face of the planet. Two main types are available:

>> Digital heat controllers are a cool way to keep your water temperature consistent. These units have an easy-to-read display and set the temperature when you plug your heater into them. Some models have dual time cycle settings that allow your fish and plants to have different temperatures depending on their needs so you don't have to constantly fiddle with knobs and take contortionist classes in order to read the numbers found on standard units.

>> Automatic feeders are another handy gadget that can dispense the right amount of food on a daily basis so you never have to worry about starving or overfeeding your fish to the point they're floating around your tank like inflated balloons.

Keep your eyes peeled for new items that are constantly entering the market so you can spend more quality time watching your fish instead of wasting all your time messing around with outdated equipment.

Chapter **25**

Ten Ways to Kill Your Fish without Even Trying

You strive to be an excellent fishkeeper, but sometimes life gets in the way, and you overlook the obvious.

The good news is you can easily remedy most mistakes if you know what to do when problems arise. You don't have to be Jacques Cousteau to know how to handle the problems in this chapter. Keep reading to discover how to avoid common pitfalls and still look cool and informed in front of your friends at the same time.

Go Away on Vacation and Forget Them

Okay, on your last day at Disneyland, you call your boss and sadly inform him that all the airplanes in California have broken down, and you're being forced to stay for an extra week. No problem. But what about your aquatic friends?

TIP

Before going on vacation, make sure you have a reliable friend who can continue to care for your pets just in case you're gone longer than originally planned. Always leave enough food with your friend to cover a time period longer than your intended stay, just in case you're delayed in getting back home.

You can choose to add equipment such as an ammonia badge to send an alert when there is a water problem. A small wireless home camera can be mounted near your tank to alert your phone or your pet sitter's phone if there are problems.

Try to find someone reliable who can turn the lights on in the morning and off at night for you (or buy an automatic timer). If you're going to be gone for an extremely long time, make sure you have someone who can dechlorinate water and top off your tank if necessary. Leave your number with that person in case he has any questions.

Another option is to purchase tablets or automatic feeders that dispense food to your fish while you're gone.

Play Doctor without a License

I once had an aunt who had a pill to cure every real or imaginary ailment known to man. The inside of her purse resembled a large pharmacy. The same ideas that are bad for humans are usually bad for fish too. As I discuss in Chapter 11, when doctoring your fish, don't overdo it.

Many new hobbyists tend to overmedicate their tanks at the first sign of disease. Many people learned this pattern during childhood. If I thought chicken soup and aspirin would help cure my fish, I'd probably dump that into the tank as well. But don't try that — it's a bad idea.

You can avoid a large number of diseases through good maintenance such as frequent water changes. (Refer to Chapter 14 for more about changing your aquarium water.) Avoid the temptation to pour medicine after medicine into your tank in hopes you'll find the right cure. Seek the advice of an advanced hobbyist or tropical fish merchant who can help you pinpoint your problem. If medication is necessary, always follow the manufacturer's instructions to the letter and use a hospital tank if possible.

Give Your Cat a Sushi Bar

Have you ever wondered why many cat foods are shaped like fish? Well, it's no accident. In your cat's tiny and distorted little brain, your new aquarium can be considered a free sushi bar. If your tank isn't covered properly, your cat can sneak in for a quick snack while you wonder why his food is collecting dust in his bowl.

REMEMBER

Take my word for it: No amount of pleading or yelling will keep some cats from this habit if they decide that fresh seafood is their favorite. Make sure that the hood you buy for your new aquarium fits properly and snugly. If you happen to own a particularly strong or fat cat, weigh the hood down with books or some other heavy objects so that your frisky feline can't pry it or flip it open. Furthermore, make sure you don't have any furniture or shelves close by that your cat can use to get on top of the tank.

Stuff Your Fish with Seven-Course Meals

Many different varieties of fish food are on the market. A good combination of flake, frozen, and live foods helps to promote good health in your wet pets. However, you need to realize that a fish's stomach is no larger than its eye, and overfeeding will rapidly foul the tank and eventually lead to disease or death. (I discuss these feeding options in greater detail in Chapter 11.)

Fish don't require seven-course meals each day to survive. If your fish are beginning to resemble a doughboy and are constantly getting stuck between rocks, then it's time to cut down on the chow. Research your individual species and feed them accordingly.

Mix Apples and Oranges

While browsing your local fish shop, you find yourself suddenly becoming attached to a large cichlid who looks as if it has been feeding on instant grow flakes for a decade. You automatically figure that this toughie will provide leadership skills for your unmotivated guppies. Within an hour of adding your new leader to the tank, you're surprised to find that all your guppies have vanished.

Mixing apples and oranges may be great for a summer fruit salad, but it doesn't work in the home aquarium. Check with your local dealer if you're unsure about the compatibility of any species.

Add Too Many Fish (the Shoehorn Syndrome)

Adding just one more fish to your home aquarium can be tempting. Nearly all hobbyists fall prey to this Shoehorn Syndrome at one time or another. If your aquarium resembles a phone booth–packing competition, then you've probably overstepped the aquarium's capacity. Remember, overcrowding can lead to bad water conditions, which can be deadly.

Don't Do Your Homework

If you want to find out more about any subject, you need to do a little research. Skilled fishkeepers do their homework before setting up a new type of system, and they investigate specific habitat requirements prior to purchasing unknown species of fish. Isn't that one of the reasons that you bought this cool book?

The Internet, your library, tropical fish magazines, your local fishkeeping club, and your nearby pet store also can provide you with a lot of extra good information that can keep you informed about the newest developments in the fishkeeping hobby.

Let the Neighbor's Unruly Kid Play with Your Fish

A mischievous kid can be every fishkeeper's nightmare. This is the same kid who always shows up at dinnertime, skateboards through your petunias, and in later years, escorts your only daughter to the senior prom.

A home aquarium is often a prime target for the neighbor's unruly kid who drops all sorts of interesting objects into the tank, such as your cat, coins, sticks, and peanut butter sandwiches. Your fish won't appreciate these offerings. Even worse, they can prove to be lethal as well. Prohibit young children from touching your aquariums without proper supervision and quickly check your tank for foreign objects at least once a day.

Become a Hypochondriac Hobbyist

Before you know it, whether you're a new hobbyist or a veteran, you'll be emotionally attached to your fish. The more you bond with them, the more you tend to overpamper them. Checking in on your fish every 30 minutes, constantly fiddling around with the equipment, and rearranging the decorations in order to achieve the perfect environment just isn't good for the fish. Maintain your aquariums, enjoy your fish, but don't fuss too much.

Buy Used or Cheap Equipment

Be careful about any used equipment you want to purchase and always test it if possible before making the final purchase. When buying new stuff from a local dealer, make sure to purchase the best equipment that your budget allows. Poorly made or worn-out equipment will inevitably lead to disaster down the road.

Be wary of old electrical aquarium pumps, hoods, and heaters at the neighbor's garage sale that look worn or have frayed wires. Don't get me wrong; I've purchased some good aquarium equipment at garage sales, but as the old saying goes, in most cases, you get what you pay for.

Chapter **26**

Ten Scientific Fish Laws

From time to time during your wonderful adventures as an aquarium hobbyist, you may notice strange phenomena in and around your fish tanks that even modern science can't explain. Seasoned hobbyists discover through experience that these strange occurrences actually have very simple explanations. Here are some examples of those strange fish laws that plague all hobbyists from time to time and how you can deal with them.

The Fish Law of Thermodynamics

The fish law of thermodynamics states that all heat in a house flows directly into your aquarium at all times. Extreme overhead house lighting also helps to turn your wet pet's home into a sauna.

Your overheating tank immediately absorbs window light so that the remaining sections of your house will convince the local astronomer that there is a black hole in the neighborhood.

TIP

To take care of these particular problems, you need to place your aquarium in an area with plenty of air movement and a consistent room temperature. Check to make sure your aquarium heater is functioning properly, and don't set your aquarium up near doors, ultrabright overhead ceiling lighting, heating vents, or windows. Remember that extreme temperature fluctuations can cause illness and death. Chapters 3 and 6 discuss the different stand placement and heaters to consider when heating your aquarium.

The Fish Law of Metamorphosis

The fish law of metamorphosis states that any fish in your tank, when given the right opportunity, will be able to instantly morph into any shape necessary to escape from the aquarium. My own fish have morphed into the shape of a French fry in order to squeeze through an air-line hole. I saw a guppy turn itself into something that resembled a tiny waffle once to squeeze through a tiny open space by the aquarium heater. The second part of this law states that after escape, this same fish will morph into either a carpet dust ball or a kitty snack.

TIP

To fix this problem, make sure that all holes in the top of the tank lid are completely covered, especially if you have species of fish that are especially prone to jumping out of aquariums. If there are small holes left after the hood and equipment are installed, cut a few small pieces of thin Plexiglas to size and attach it with aquarium silicone to seal the hole. Chapter 6 provides more information on how to make your hood escape proof.

The Fish Law of Motion

The fish law of motion states that any sluggish or ill-looking fish will instantly be able to dash madly at twice the speed of light when a net is inserted into the aquarium. The fish will always move directly at right angles to the net's strategic placement — a maneuver that will leave you with wet clothes, a lot of frustration, a tank full of displaced decorations, torn-up live plants, and piles of gravel.

TIP

To avoid this problem, try adding a little food to coax your fish to the top of the tank when you need to catch one. Gently lift out large aquarium decorations, such as rocks, before you attempt to capture your fish. Doing so provides you with more space and maneuverability.

The Fish Law of Anti-Matter

The fish law of anti-matter states that fish are the only animals on earth that are capable of hiding their own body matter after death so that they can never be found. On a good day, Sherlock Holmes wouldn't be able to find a dead guppy in a 1-gallon bowl because of this law.

REMEMBER

Having a good filtration in your tank is important; make sure you frequently change the water because of this unusual problem. If you can't locate a dead fish, then a buildup of waste will occur and cause water fouling and disease.

TIP

Keep track of the number of fish you have so that you can look for any that have been missing. Fish often die beneath caves, rocks, plants, and other decorations, because they go there to get away from their tankmates when they're ill or old. Try to avoid decorations with tiny holes that lead to the inside of the piece so that your fish won't be able to go in and get stuck or die unnoticed. An inexpensive ammonia sensor can be purchased and placed inside the tank to help alert you when ammonia levels rise to a high level so that you have to respond before disaster strikes.

The Fish Law of Nutrition

The fish law of nutrition states that your fish will eat all food that is unfit for aquatic consumption, so make sure that you routinely check your tank for foreign objects that may have fallen into the water. The second part of this law states that any uneaten food will fall directly into an area that the human eye can't see. Because of this problem, it's important to feed your fish small meals several times per day, instead of dumping half a can of flake food into the tank all at once.

TIP

Watch what they eat and stop feeding them immediately when they show no interest in the food. And don't worry, your fish won't go into a coma if they have to skip a meal, because it's common in their natural environment. Keep the tank clean by vacuuming on a consistent basis to avoid buildup of debris caused by uneaten food.

The Fish Law of Company

The fish law of company states that all aquarium fish lethargically lurk in a corner or disappear behind decorations at the exact moment when your visitors arrive to see them. The fish will return to their normal activity level after dark, even if they aren't nocturnal.

REMEMBER

If you want to successfully show your fish to your company, arrange to have your friends come over at a time when you'd normally give your fish a special treat. Doing so allows your friends to get a glimpse of your prize pets. If you wiggle your fingers near the glass, you may be surprised how your fish love to come and investigate.

The Fish Law of Potential Energy

The fish law of potential energy states that a fish's energy can be stored indefinitely and will only be released when the aquarium hood is opened and a direct escape route is in sight.

REMEMBER

To avoid this problem, make sure that your aquarium hood fits securely. Close any holes that the hood doesn't completely cover. Flip to Chapter 6 for more detailed information about hoods.

The Fish Law of Psychic Felines

The fish law of psychic felines states that any cat within a hundred miles of your aquarium will be able to zero in on, sneak through an open window or door to get at, and physically engulf any fish that has jumped from your tank — before you can cross the room to save it. Your wet pets are fair game, so make sure to keep a distrustful eye on any other pets that are living in the same household or neighborhood.

REMEMBER

These ways can keep your fish safe from prowling felines:

>> Make sure the tank covers the entire top of the stand with no leftover area for them to jump up.

>> Don't put your tank too close to furniture, shelves, or other objects that your cat can use to get on top of the tank.

>> Don't draw unwanted attention by lifting your cat to show them the fish. Doing so is like waving donuts in front of me the first thing in the morning.

The Fish Law of Aggression

The fish law of aggression states that any two fish can show aggression toward each other without just cause at any given moment of time. For this reason, it's vital that you keep track of your fish's social habits to make sure that a minor scuffle doesn't end up turning into a major war. Rearranging a few tank decorations every few months helps break down pre-established territories and reduce potential aggression.

TIP

Feed your fish at different areas of the tank periodically so fish that occupy a certain space don't try to claim it all.

The Fish Law of Time

The fish law of time states that a fish will be prone to contract an illness the day before your vacation starts or at the beginning of a holiday weekend when all the pet shops are closed.

That's why it's important to have extra medication on hand for such emergencies. Training a friend, neighbor, or relative in the basics of fish disease and treatment comes in handy if you happen to be on vacation when disaster strikes. If one isn't available, contact a pet or house sitter. Instruct the employee on how to take care of your specific species of fish while you're gone. Chapter 11 gives you the lowdown on taking care of sick fish.

Chapter **27**

Ten Aquatic New Year's Resolutions

"**I**, (state your name), promise to do the following in the new year:

Feed the Fish the Good Stuff

I promise to feed my fish properly and throw away the cans of food that have been in the attic since the Gulf War. I promise to feed a proper diet for each species.

TIP

To make sure you're feeding your fish what they want, research your species to see the types of foods such as flake, worms, bits of vegetables, and other exciting edibles that will help them thrive. Chapter 10 can help you get started.

Clean the Tank Frequently

I promise to clean my tank regularly and maintain it properly with frequent water changes and an aquarium vacuum on a regular basis.

REMEMBER

Your tank is your fish's house. Cleanliness is next to godliness. I recommend vacuuming your tank at least once a week. Change 20 percent of the water every two weeks. See Chapter 12 for more information on maintenance.

Reduce Celibacy

I promise to buy my ten male swordtails several females and keep the correct mix of males and females in the tank (with standard exceptions, such as the betta).

REMEMBER

Make sure you know how many males and females will cohabit peacefully for your species before you buy. Chapters 19 and 20 provide some insight into breeding your fish.

Remove Algae

I promise to remove excess algae from the aquarium glass once a week and to maintain good water conditions and proper lighting.

TIP

Keeping your water conditions pristine and proper feeding are the best defenses against algae. See Chapters 10 and 16 for more information on feeding and algae control.

Monitor Filter Mediums

I promise to replace clogged filter pads and change them when needed. I also promise to follow the manufacturer's instructions on all filter mediums I use.

REMEMBER

Filter mediums vary from filter to filter, so make sure you ask your local dealer about maintenance on a particular medium if you are unsure. See Chapter 6 for more information on equipment.

Turn on the Lights

I promise to turn on my aquarium lights daily and to slowly increase the room lights before switching the tank light on so that I won't be forced to give my fish CPR.

REMEMBER

Many types of lighting are available. Which type you choose depends on your tank setup. See Chapter 6 for more on lighting.

Use My Test Kits

I promise to brush the dust off of my test kits and use them faithfully once a week and regularly test for excessive nitrates and ammonia and keep an eye on the pH. I also promise to not use any kit that is outdated.

REMEMBER

Test kits are vital to keeping your water condition's pristine. Your fish will be healthier and live longer if you test your water conditions and adjust them accordingly on a regular basis. Chapter 14 explains the ins and outs of information on water testing.

Pay Attention to My Fish

I promise to spend more quality time with my fish, such as wiggling my fingers near the glass. I will acknowledge my fish's presence at least twice a day. On the flip side, I won't go overboard by constantly bothering my fish every hour.

REMEMBER

Fish need stimulation just like humans. When fish are removed from the naturally occurring daily events in their home environment, they can become listless. Spending time with them helps them to remain alert and active.

Redecorate the Tank

I promise to rearrange the tank decorations at least twice a year and add new plants now and then. Then my fish won't look bored and will stop spitting gravel at me.

REMEMBER

Redecorating an aquarium once in a while will keep your fish from becoming territorial and will reduce fighting during feeding. Chapter 5 examines many good decorating ideas.

Share with Others

I promise to share my aquarium information and ideas with family, friends, and other fishkeepers, so that my hobby will continue to thrive for future generations.

TIP

The only way to keep the aquarium hobby strong is by sharing it with others so that future generations will have an interest in keeping fish. Talking to and including children in your hobby will help to create future hobbyists. Look at Chapter 22 for different ways to share your hobby.

Index

A

accessories, 9, 329–334

acclimation, for live plants, 226

acidity, 209

acriflavine, 181

acrylic aquariums, 41–42

actinic blue bulbs, 84

activated charcoal, 70

activated zeolite, 70

adaptability, of systems, 324

adding
  substrates, 56–57
  water to aquariums, 190–191

additives, nitrogen cycle and, 206

adipose fin, 92

aequidens maronii (keyhole), 124

African cichlids, 120–121

aggression, 252–253, 274, 345

air pumps, 79–80

air-line tubing, 81–82

airstones, 79–81, 187

algae, 228, 348

algae cleaners, 330

algae control, 199

alkalinity, 209

all-in-one tanks, 45

aluminum stands, 49

Amazon frogbit *(limnobium laevigatum),* 245

Amazon sword *(echinodorus amazonicus),* 238–239, 247

Amazon swordplant *(echinodorus bleheri),* 268

American cichlids, 121–125

ammonia
  about, 202
  testing, 207–210

ammonia control granules, 197–198

anabantids, 94–95, 106–108

anal fin, 91, 108

anchoring wood, 59

angelfish *(pterophyllum scalare),* 121–122, 286

angle iron stands, 48–49

antibiotics, 200

appearance, of systems, 325–326

aqua soil, 54

aquarium claw, 329–330

aquarium clubs, 314

aquarium keeping
  about, 15–16
  benefits of, 16–17
  organization, 23
  water systems, 18–22

aquarium salt, 198

aquarium sealer, 332

aquarium smart controllers, 334

aquarium webcams, 294

aquariums
  about, 8–9, 133
  acrylic, 41–42
  adding water to, 190–191
  all-in-one, 45
  appearance of in stores, 140–141
  Betta, 45
  for breeding, 264
  building, 40
  buying, 33–39
  carrying capacity of, 47
  children and, 37
  choosing, 46–47
  cleaning, 348
  conditioning, 202–203

cost
  about, 14
  of acrylic tanks, 41
  as a benefit of fishkeeping, 17
  of systems, 325
  tanks, 35
crushed coral/shells, 55
cryptocorn (*cryptocoryne affinis*), 268
cryptocoryne (*cryptocoryne balanssae/wendetti*),
    220, 233–234
ctenoid scales, 101
cuttings, 222
cycling chemicals, 196, 202
cycloid scales, 101
cyprinids, 125–127
cyprinodonts, 108–111

D

dead areas, 59
dechlorinator, 30, 186–187, 195–196
decorations
  about, 62–63, 349–350
  for breeding, 264–265
  troubleshooting, 256–257
dH (hardness)
  for breeding, 269
  testing, 210
diatom filters, 74–75
diatomaceous earth, 74
diet and nutrition
  about, 151–152, 153
  fish and, 343
  fry, 162
  identifying food types, 157–162
  improper diet as cause of disease, 176
  needs for, 152–154
  overfeeding, 153
  types of eaters, 155–157
  underfeeding, 153

digital heaters, 77
digital photography, 292–294
digital thermometers, 78
digital water testing, 333
disco gravel, 55–56
discoloration, of plastic tanks, 42
discus (*symphysodon* varieties), 123–124
disease
  causes of, 174–176
  classifications of, 167
  hospital tanks, 180
  identifying illnesses, 168–174
  medications, 180–181
  monitoring for, 177–178
  preventing, 163–168
  quarantine tanks, 178–179
  salt bath, 177
  stress and, 167
distilled water, 189
distortion
  of acrylic tanks, 41
  of plastic tanks, 42
distractions, as a benefit of fishkeeping, 16
do-it-yourself stands, 49
doors, 28
dorsal fin, 90–91
dragon-eye goldfish (*carassius auratus*),
    129, 131–132
dropsy, 169
duckweed (*lemna minor*), 245
dwarf anubias (*anubias nana*), 234
dwarf four-leaf clover (*marsilia hirsute*),
    234–235
dwarf sagittaria (*sagittaria subulata*),
    237–238
dwarf swordplant (*echinodorus tenellus*),
    247
dye dipping, 103

gill parasites, 171

glass aquariums, 40

glass catfish *(kryptopterus bicirrhis),* 113

glass cleaner, 195

glass flakes, 55

glowlight tetra *(hemigrammus erythrozonus),* 115–116

goldfish *(carassius auratus),* 129–130

gonopodium, 91, 108, 277

GPH (gallons per hour), 69

gravel
  about, 54, 56
  automatic cleaners for, 333–334
  mature, 206

green algae, 228, 258

green barb *(barbus tetrazona),* 125

green cabomba *(cabomba caroliniana),* 248

ground-fault circuit interrupter (GFCI), 31

growout tank, 281

growth food, 162

guppy *(poecilia reticulata),* 108–109, 284

H

hairgrass *(eleocharis acicularis),* 247

hanging lighting, 86

hanging thermometers, 78

hang-on-back filters, 72–73

hard water, 188

hardness (dH)
  for breeding, 269
  testing, 210

hardwood floor, 26

harlequin rasbora *(rasbora heteromorpha),* 126–127

hearing, 97

heaters
  about, 77–79
  for breeding, 266
  troubleshooting, 254–255

herbivore, 106

high traffic areas, 28–29

high-powered mercury vapor lights, 84

history, 18

holding tank, for shows, 308

hole in the head, 171

hoodlights, 299

hoods
  about, 83, 85–86
  for breeding, 264
  troubleshooting, 342, 344

hornwort *(ceratophyllum demersum),* 241–242, 247, 268, 320

hospital tanks, 180

I

ichthyologists, 97, 100

icons, explained, 3

identifying
  fish, 99–103
  illnesses, 168–174
  water systems, 18–22

illnesses, identifying, 168–174

inbreeding, 283–284

incandescent (Tungsten) lighting, 84, 299

indoor goldfish pond, setting up, 216

indoor pond barrels, 45

infusoria, 161

injected dye, 103

injuries, 253

internet resources
  aquarium clubs, 314
  buying fish online, 226
  city water report, 30
  classified ad, 38
  Marineland, 85

intestinal parasites, 172

invertebrates. *See also* coldwater fish/invertebrates

malachite green, 181, 200

mangrove (*brugiuera* species), 248

marbles, 55

marginal plants, 220

marine community tank, 53

marine coral reef, 53

marine dolomite, 55

marine systems

about, 21–22, 211–212

coldwater, 20–21, 215–216, 321

freshwater systems, 19–21, 324–326

indoor goldfish pond, 216

saltwater systems, 324–326

setting up, 320–324

small plant tank, 214–215

tropical freshwater, 212–214

Marineland (website), 85

Marineland Internal Polishing filter, 72, 75

marisa cornuarietis (*ramshorn snail*), 128

material-based stands, 49

mechanical filtration, 69

medications

about, 180–181

chemicals for, 200

live plants and, 228

melanochromis johanni (blue johanni), 121

melting, of plastic tanks, 42

metal halide lights, 84

metal poisoning, 175

metals, in tap water, 187

methylene blue, 181

microworms (*anguillula silusiae*), 162

midwater feeders, 101

midwater plants, 237–238

mollies (*poecilia sphenops*), 285

monitoring

during conditioning, 205

equipment, 164

fish, 165

salinity, 21

temperature, 79, 164–165

water, 165–166

mopani wood, 59

mosquito larvae, 161–162

mosses, 221

mouth fungus, 172

mouth location, classification based on, 101

mouthbrooders, 279

moving tanks, 50

mutation, 283

N

nares, 97

natural environment, 52–53

natural filtration, with plants, 75

neon tetra (*paracheirodon innesi*), 116

nerite snail (*neritina natalensis*), 132–133

neuromasts, 96

new tank syndrome, 207

nitrates, testing, 207–210

nitrites, testing, 207–210

nitrobacter, 205

nitrogen cycle

about, 196

starting, 203–207

water testing and, 201–210

nitrosamonas, 203–204

nocturnal, 112

noise

as a benefit of fishkeeping, 16

with filters, 76

nonsubmersible heaters, 77

nutrition and diet

about, 151–152, 153

fish and, 343

fry, 162

identifying food types, 157–162

About the Author

Madelaine Francis Heleine is a contributing writer to many aquatic magazines, including *Tropical Fish Hobbyist* and *Aquarium Fish,* and is also the author of several aquarium books. She has been in the writing industry for more than 40 years.

Her interest in fish began when she was five years old. She often dreamed of keeping fish at home as she watched the local fishermen bring in their daily catch in her hometown. She began keeping aquariums at age seven and began breeding fish at age ten. She built her aquarium collection by selling and trading her newborn fry to local aquarium stores in exchange for aquariums and equipment as she was growing up.

Her passion for aquarium fish continued after she finished her college degree in journalism and began writing aquarium-keeping articles for print and online aquatic magazines. Eventually, she wrote several aquarium columns and began writing fishkeeping books to help other hobbyists enjoy keeping aquariums at home as much as she did. Her love of fish has also appeared in her greeting cards, cartoons, and other artwork.

Maddy enjoys breeding fish, scuba diving, cooking, woodworking, and playing MMORPG computer games.

Dedication

This book is dedicated to my brother Don who was lost for 59 years across the sea, but then was found. He has made me whole, and our two hearts now beat as one. Together, we keep perfect time. I love you, Skipper.

Author's Acknowledgments

I want to thank my sisters Rose and Mary, my cousins Linda, Sally, and Helen for always being there, and my sister-in-law Marina for her never-ending support.

Publisher's Acknowledgments

Acquisition Editor: Ashley Coffey

Project Editor: Chad R. Sievers

Copy Editor: Chad R. Sievers

Proofreader: Debbye Butler

Technical Editor: Mark Valderrama

Production Editor: Mohammed Zafar Ali

Cover Image: © Sukpaiboonwat /Shutterstock

Leverage the power

Dummies is the global leader in the reference category and one of the most trusted and highly regarded brands in the world. No longer just focused on books, customers now have access to the dummies content they need in the format they want. Together we'll craft a solution that engages your customers, stands out from the competition, and helps you meet your goals.

Advertising & Sponsorships

Connect with an engaged audience on a powerful multimedia site, and position your message alongside expert how-to content. Dummies.com is a one-stop shop for free, online information and know-how curated by a team of experts.

- Targeted ads
- Video
- Email Marketing

- Microsites
- Sweepstakes sponsorship

20 MILLION PAGE VIEWS EVERY SINGLE MONTH

15 MILLION UNIQUE VISITORS PER MONTH

43% OF ALL VISITORS ACCESS THE SITE VIA THEIR MOBILE DEVICES

700,000 NEWSLETTER SUBSCRIPTIONS TO THE INBOXES OF

300,000 UNIQUE INDIVIDUALS EVERY WEEK

Custom Publishing

Reach a global audience in any language by creating a solution that will differentiate you from competitors, amplify your message, and encourage customers to make a buying decision.

- Apps
- Books
- eBooks
- Video
- Audio
- Webinars

Brand Licensing & Content

Leverage the strength of the world's most popular reference brand to reach new audiences and channels of distribution.

For more information, visit dummies.com/biz

PERSONAL ENRICHMENT

Staying Sharp	Facebook	Guitar	Investing	Beekeeping	Digital Photography
9781119187790	9781119179030	9781119293354	9781119293347	9781119310068	9781119235606
USA $26.00	USA $21.99	USA $24.99	USA $22.99	USA $22.99	USA $24.99
CAN $31.99	CAN $25.99	CAN $29.99	CAN $27.99	CAN $27.99	CAN $29.99
UK £19.99	UK £16.99	UK £17.99	UK £16.99	UK £16.99	UK £17.99

Meditation	Pregnancy	Samsung Galaxy S7	iPhone	Crocheting	Nutrition
9781119251163	9781119235491	9781119279952	9781119283133	9781119287117	9781119130246
USA $24.99	USA $26.99	USA $24.99	USA $24.99	USA $24.99	USA $22.99
CAN $29.99	CAN $31.99	CAN $29.99	CAN $29.99	CAN $29.99	CAN $27.99
UK £17.99	UK £19.99	UK £17.99	UK £17.99	UK £16.99	UK £16.99

PROFESSIONAL DEVELOPMENT

Windows 10	AutoCAD	Excel 2016	QuickBooks 2017	macOS Sierra	LinkedIn	Windows 10
9781119311041	9781119255796	9781119293439	9781119281467	9781119280651	9781119251132	9781119310563
USA $24.99	USA $39.99	USA $26.99	USA $26.99	USA $29.99	USA $24.99	USA $34.00
CAN $29.99	CAN $47.99	CAN $31.99	CAN $31.99	CAN $35.99	CAN $29.99	CAN $41.99
UK £17.99	UK £27.99	UK £19.99	UK £19.99	UK £21.99	UK £17.99	UK £24.99

SharePoint 2016	Fundamental Analysis	Networking	Office 2016	Office 365	Salesforce.com	Coding
9781119181705	9781119263593	9781119257769	9781119293477	9781119265313	9781119239314	9781119293323
USA $29.99	USA $26.99	USA $29.99	USA $26.99	USA $24.99	USA $29.99	USA $29.99
CAN $35.99	CAN $31.99	CAN $35.99	CAN $31.99	CAN $29.99	CAN $35.99	CAN $35.99
UK £21.99	UK £19.99	UK £21.99	UK £19.99	UK £17.99	UK £21.99	UK £21.99

dummies.com

dummies®
A Wiley Brand

Learning Made Easy

ACADEMIC

Algebra I dummies

Mary Jane Sterling

9781119293576
USA $19.99
CAN $23.99
UK £15.99

Basic Math & Pre-Algebra dummies

Mark Zegarelli

9781119293637
USA $19.99
CAN $23.99
UK £15.99

Calculus dummies

Mark Ryan

9781119293491
USA $19.99
CAN $23.99
UK £15.99

Chemistry dummies

John T. Moore, EdD

9781119293460
USA $19.99
CAN $23.99
UK £15.99

Physics I dummies

Steven Holzner, PhD

9781119293590
USA $19.99
CAN $23.99
UK £15.99

1,001 Practice Questions
SAT dummies

Ron Woldoff

9781119215844
USA $26.99
CAN $31.99
UK £19.99

Organic Chemistry I dummies

Arthur Winter

9781119293378
USA $22.99
CAN $27.99
UK £16.99

Statistics dummies

Deborah J. Rumsey, PhD

9781119293521
USA $19.99
CAN $23.99
UK £15.99

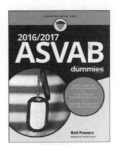

2016/2017
ASVAB dummies

Rod Powers

9781119239178
USA $18.99
CAN $22.99
UK £14.99

Includes Online Practice Tests
1,001 Practice Questions
Praxis Core dummies

Carla Kirkland
Chan Cleveland

9781119263883
USA $26.99
CAN $31.99
UK £19.99

Available Everywhere Books Are Sold

dummies.com

dummies
A Wiley Brand

Small books for big imaginations

GETTING STARTED WITH Coding
Get Creative with Code!
Camille McCue, PhD

9781119177173
USA $9.99
CAN $9.99
UK £8.99

MODDING Minecraft
Build Your Own Minecraft Mods!
Sarah Guthals, PhD
Stephen Foster, PhD
Lindsey Handley, PhD

9781119177272
USA $9.99
CAN $9.99
UK £8.99

MAKING YouTube VIDEOS
Star in Your Own Video!
Nick Willoughby

9781119177241
USA $9.99
CAN $9.99
UK £8.99

DESIGNING Digital Games
Create Games with Scratch!
Derek Breen

9781119177210
USA $9.99
CAN $9.99
UK £8.99

GETTING STARTED WITH Raspberry Pi
Program Your Raspberry Pi!
Richard Wentk

9781119262657
USA $9.99
CAN $9.99
UK £6.99

EXPERIMENTING WITH Science
Think, Test, and Learn!
Olivia J. Mullins, PhD

9781119291336
USA $9.99
CAN $9.99
UK £6.99

CREATING Digital Animations
Animate Stories with Scratch!
Derek Breen

9781119233527
USA $9.99
CAN $9.99
UK £6.99

GETTING STARTED WITH Engineering
Think Like an Engineer!
Camille McCue, PhD

9781119291220
USA $9.99
CAN $9.99
UK £6.99

WRITING Computer Code
Learn the Language of Computers!
Chris Minnick and Eva Holland

9781119177302
USA $9.99
CAN $9.99
UK £8.99

Unleash Their Creativity